Design and Violence

Design and Violence

Paola Antonelli and Jamer Hunt

The Museum of Modern Art, New York

Contents

7   Foreword

9   Design and Violence

Hack

19   The Box Cutter
John Hockenberry

22   Stuxnet: Anatomy of a
Computer Virus
Lev Manovich

26   Pivot: Design against Trafficking
*Shandra Woworuntu and
Christopher L. Heuertz*

30   Hacked Protest Objects
*Carlotta Werner and
Johanna Sunder-Plassmann*

36   The Crisis of Credit Visualized
Gillian Tett

40   The Liberator
Rob Walker

46   HonestAds
Leslie Savan

48   IR8
Bruce Nussbaum

52   Menstruation Machine
Elizabeth Grosz

Control

57   Nirbheek Pistol
Nivedita Menon

60   Republic of Salivation
John Thackara

64   Plastic Handcuffs and Anti-Bite/
Spit Masks
Shira A. Scheindlin

68   Thomson Correctional Center
Raphael Sperry

74	**Magnasanti** *Ayssar Arida*	154	**Five Classified Aircraft** *William Gibson*
78	**Borderwall as Architecture** *Judith Torrea*	160	**Army Field Manual 5-0:** **The Operations Process** *Harry Jones*
84	**Technicals** *Aminatta Forna*		
88	**Operation Sovereign Borders** **Graphic Storyboard** *Ahmed Ansari*		**Annihilate**
96	**Female Genital Mutilation** **Awareness Poster Campaign** *Angélique Kidjo*	165	**Mountaintop Removal** *Laura Antrim Caskey*
		170	**Mine Kafon** *Jody Williams*
100	**Prospectus for a Future Body** *André Lepecki*	176	**M855A1 Enhanced** **Performance Round** *Clive Dilnot*
108	**Scary Beautiful** *Alison Bancroft*	180	**How to Kill People: A Problem** **of Design** *Alice Rawsthorn*
	Trace	184	**Natural Deselection** *JC Cahill*
113	**Vice/Virtue Water Glass Series** *Susan Yelavich*	188	**Serpentine Ramp** *Ingrid Newkirk*
118	**Violence** *Anne-Marie Slaughter*	194	**Euthanasia Coaster** *Antonio Damasio*
122	**The Stiletto Heel** *Camille Paglia*	198	**Beetle Wrestler** *Hugh Raffles*
126	**Head Hand Bag** *Cintra Wilson*	202	**Salty's Dream Cast Casino** *Jamin Warren*
128	**Drone Shadows** *Arianna Huffington*	206	**Ninja Star** *Brian Ashcraft*
134	**Digital Attack Map** *Gabriella Coleman*	210	**Glassphemy!** *Geoff Manaugh*
140	**Million Dollar Blocks** *Steven Pinker*	214	**AK-47** *China Keitetsi*
144	**The Refugee Project** *António Guterres*	220	**The Design and Violence Debates**
		223	**Acknowledgments**
148	**Blue Bra Graffiti** *Nama Khalil*	226	**Contributors**
		230	**Index and Credits**

Published in conjunction with the exhibition
Design and Violence, online on the website
of The Museum of Modern Art, New York,
at http://designandviolence.moma.org, and
organized by Paola Antonelli, Senior Curator,
Department of Architecture and Design, and
Director of R&D, The Museum of Modern Art,
and Jamer Hunt, Director, Graduate Program
in Transdisciplinary Design, Parsons The New
School for Design, New York, with Michelle
Millar Fisher, Curatorial Assistant, The Museum
of Modern Art.

Produced by the Department of Publications,
The Museum of Modern Art, New York

Christopher Hudson, Publisher
Chul R. Kim, Associate Publisher
David Frankel, Editorial Director
Marc Sapir, Production Director

Edited by Sarah Resnick
Designed by Shaz Madani
Production by Matthew Pimm
Printed and bound by Ofset Yapimevi, Istanbul

This book is typeset in Bureau Grotesque and
Helvetica. The paper is 130gsm Amber Graphic.

Library of Congress Control Number:
2015931936
ISBN: 978-0-87070-968-5

Published by The Museum of Modern Art
11 West 53 Street
New York, New York 10019
www.moma.org

Distributed in the United States and Canada
by ARTBOOK I D.A.P., New York
155 Sixth Avenue, 2nd floor, New York, NY 10013
www.artbook.com

Distributed outside the United States and
Canada by Thames & Hudson ltd
181A High Holborn, London WC1V 7QX
www.thamesandhudson.com

Printed in Turkey

Foreword

This book represents the culmination of a pioneering curatorial experiment at The Museum of Modern Art exploring the intersection of contemporary design and violence in its myriad forms. Born first as an online platform, and then as a series of public debates, *Design and Violence*, organized by Paola Antonelli and Jamer Hunt, examines the ways in which violence manifests in the post-2001 landscape and asks what makes these manifestations unique to their era. The project is not only emblematic of our contemporary moment; its unusual format and challenging, provocative content test the boundaries of traditional exhibition making and represent a paradigm shift at the Museum.

Today, humankind enjoys better health, longer life spans, and greater access to material goods than ever before. Connecting to friends and strangers across both short and vast distances has likewise never been easier. The field of design, whether through applied medicine or mechanical engineering or computer science, has helped to propel these advances. As such, design has been rightfully trumpeted as a force for good, a facet of creative production that touches all of our lives.

Yet, this narrative, albeit comforting and easy to digest, troubles in its simplicity. Throughout history, design has both perpetuated and mediated violence, giving rise to tools that harm, control, manipulate, and annihilate—from the simple, handheld weapons of ancestral times to the undetectable, self-propagating computer malware of contemporary ones. The potential violence wrought by these tools is compounded by systemic power imbalances and their reification in our bureaucratic, social, and economic structures. It is the reexamination of this omnipresent yet shadowy narrative that drives the investigation at the heart of *Design and Violence*.

Over the last decade, several of the Museum's design exhibitions, including *Safe: Design Takes on Risk* (2005), *Design and the Elastic Mind* (2008), and *Talk to Me* (2011), have staked the claim that design encompasses not only tangible objects but also information architectures, user interfaces, and communications protocol. *Design and Violence* is born of this legacy, engaging with graphic, industrial, speculative, and architectural design, among other forms. The essays in this book, commissioned from a roster of talented writers, activists, and scholars, cast a suitably wide net. Among the various objects considered, some are designed to propagate violence, others to subvert it; mass-produced plastic handcuffs used by law enforcement and spray bottles repurposed as protest tools succinctly illustrate the two poles on this spectrum. Still other ideas presented in these pages animate violence in order to condemn it, such as the roller coaster designed to induce euphoria at the same time that it euthanizes its passengers. The terror evoked by guns and by prison architecture may be palpable and incontestable; but as with interface designs that engage with political lies or that celebrate the fraught processes of natural selection, violence can also present in subtle and ambiguous ways, empowering and disempowering simultaneously.

Since its inception in 1932, the Department of Architecture and Design has provided a platform for groundbreaking exhibitions and projects. *Design and Violence,* insofar as it bravely charts novel territory, represents yet another example of the department's ambition. The design concepts in this volume often provoke discomfort, not only because they cast a harsh light on contemporary humankind—for whom death, destruction, and the deliberate infliction of harm are by no means unfamiliar—but also because they bring into relief our own often unwitting, and sometimes willing, complicity in the field's darker recesses. The Museum is proud to support this project as part of its commitment to facilitating engagement with a broad cross section of contemporary art, architecture, and design discourses, no matter how challenging they may be. *Design and Violence* does not always make for easy reading, but the dialogue it provokes should not be shied away from.

Glenn D. Lowry
Director, The Museum of Modern Art

Design and Violence

In violence we forget who we are.
—Mary McCarthy[1]

In 2011, acclaimed scholar Steven Pinker published *The Better Angels of Our Nature: Why Violence Has Declined*, a commanding attempt to correct what he sees as a widespread misconception: that the world is more violent today than ever before.[2] On the contrary, Pinker argues, violence has for centuries been on an evident decline. Perhaps intuiting the knee-jerk skepticism of future readers, he mounts an exhaustive defense, patiently and convincingly steering his argument through reams of data and mountains of statistical evidence.

Pinker's argument is undoubtedly seductive. Certainly, public executions, once a widespread form of punishment, are no longer as prevalent. Nor is, for example, legal impunity toward the killing of wives. We have undeniably curbed some of our instinctual tendencies toward brutality. Yet what if violence were merely mutating rather than disappearing? What to make of the fact that in the United States African American males are six times more likely to go to prison than white males (despite comprising a much smaller proportion of the overall population); and that, if trends continue, one in every three black American males will face incarceration in his lifetime?[3] Or that, because of our thirst for fossil fuels and our appetite for material possessions, the temperature of the planet is rising, possibly irrecoverably, to dangerous new highs, launching us on a course toward new conflicts? How, in other words, do we even begin to explore the unanticipated consequences of our collective actions? These may take subtler, less measurable forms, but they are violence nonetheless.

Not only does violence appear to be morphing, but how we experience, perceive, and assess it is also shifting. Since at least the 1960s (and more likely as far back as the abolitionist and suffragette movements of the nineteenth and early twentieth centuries), minority-, gay-, and disability-rights struggles, along with feminist and anticolonialist ones, have each illuminated the pernicious ways in which unequal access to basic human rights such as education, employment, and housing are themselves insidious forms of violence. Phrases such as "stick it to the Man" emerged as fierce pushback against assaults by big business, paternalistic government, and conformist institutions. In her treatise *On Violence*, Hannah Arendt diagnosed this inability "to localize responsibility and to identify the enemy" as a kind of tyranny, calling it "among the most potent causes of the worldwide rebellious unrest," and highlighting "its chaotic nature, and its dangerous tendency to get out of control and run amuck."[4] Protesters in the 1960s and 1970s, from Parisian students to the Black Panthers, from punks to the Sanbabilini,[5] conjured threats and acts of violence both as catharsis and as confrontation. Pinker refers to the loose grouping of movements that rose up against these polymorphous forms of discrimination as the "rights struggles." And while he credits these struggles with redefining violence as we know it, his argument does not extend far enough to convincingly account for the impact of such violence on those forced to contend with it day in and day out.[6]

***

Where there is transformation, there is design: indeed, the reshaping of everyday experience is at the core of the designer's work. Whether under the guise of urban renewal or the cliché of disruptive innovation, designers—of buildings, infrastructures, garments, products, graphics, interfaces, and even experiences—have often played invisible or ambiguous roles, reconfiguring everything from our ecosystems to our moral philosophies to our ways of life. Traditionally designers have set out to better society, their objectives ranging from the quotidian (spoons) to the autocratic (cities).[7] Yet at times they may find it all too easy to overstep, indulge in temptation, or succumb to the dark side of a moral dilemma; they may also simply err. With characteristic polemics and drama, design activist Victor Papanek thundered in 1971, "There are professions more harmful than industrial design, but only a very few of them."[8] From the Three Gorges Dam to the Cross-Bronx Expressway, from police batons to high-heeled shoes, designers often generate forms for social, psychological, and material violence.

Nevertheless, within the profession, voices that trumpet design's commercial and aesthetic successes have dominated. Design's history of violence, unless linked overtly to political and social suppression, too often goes unexplored. How is it possible, for example, that Mikhail Kalashnikov, designer of the AK-47 assault rifle, now considered the most widely adopted firearm in the world (and used by armed forces in more than eighty countries), could naively reflect in his later years, "My spiritual pain is unbearable. . . . If my rifle claimed people's lives, then can it be that I . . . a Christian and an Orthodox believer, was to blame for their deaths?"[9] Turning a blind eye to the depth of design's complicity in destroying as much as (or more than) it creates, our profession has been institutionally incapable of gauging the full extent of its impact. *Design and Violence* confronts this head-on. It considers the manifestations of violence in contemporary society through the lens of design, contemplating the ambiguous relationships between creation, destruction, and everyday experience.

Launched in 2013 as an online curatorial experiment, *Design and Violence* features controversial, provocative, and compelling projects that raise unsettling questions about designers and their complicity in violence. Each week, over the course of a year and a half, we invited one author to respond in writing to a selected design (occasionally contributions have included illustration, animation, and even sound art). We then published the encounter online, alongside a leading question that distills issues raised in the author's response, and invited the public to respond. In doing so, we opened a space for comment, reflection, and active (sometimes fierce) debate. As designers and curators we aspired to challenge ourselves and a wider community to consider whether and how contemporary violence has mutated, as well as the role of design in engendering these new forms—or not.

Violence evades easy definition primarily because the term accommodates so many configurations, spanning the symbolic and the real, the individual and the collective. As we define it for this project, violence is a manifestation of the power to alter the circumstances around us, against the will of others and to their detriment. In its various guises, violence tempts us all. Once more we invoke Arendt, for whom power belongs to the order of politics and manifests only in the aggregation of people and political agency. Violence, on the other hand, is of a completely different order. She writes, "Violence, we must remember, does not depend on numbers or opinion but on implements, and the implements of violence share with all other tools that they increase and multiply human strength. Those who oppose violence with mere power will soon find out that they are confronted not with men but with men's artifacts, whose inhumanity and destructive effectiveness increase in proportion to the distance that separates the opponents."[10]

***

With few exceptions, *Design and Violence* focuses on the myriad ways violence has manifested since 2001, a watershed moment in the American collective experience and a traumatic one for the world. September 11, 2001, was a turning point in the socio-technical construction of violence; it is for this reason that we situate this project in the years since this cataclysm. Two related and equally tectonic shifts make a contemporary exploration of design and violence since 2001 particularly revealing: the dematerialization of the means of warfare, from clubs, knives, guns, and bombs to propaganda, counterinsurgency, and cyberwarfare; and the shift from symmetric, nation-based war strategies to asymmetric, decentralized ones.

   In the wake of the attacks of September 11, 2001, the U.S. government under George W. Bush launched a global "war on terror." Rooted in political pretzel logic, the war rationalized an all-out assault on whomever, whenever, and for whatever reasons. The approach has also redefined war as we know it, entailing not a collision of nation-states or superpowers, their battalions waging attacks in fields, skies, and oceans, but rather a continuous struggle to root out an enemy that is everywhere and nowhere: the caves of Afghanistan; the religious centers of London; the jogging path of the Buttes-Chaumont park in Paris; or the tract homes of suburban New Jersey. The government also rewrote the rules of engagement: "enhanced interrogation techniques," the usurpation of sovereign airspace, remote-controlled drone attacks, and targeted assassination have revived torture and tossed aside the Geneva Conventions. With no easily defined enemy or endgame, the conflict may never end.

   Much of the post-9/11 havoc came about because "terror's" earliest incarnation in the United States' collective imaginary, Al Qaeda, presented a new form of opponent: stateless, distributed, decentralized, and highly networked. For a conventional military power, there were no longer borders to cross, territories to seize, or populations to pacify. A 1996 Rand Corporation monograph, *The Advent of Netwar*, foresaw as a consequence of the information revolution's networked organization a shift toward decentralized, amorphous, and diffuse forms of conflict. The term "netwar" depicts "societal conflict and crime, short of war, in which the antagonists are organized more as sprawling, leaderless networks than as tight-knit hierarchies."[11] The Rand researchers suggested that netwar capabilities were being developed by terrorists, criminals, fundamentalists, ethno-nationalists, revolutionaries, and militant radicals alike, with new doctrines, strategies, and technologies emphasizing networked forms of organization.

"Netwar may be the dominant mode of societal conflict in the 21st century," they concluded.[12] Nonstate combatants integrating network theory reveal that asymmetrical strategies can confound much more powerful, albeit lumbering adversaries.

The U.S. and NATO occupations of Iraq and Afghanistan following 9/11 also rewrote the terms of combat. With overwhelming force no longer the objective—it would only further destroy Afghanistan's social and political infrastructure—a different tactic was in order: "Protracted popular war is best countered by winning the 'hearts and minds' of the populace," reads the 2006 *U.S. Army/Marine Corps Counterinsurgency Field Manual*.[13] The shift in strategy from overwhelming force to counterinsurgency means that foot soldiers today act more like anthropologists and less like combatants. Their aim (apart from their own survival in a combat zone) is social and political accommodation, not military conquest. These changes in strategy are redefining violence and force as we know them. Mass armed warfare begins to look more like violence in its everyday guises: insidious, invisible, and immaterial.

As further evidence of the quicksilver nature of warfare, in 2005 the U.S. Air Force adapted its mission statement to include, along with air and space, a new dimension of control: cyberspace.[14] Increasingly, it seems, the terms of warfare, espionage, and conflict are played out via immaterial electrons circulating across information networks and not in our material world of bludgeons, bullets, and bodies. The precipitous rise of cybercrime, cyberterror, and cyberwarfare in the twenty-first century assumes forms such as malware, viruses, worms, distributed-denial-of-service (DDoS) attacks, and massive, state-sponsored information offensives. In 2010, for example, the U.S. government, in partnership with Israel, crippled centrifuges at the Natanz nuclear enrichment facility in Iran by unleashing the devious computer worm Stuxnet (p. 22), its sole objective to make the facility's centrifuges spin out of control and effectively destroy themselves (neither government has admitted its involvement).

DDoS attacks incapacitate target websites by directing to them high volumes of network traffic. The tactic has existed since the mid-1990s, but was popularized in recent years by the hacker collective Anonymous, who has often used the strategy as a form of electronic civil disobedience. In 2013, Google introduced the Digital Attack Map (p. 134), a real-time tool that visually maps the origin, target, and geographical distribution of DDoS attacks. Dotted tracers light up like fireworks over a map of the world, visualizing the profusion of attacks at any one moment (as well as over time) and their near-worldwide ubiquity. No institution or organization is immune.[15] As of late 2014, cyberattacks have been successfully launched against banks (JPMorgan Chase); newspapers (*New York Times*); retailers (Home Depot, Target, Neiman Marcus); service providers (Apple's iCloud); governments (China, Pakistan, Canada); and even the U.S. Pentagon, headquarters of the Department of Defense. We have, by all appearances, entered a very different era of warfare, terror, espionage, crime, and violence.

***

Design and Violence is not a gallery-based exhibition simply translated online. From our earliest conversations, we conceived it as a platform for multiple projects—a series of public debates, a set of academic course materials, a symposium, and this book, for instance—with the website as anchor. Unlike traditional exhibitions, which do not easily accommodate direct dialogue, the project's multiple formats invite commentary, feedback, questions, and even discord from audiences. Among the many benefits of this approach, the exhibition is accessible to visitors who may never cross the physical threshold of the Museum, and clearly indicates the institution's interest in the opinions of its audiences. We called the project a "curatorial experiment" to signal its inherent adaptability and responsiveness, traits we hoped could be developed to launch the conversation into public awareness.

We have strived to make *Design and Violence* an open invitation to discussion rather than the last word on any one subject, although this stance is often hard to negotiate. To better understand the broader impact of design, we invited authors from outside the field to write about many of the projects we selected, hoping they might jolt us out of complacency, professional blindness, and simple overfamiliarity. Our respondents bring perspectives diverse and unique. Pinker himself discusses Spatial Information Design Lab's information visualization Million Dollar Blocks (p. 140). Nobel Peace Prize winner Jody Williams comments on Massoud Hassani's demining tool, Mine Kafon (p. 170). New York District Court judge Shira Scheindlin, who famously declared the NYPD's stop-and-frisk procedures unconstitutional, takes on plastic handcuffs and the anti-bite or anti-spit mask (p. 64). Former Ugandan child soldier China Keitetsi reflects on the AK-47 rifle (p. 214). United Nations High Commissioner for Refugees, António Guterres, considers Hyperakt and Ekene Ijeoma's Refugee Project (p. 144). Sex-trafficking survivor Shandra Woworuntu responds to the stealthy Pivot project by Public Practice Studio (p. 26). And musician and activist Angélique Kidjo examines Amnesty International's campaign posters intended to stop feminine genital mutilation (p. 96).

To expand the range of voices even further, we opened each post to comments from the reading public, invited the object's designer to weigh in, and encouraged both author and designer to share the post and solicit comments through social media. The results have often been surprising. Two designs in particular have become lightning rods for discussion and dissent. The post on Temple Grandin's Serpentine Ramp (p. 188), featuring a powerful response by PETA's president Ingrid Newkirk, brought heated discussion over the ethics of meat production and consumption to one of our public debates (p. 220) and precipitated our longest comment thread to date. John Thackara's no-holds-barred critique of Michael Burton and Michiko Nitta's speculative design project, Republic of Salivation (p. 60), engendered a similarly intense discussion in the comments section. Drawing in voices from around the world, the dialogue shed as much light as heat on the global politics and ethics of speculative and critical design.

One remarkable comment on the website may best demonstrate the value of inviting into the Museum the participation of outside voices. In April 2014, we published a post on the Euthanasia Coaster, an intentionally provocative conceptual design by Julijonas Urbonas (p. 194). Urbonas's roller coaster features seven loops, each tighter than the one before, propelling the rider through successive degrees of g-force acceleration until a final, inescapable death. Urbonas's design aspires to offer agency to the fatally ill, an antidote to an otherwise grim end. Respondent Antonio Damasio, leading professor of neuroscience at the University of Southern California, gently critiqued this speculative fiction: "Euthanasia is death . . . compounded by myriad questions regarding the circumstances in which it may or not be acceptable." His objection to the possibility of a "joyful euthanasia" lay in the very chilling possibilities for its misuse by an increasingly technocratic society. In a comment, one reader countered with the following:

> Your post extends from a singular premise—that death is necessarily a tragedy. As somebody who is in pain every day, I do not believe this is the case. Sometimes life is the tragedy. When one's only experience is overwhelming pain, it is a tragedy to be prevented release. For many there is only one option for release and that is the final option. I feel it likely that one day in the distant future I may choose this option myself. Doing so through the experience of something so amazing that the human body cannot withstand it sounds a whole lot better to me than a boring gray room.
>
> To remove all violence from humanity would be to utterly sanitize life, to remove the experience of anything but grays. Certainly the specter of interpersonal violence is undesirable, but I WISH to be violently happy, violently sad, violently moved. I wish to feel violent acceleration and violent relief. Conflating violence with anything that challenges us is to remove all value from the human experience, to paint the world gray.[16]

Profound, wrenching, revelatory, this comment reframes certain experiences of violence and affirms the worth and necessity, even, of the project's open, participatory framework.

Many commenters have shifted the evolution of *Design and Violence* and along with it our thinking. Free of the time-based constraints of a gallery exhibition that begins and ends on specific days, we launched the project with an open-ended checklist, an unusual curatorial freedom. This extraordinary flexibility has allowed us to contemplate our ongoing exchanges, both with each other and the public, and extend the period of research and development far beyond what is normally available. When we initially conceived *Design and Violence*, we focused on projects that challenged our understanding of violence. These works—Diller + Scofidio's Vice/Virtue water glass series (p. 113), for instance, or James Bridle's Drone Shadows (p. 128)—fall for the most part in the category of critical design; that is, conceptual projects that ask us to consider the future we are creating through design, or that compel us to grapple with design's ability to reshape our experiences.

But as *Design and Violence* developed, commenters helped us to recognize that we were too often featuring projects with abstracted or symbolic notions of violence. Over the course of several months, the projects we selected shifted in orientation; we turned to designs and to authors who could speak more directly to the distorting cruelty of designed violence. By no means are we implying that some forms of violence are more authentic than others, or that some authors have more authority to speak on these issues; only that design shapes violence in various ways, and we had been omitting those experiences most immediately felt. To put it in concrete terms: the visionary prospect offered by Sputniko!'s Menstruation Machine of a world in which all genders understand one another (p. 52) differs markedly from the sanitary napkin designed by Public Practice Studio to counter female sex trafficking even though both illuminate forms of violence.

We recognized from the very outset that a project on violence hosted by

The Museum of Modern Art posed an inherent risk: aestheticizing violence and recasting it as this week's outré object. Our critics were not slow to suggest this. "Patrick," for instance, inveighed against the Museum under William Gibson's response to Trevor Paglen's *Five Classified Aircraft* (p. 154), a collection of unofficial embroidered patches from the "black world" of classified intelligence:

Today army pins, yesterday heels. The Internet requires an extremely warped sense of gimmickry and violence certainly fits the bill. But it's just another meaningless brand wrapped on multiple justifications. Perhaps museums can now classify the new hot style of the month. Violence . . . So chic. So 2013.

Once an object is stamped "violent" by MoMA, does that make it so?

The inherent problem with showing symbols and pictures of violent design [outside of their] context is an extreme fetishization of those symbols. It's like gratuitous, sexed-up violence without the "story" (insert unchallenging content). One wonders if "chicks with guns" is around the corner.

The blog format of this project seems only to heighten the state of fetishism and separation from context, more flattened imagery in an already crowded landscape.

Indeed, "Patrick" vividly outlines the very hazards we have been trying to circumvent from the outset: the stylizing of violence, the flattening of affect, and the frisson of risk and danger in the comfortable context of a safe institution. Granted, Paglen's work was only the fourth in our series of posts, and we had not yet reached a critical mass of examples. The reaction led us to fine-tune the way we wrestled with the concept of violence and its impact, while acknowledging its relevancy to design discourse and to culture. What more opportune channel for dialogue than through a free and accessible Internet site at a highly visible and influential establishment like The Museum of Modern Art?

***

This book is not a literal transposition of the website. Instead, you are reading a curated condensation of our experiment. Here we include a selection of more than forty design artifacts, each entry composed of images, the author's response, the leading question, and a selection of comments that illuminate new avenues for discussion. Certain projects live more comfortably in an electronic environment, so we opted not to reproduce them: Christoph Niemann's antic animated GIFs; Jad Abumrad's dazzling sound piece; and many of the data visualizations. Unlike on the website, we have organized the selected entries into four animating categories: Hack/Infect (to utilize the structure or code of an object or system against itself either through subversive reconfiguration or by the introduction of an active foreign element); Control (to use power or violence in order to discipline, dominate, or restrict one's own or another's ability to act with free will); Trace (to make visible, before or after the fact, the immaterial legacy of violence upon our mental and physical landscapes); and Annihilate (to seek out total obliteration of an obstacle or adversary by any means available, whether human made or naturally occurring). These categories identify patterns across the various manifestations of violence, and knit together projects to create contrasting and divergent associations.

Throughout this experiment, one simple mission has inspired us: to wade into the ethical mire that design, and every act of human intention, draws us into. Considering the broad influence of design on the world and the contemporary pace of innovation—requiring continuous alterations and adaptations—design shoulders a heavy, yet shadowy responsibility. It needs to be brought into the light and grappled with. This project is our attempt.

Paola Antonelli
Senior Curator, Department of Architecture and Design,
The Museum of Modern Art
and Director of R&D

Jamer Hunt
Director, Graduate Program in Transdisciplinary Design,
Parsons The New School for Design

A complete archive of *Design and Violence* lives at the original URL: http://designandviolence.moma.org.

1. Mary McCarthy, "Characters in Fiction," *Partisan Review* 28, no. 2 (1961): 171–91.
2. Steven Pinker, *The Better Angels of Our Nature: Why Violence Has Declined* (New York: Viking, 2011).
3. E. Ann Carson and William J. Sabol, *Prisoners in 2011*, U.S. Department of Justice, Office of Justice Programs, Bureau of Justice Statistics, 2012, p. 8. As quoted in the Sentencing Project, *Report of the Sentencing Project to the United Nations Human Rights Committee: Regarding Racial Disparities in the United States Criminal Justice System*, Sentencing Project: Research and Advocacy for Reform, 2013, http://sentencingproject.org/doc/publications/rd_ICCPR%20Race%20and%20Justice%20Shadow%20Report.pdf.
4. Hannah Arendt, *On Violence* (New York: Harcourt, Brace and World, 1970), p. 38–39.
5. Sanbabilini is a far-right movement from the 1970s, so called because its members used to gather around Piazza San Babila in Milan, Italy.
6. Paola, the Italian half of this author duo, experienced adolescence in Milan amid armed extremists warring among themselves and with the police. Her walk to school was rerouted almost daily to avoid danger zones that would often shift overnight.
7. "Dal cucchiaio alla città" (From the spoon to the city) is a slogan coined by Italian architect and critic Ernesto Nathan Rogers to describe the Milanese architectural and design process, which at the time encompassed all scales—and still does, unfortunately to a lesser extent. There is some disagreement about when Rogers said this. Deyan Sudjic notes that Rogers wrote something like it in a 1952 editorial for *Domus. The Language of Things: Understanding the World of Desirable Objects* (New York: W. W. Norton, 2009), p. 34.
8. Victor Papanek, "Preface," *Design for the Real World: Human Ecology and Social Change* (New York: Pantheon Books, 1971).
9. Mikhail Kalashnikov in an April 2013 letter to the head of Russia's Orthodox Church written shortly before his death. Excerpt published in Luke Harding, "Kalashnikov Inventor Haunted by Unbearable Pain of Dead Millions," *Guardian*, January 13, 2014.
10. Hannah Arendt, "Reflections on Violence," *New York Review of Books*, February 27, 1969.
11. John Arquilla and David Ronfeldt, *The Advent of Netwar*, RAND Monograph Report (Santa Monica, Calif.: RAND Corporation, 1996), http://www.rand.org/pubs/monograph_reports/MR789.html.
12. Ibid.
13. *U.S. Army/Marine Corps Counterinsurgency Field Manual* (Chicago: University of Chicago Press, 2007) quoted in Elizabeth Dickinson, "A Bright Shining Slogan: How Hearts and Minds Came to Be," *Foreign Policy*, August 24, 2009, http://www.foreignpolicy.com/articles/2009/08/13/a_bright_shining_slogan.
14. Pamela L. Woolley, "Defining Cyberspace as a United States Air Force Mission" (unpublished graduate research project, Department of the Air Force Air University, Air Force Institute of Technology). The term "cyberspace" was added to the U.S. Air Force's mission statement on December 7, 2005. Woolley writes, "On December 7, 2005 the Air Force (AF) Chief of Staff released the following new mission statement for the AF: 'The mission of the United States Air Force is to deliver sovereign options for the defense of the United States of America and its global interests—to fly and fight in the Air, Space, and Cyberspace.' The addition of 'Cyberspace' to the mission statement let [*sic*] many to ask, what is Cyberspace? And what does it mean to have cyberspace as a mission area?"
15. Except, as Gabriella Coleman points out in her essay for this book (p. 134), those territories without the infrastructure of the Internet, itself a different measure of social, political, and economic violence.
16. Here as elsewhere in this volume, comments extracted from the *Design and Violence* website may be truncated (indicated by an ellipsis). Save for minimal editing, usually for reasons of space and comprehension, comments are otherwise quoted as they appear online—warts and all.

Hack

To utilize the structure or code of an object or system against itself either through subversive reconfiguration or by the introduction of an active foreign element.

The Box Cutter
(Designer unknown, c. 1920)

The single-edge razor blade enclosed in a protective handle, now known colloquially as a box cutter, is believed to have originated in the 1920s as a hand tool derived from much earlier utility knives and straight razors. The model pictured here (p. 20) was first patented in the 1950s in the United States. In the United Kingdom, a slightly different model, referred to as the Stanley knife, was named after the company that began manufacturing it in the 1920s. The box cutter continues to be redesigned by many companies and manufacturers interested in leaving their mark on the classic and widely used blade. The tool earned notoriety in the early twenty-first century after the *9/11 Commission Report* revealed that it may have been used by the hijackers in the September 11, 2001, terrorist attacks on the World Trade Center. The exact design of the allegedly used blades was never verified.

John Hockenberry

A box cutter is the perfect tool for our time, for thinking "out of the box." We create boxes that require a blade to liberate ourselves and the other things we place in them. These self-referencing iterations of irony transform the utility knife into the clown acrobat of industrial capitalism. The blade punctures the fiction like a hammer smashing a nested set of Russian dolls.

The fashionable out-of-the-box thinking of the late twentieth century put a utility knife into each of our hands and set aside all of the carefully crafted blades we had carried for thousands of years. A traditional knife is an extension of the hand, cutting and shaping the materials preindustrial humans consumed as food, wore as clothing, and constructed as shelter. The utility blade can do nothing in a world of hunters, builders, and farmers.

The utility knife is invisible and useless in this traditional world, and yet the tribal postindustrial assault on boxes needed a sacred tool. Out-of-the-box thinking required a ceremonial weapon.

Men in planes screaming about God performed the initiation ceremony of the box cutter. On a day in September 2001 it became the postindustrial murder weapon. Cutting itself out of this final box, the utility knife slashed its way out of the twentieth century, never to return.

Online packagers seem careful to use soft tape for their boxes so consumers won't have to reach for the twenty-first century's murder weapon to see the lovely things they have purchased.

In a world where shoes are bombs and shampoos can bring down jetliners, you may still find a utility knife in your own drawer, in your own kitchen. See if I'm right. I'm betting that it is no longer invisible.

John Hockenberry is an Emmy and Peabody Award–winning journalist and host of public radio's live morning news program *The Takeaway*.

Q: Which other "invisible" everyday objects can become lethal weapons?

COMMENT 1. Susan Yelavich:
I am struck by how remote violence is from all of us contributing to this site. We are either the lucky survivors expunging our guilt or we're harboring wounds too deep to share.

Designer unknown. Box Cutter. c. 1950s.
Stainless steel, 4 ³⁄₁₆ x 2 ⅛ x ⅛"
(10.6 x 5.4 x 0.3 cm)

Stuxnet: Anatomy of a Computer Virus
(Patrick Clair, 2011)

Patrick Clair's motion infographic *Stuxnet: Anatomy of a Computer Virus* thoughtfully animates the inner workings of the elusive malware Stuxnet. This intricately constructed computer virus, consisting of a worm, a file shortcut, and a rootkit, was designed to disrupt programmable logic controllers, or PLCs, run on Microsoft Windows operating systems. PLCs typically control automated manufacturing and monitoring processes, such as industrial-plant assembly lines. The Stuxnet virus works in two waves: first, it maps a blueprint of the plant operating systems; second, it disrupts these systems. By exploiting unknown security gaps, the virus was able to destroy 20 percent of Iran's nuclear centrifuges, while simultaneously relaying normal readings to the plant operators. The attack was delivered via USB thumb drive, and although it was first detected in June 2010, it may have been circulating for up to a year prior. The malware, which has been linked to a policy of covert warfare allying the United States and Israel against Iran's nuclear armament, is considered to be the world's first weaponized piece of software and heralds a change in twenty-first-century global military strategy. Its creators remain unidentified.

Lev Manovich

My own first encounter with design and violence was at the age of fifteen. As a high-school student in Moscow, I was required to take two years of mandatory classes in military education. Over many months, we practiced disassembling and reassembling the masterpiece of the "design meets violence" genre: the legendary Kalashnikov rifle. Because it consists of only a handful of pieces, I was able to dismantle it in eleven seconds, and put it back together in sixteen. (Dismantling the rifle within a certain time was required for passing the course.)

I suppose this background gives me some qualification to reflect on projects in the *Design and Violence* initiative, such as Patrick Clair's video infographic on Stuxnet, a computer worm unleashed on Iran's nuclear program, among other target sites, and discovered in June 2010. Computer worms, as with viruses and executable scripts, constitute part of the various tools and techniques in the arsenal of cyberwarfare and cyberspying. If mid-twentieth-century non-networked weapons such as the Kalashnikov are location specific, operating only within their user's immediate line of sight, viruses and worms are not hampered by geography: worms such as Stuxnet can replicate and move from computer to computer around the world, attacking not only the host system but also its hardware and the other computers it controls.

Stuxnet is the first known computer worm to spy on and reprogram industrial systems. It indiscriminately hops across computers that run Windows-based operating systems, but its malware specifically targets industrial software from Siemens that is used to control a variety of large-scale infrastructure systems, including manufacturing plants. Stuxnet affected facilities in a number of countries, including Iran, Indonesia, India, and the United States. Due to its size, and the unusual complexity of its code, it has been speculated that the worm was developed by a nation-state. (According to a 2012 *New York Times* op-ed, the United States and Israel collaborated on its design.[1])

Because Stuxnet has been in and out of the news for several years now, there are a number of well-designed media presentations explaining its history, effects, and operations (besides dozens of articles). These include a compelling diagram by Guilbert Gates that accompanied a *New York Times* op-ed,[2] and a

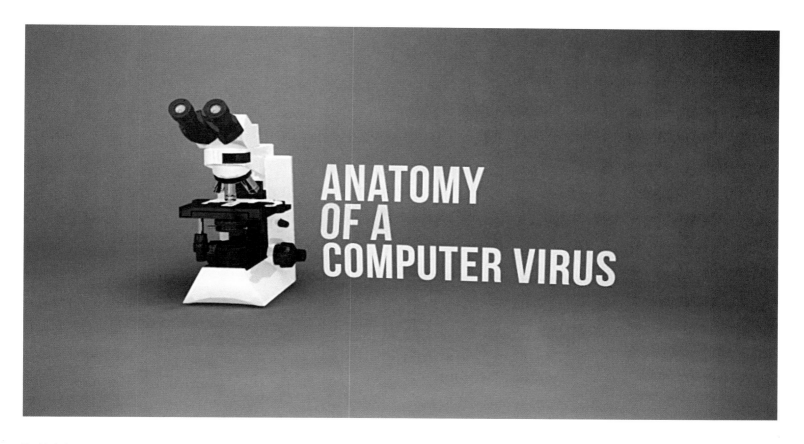

Patrick Clair (Australian, born 1982).
Stuxnet: Anatomy of a Computer Virus.
2011. Digital video (color, sound),
3:21 min.

dynamic 2011 TED video from the German scientist Ralph Langner, who worked on an analysis of the worm.[3] (At the time of writing, the video had received over one million views.) As always, the most detailed single source is the *Wikipedia* page, which, as of December 2014, has been edited 1,529 times by 716 distinct authors, and has received over 62,035 views in the last thirty days alone.

Knowing about all this coverage of the Stuxnet worm helps in thinking about Patrick Clair's video, produced for an Australian TV program in 2012. In contrast to the more complete historical narrative presented on *Wikipedia*, Clair's video presents only one of its dramatic episodes: the discovery that Stuxnet affected Iranian nuclear reactors. The video uses the contemporary language of motion graphics, with animated 2-D and 3-D text, unexpected 90-degree camera turns, superfast zooms, and 3-D vector graphics. As is typical of such videos, the movement never stops; forms are transposed, transfigured, added, and multiplied without pause. This constant movement is visually engaging but also troubling. The constantly flowing animation works differently than broadcast-news segments that typically cut between the newscaster's narration, live and recorded interviews, and on-the-scene reporting. These cuts or breaks may interrupt the viewer's immersion in the story, but they also leave space for the viewer to digest and better understand the information presented. In the motion-graphics narrative, however, there are no such breaks or juxtapositions of media types; instead the story unfolds in one continuous three-minute-long animation accompanied by a constant music beat in the background. The color wireframes and robotic-camera moves look cool, but all too often at the expense of the important facts and details of the events being described.

Branding Stuxnet as "the first weapon made entirely out of code" (this may be true or not, depending on one's definition), the video tries to convey the

Patrick Clair. *Stuxnet: Anatomy of a Computer Virus.* 2011

worm's operation through visual forms and metaphors. For example, at 1 minute, 30 seconds, the familiar Kalashnikov rifle appears on the screen, presented as a wireframe model. The rifle multiplies and shrinks to form the word "code," linking the physical and electronic forms of assault weaponry. (It reminds me of how, at the end of our course in my Moscow high school, we were taken to a real military range out of town to practice what we had learned. My fellow students and I, each with a heavy Kalashnikov in hand, lined up across a white winter field and then shot at the targets.)

Projects such as Clair's exist within a paradigm I call "info-aesthetics." These projects, which arise not only from the field of data visualization but also from motion graphics, human-computer interaction (HCI), architecture, music, and custom hardware, to name a few, have as their true subject the "stuff" our software society is made from—data (big and small), algorithms, distributed client-server systems, global networks, networked hardware. And, as with these other works, Clair's video tries to give this stuff a visible form in order to make sense of it and to produce knowledge from it. But because data and code largely exist at a scale outside of that of the human body and perception—because they are too big, or too fast, or too dispersed—the task is quite hard.

Which leaves me with the same questions I've been asking for years: Can our information society be represented iconically, if all its most characteristic activities are dynamic processes? How can the superhuman scale of our information structures be translated to the scale of human perception and cognition? Clair's video dramatizes how challenging a task this is for contemporary designers. Were we to remove the video's familiar objects—the microscope, the schematic diagram of a nuclear plant, the rifles, and the text—what would be left? Is it possible to visually represent a software "thing"—in this case, Stuxnet—that operates on a scale radically different from the old, familiar Kalashnikov rifle?

Lev Manovich is the author of three books, including *The Language of New Media* (Cambridge, Mass.: The MIT Press, 2001), and a professor at The Graduate Center, CUNY.

1. Misha Glenny, "A Weapon We Can't Control," *New York Times*, June 24, 2012, http://www.nytimes.com/2012/06/25/opinion/stuxnet-will-come-back-to-haunt-us.html.
2. Guilbert Gates, "How a Secret Cyberwar Program Worked," *New York Times,* June 1, 2012, http://www.nytimes.com/interactive/2012/06/01/world/middleeast/how-a-secret-cyberwar-program-worked.html.
3. Ralph Langner, "Cracking Stuxnet, a 21st-century Cyber Weapon," filmed March 2011, TED video, 10:40, http://www.ted.com/talks/ralph_langner_cracking_stuxnet_a_21st_century_cyberweapon.

Q: Can malware ever be used for positive ends, or is it inherently a weapon for wrongdoing?

COMMENT 1. Jason Persse:
The notion of any weapon being used for "positive" outcomes is so problematic that it makes the question seem ludicrous. The better the weapon's design, the more assuredly it will outstrip even the most noble of intentions and lead to widespread harm. Stuxnet and the AK-47 are both especially apt examples: when applied to weaponry, "user-friendly and supremely durable," the one-two punch that every designer hopes to land, becomes a genie you can never push back into the bottle. All weapons are inherently intended for wrongdoing; designing them well just means more people can do wrong to more people with greater reliability.

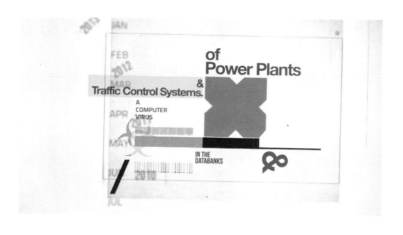

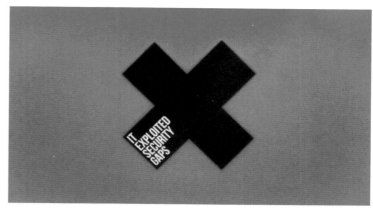

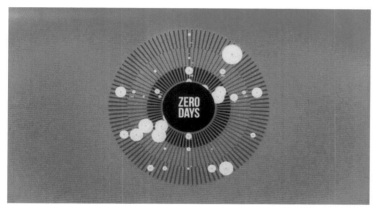

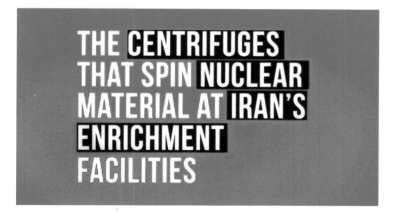

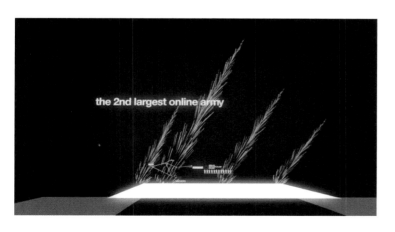

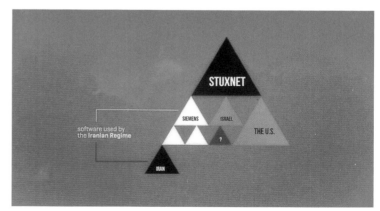

Pivot: Design against Trafficking
(Public Practice Studio, 2012–13)

Human trafficking happens to men, women, and children of all ages, and occurs in many different industries and geographic locations. In 2009, the United Nations Office on Drugs and Crime reported that approximately 79 percent of human-trafficking incidents worldwide involve sexual exploitation; most of the victims are women and girls. The women involved are rarely left alone, making it difficult to pass information to them. The Public Practice Studio at the University of Washington, Seattle, attempts to confront this coercive violence with Pivot, a feminine-hygiene product designed to communicate rescue information to trafficked women. Pivot consists of two sanitary pads in a box with nondescript, functional packing. Sandwiched between the pads is an insert whose simple illustration depicts how trafficked women wishing to seek help may do so. The insert contains a detachable slip, disguised as a fortune-cookie message, with the telephone number for a national portal to services and counseling. Pivot allows women to access this information at the one moment they may be left alone by their captors—in the bathroom—and then to flush away all but the telephone number, which can be pocketed for future use. Pivot is designed to be distributed by shelters, doctors, and community centers. Public Practice Studio is led by Tad Hirsch, assistant professor of interaction design, and, at the time Pivot was conceptualized, the studio's members included Mike Fretto, Kari Gaynor, Josh Nelson, Adriel Rollins, and Melanie Wang—all students in the University of Washington's Division of Design.

Shandra Woworuntu and Christopher L. Heuertz

I'm a little girl dancing with butterflies in the garden. I hold a blossom and lift up the corner of my tiny, floral-print summer dress while singing, "Little butterfly, where do you go?" I'm a typical ten-year-old girl who loves to play in the river, letting the current take me out to sea. Climbing to the top of an oak tree, looking down at what seems to be the bottom of the earth, I reach out to grab the stars under the moonlight of the Indonesian night sky.

Everything is beautiful.

Everything is perfect.

Suddenly I awake. Not in a garden or by the banks of a river, and certainly not in an old oak tree. Not even in Indonesia. I find myself locked in a cold, dark room. Cigarette smoke burns my eyes. The smell of sweat on the sheet I lie on is repulsive.

From a dream to a living nightmare, in an instant.

Just months earlier my anxious fingers danced on the keyboard at the international bank where I worked. Then my concern was tracking the stock market's pulse. Currency and exchange-rate speculation kept me awake at night. Now what keeps me up is fear.

I'm not alone. I scan the room and notice that many of the other trapped women are much younger than I am. I'm no longer surprised to see their bruised faces, fresh wounds, and pale complexions due to untreated illnesses and malnourishment. One of the younger girls starts sobbing. There's nothing I can do; there's nothing anyone can do. Unlike her, I've learned to cry on the inside, keeping my tears to myself.

And the guns. My traffickers think the guns are what scare us, what keep us subservient. But for some of us a bullet would bring relief. At least death by bullet would offer a quicker, more humane death than the one we die slowly as sex slaves. Still the guns are a symbol of control, an illusion of power.

The humiliation I feel from strangers gazing at my naked body forces me back to the dream. The memories of dancing with those butterflies keep me distracted, keep part of me alive. When they put a gun to my head, I return to those butterflies, asking them to chase the fear away.

I feel so small.

I am nothing.

I am lost.

My life is over.

What have they done to me? Deprived of food, locked in darkness, barely clothed . . . I am powerless.

My nose is filled with the residue of the cocaine they've forced me to sniff, the lingering odor of marijuana smoke hanging in the air, and the bittersweet traces of the crack I was made to smoke. My throat burns with the taste of stiff, cheap whiskey—one of the only things they offer to nourish my weak body.

Sleep deprived and fading in and out of consciousness, I'm forced to serve any paying client, men old and young, fat and lean—their money unites them as buyers, reducing me to a commodity.

They throw me down on the dirty mattress; the stench of it has made me vomit more than once. Sometimes they turn me around and have their way with me; at least like this, I don't have to see the evil in their eyes. When I'm on my back, I blankly stare at the ceiling, allowing my tears to fall down the sides of my face while praying the clients will finish quickly. I've become their human rag doll, one with a $30,000 debt.

When they're finished, I'm moved to another room; maybe it's a hotel or an apartment building. All I know is that my captors' routine is to transfer me under a cloak of darkness. Always at night when the city seems so quiet, so distant.

I wonder: How many others suffer this same hell? How many more were lied to? How many young women in New York are hidden away and forced to give up tiny pieces of their soul one trick at a time?

And then—a glimmer of hope. A spark of courage ignites something within me. I am determined. I will find a way out. I will find my way home.

From a tiny bathroom window in a second-story apartment building I jump. The fresh air. A split-second of freedom. I am that butterfly from my dreams.

I am free.

Shandra Woworuntu is a legislative lobbyist in Washington, D.C., and an advocate on behalf of anti-human-trafficking groups. Christopher L. Heuertz is an activist who has worked alongside organizations in Bolivia, India, Moldova, Romania, and Thailand to establish small businesses and microenterprise initiatives as alternative incomes for women working in the sex industry.

Q: Can humankind's capacity to enslave fellow humans ever be mitigated or stopped through design?

COMMENT 1. Kristina Parsons:
Perhaps effectively combating this violence is a question of access and disruption. Pivot addresses the issue of communicating help to those who are brutally and forcibly cut off from the world through a simple, informative graphic. This covert slip of paper is able to infiltrate a system that subjugates and dehumanizes people through the human-trafficking trade. What if we could imagine a world where disruptive innovation isn't just targeted toward subverting commercial systems like taxi or entertainment services, but rather toward dismantling the ubiquitous violence that too often goes unseen? In the end, disrupting the trafficking industry not only has the ability to rescue and empower, but to liberate.

Opposite and right: Mike Fretto (American, born 1982), Kari Gaynor (American, born 1984), Tad Hirsch (American, born 1970), Josh Nelson (American, born 1978), Adriel Rollins (American, born 1976), and Melanie Wang (American, born 1975) of Public Practice Studio (USA, est. 2012). Pivot. 2012–13. Sanitary pad, water-soluble paper, cardboard box, overall 4 ⅜ x 3 x 1" (11.1 x 7.6 x 2.5 cm)

Below: Contact information for a national human-trafficking hotline disguised as a fortune-cookie slip

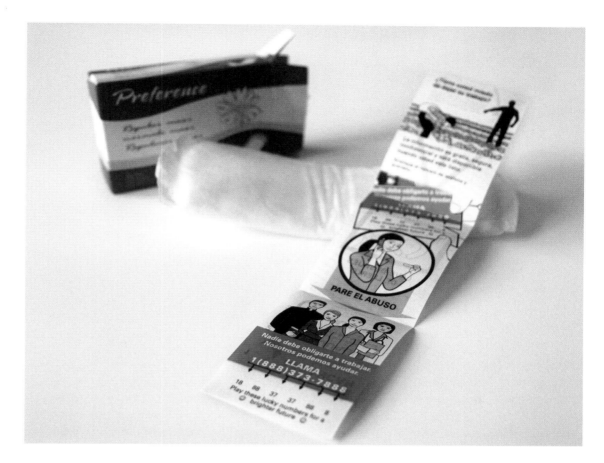

Hacked Protest Objects
(Various designers, ongoing)

Tunisian street vendor Mohamed Bouazizi set himself alight on December 17, 2010, after being repeatedly harassed by Tunisian authorities. His act galvanized the Tunisian revolution, the wider Arab Spring, and, in part, the Occupy protests across Europe and America. Although each of these movements adopted a unique set of goals and yielded varied consequences, the protests remain connected in many ways, including, as designer Carlotta Werner and artist Johanna Sunder-Plassmann highlight here, their use of everyday objects that have been hacked. These objects take many forms and are created for various ends. In Cairo, chemical spray bottles held to the eyes of protesters may at first suggest violence but are revealed instead to mitigate its effects. In Hamburg, the seemingly benign toilet brush symbolizes public anger. In Kiev, the baseball bat morphs from a sporting implement into a punitive weapon decorated with protest slogans. Bouazizi's self-immolation underscores the grassroots and often desperate nature of these acts of repurposing: as unrest continues in Syria, Nigeria, Thailand, and elsewhere, protesters will use any means at their disposal, from mundane objects to their own invaluable lives.

Carlotta Werner and Johanna Sunder-Plassmann

Istanbul, September 2013, nighttime: I find myself among a crowd, unaware that the ongoing Taksim Gezi Park protests against Prime Minister Recep Tayyip Erdoğan's government have shifted to the Asian quarter of the city. Tear gas— my lungs are burning. A man next to me holds a bottle of household cleaner and sprays its contents into his girlfriend's eyes. I am shocked by his violent act but no one else is, and soon it's clear why: the cleaning agent is actually milk mixed with water and is used to ease the effect of tear gas on the eyes.

During the next few days, I notice that many more everyday objects have been modified or hacked for use in the protests. Although I am visiting from my native Germany, from 2010 to 2011 I lived in Istanbul, and so share with my Turkish friends a common understanding of the objects around us. Since the protests started, however, many everyday objects have taken on an added layer of meaning. Cleaning-spray bottles have turned into medical supplies. Painting respirators have become teargas protectors, as well as fashionable accessories that identify people as protesters. Later, these respirators would become decorative objects in the protesters' flats. Goggles, scarves, and plastic bottles— their intended uses have also changed.

The emergence of these modified everyday objects is an epiphenomenon of the political protests in Istanbul. Born of necessity, these newly transformed objects help the protesters cope with many different tasks. They protect the body and provide first aid. They allow individuals to announce events and to organize demonstrations; to identify with or dissociate from a group; to defend, attack, and provoke.

Designed by individuals outgunned and facing professional, well-equipped forces, the hacked objects share some common features: they are readily and cheaply available, and they appear and disappear as they change their symbolic and practical meanings. Made in reaction to suddenly changing social circumstances, these objects convey information about the mode and nature of the protests themselves, including their level of violence; their subgroups and organizational forms; and the protestors' means of communication. They also recall, or stand in as symbols for, past events of particular significance, as well

as the changed nature of civic and social relationships among protesters and in the city at large.

The phenomenon of hacked objects is not unique to Taksim. Protesters in Tahrir Square in Cairo used reflective safety vests to identify themselves as members of the self-organized community group Tahrir Bodyguards. Reacting to the numerous instances of sexual harassment that occurred during the protests, the group organized in order to protect female demonstrators. In Maidan, the central square in Kiev, self-made and archaic-looking weapons speak to the brutal violence of this protest-turned-conflict. Some of the altered clubs and bats are decorated with nationalistic writings or Christian symbols, revealing the personal attachments of the owners to their objects. In Hamburg's so-called danger zone, toilet brushes became an ironic symbol of unjustified police control. Hours after a short video aired on national television showing a policeman confiscating a toilet brush from a demonstrator—the person had legally obtained the brush and was doing no harm with it—toilet brushes sold out of stores as demonstrators carried them into the streets. This event evoked a creative wave of digital image alterations, graphic illustrations, and caricatures.

The sheer variety of repurposed objects is proof of the creativity and ingenuity that arise in mass movements. What do these objects reveal about both the differences and similarities among the various protests and their respective geographic locations? How do social media influence the distribution of these objects and their local adaptations?

The research project Hacked Objects in Political Protests invites everyone to contribute images, videos, objects, and stories of participation from protests around the world, along with the designs born in tandem with these protests. The project will discuss and reflect on this globally crowdsourced design process. A spray bottle is not just a spray bottle anymore.

Carlotta Werner and Johanna Sunder-Plassmann are a German product-designer and media-artist team.

Q: Do you know of any other seemingly neutral objects that can step up and become heroes in times of need?

COMMENT 1. Josh MacPhee:
Social movements have been repurposing everyday items for as long as capitalism has been producing them. The wooden shoe, or sabot, was shoved into early machinery at the advent of the Industrial Revolution. The mass-produced glass bottle was likely converted into the molotov cocktail early on in its lifespan (at least as early as the 1930s). For that matter, the Christian cross was repurposed by the Romans as a tool to punish enemies of the state—long before the advent of capitalism or mass production. . . . Struggles to create and uphold systems of value other than monetary profit are always in tension with the capitalist economic imperative to crush and/or to recuperate these alternative systems.

Assorted consumer-product bottles
hacked for use in protests, Istanbul,
Turkey. 2014

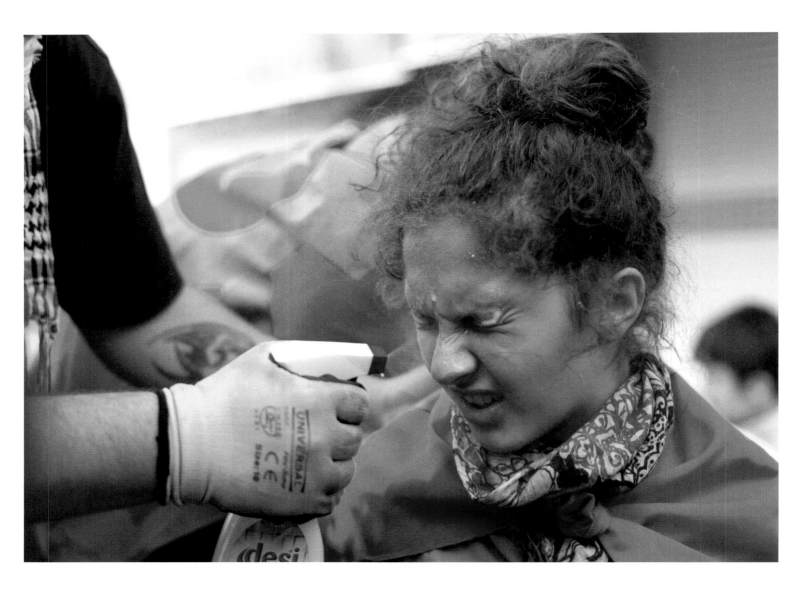

Toilet brush at a protest, Hamburg,
Germany. 2014

The Crisis of Credit Visualized
(Jonathan Jarvis, 2009)

It is hard to think of a single institution or individual who has not been affected by the global economic crisis that began in 2007. Yet, for many, including those who suffered the consequences most directly, deciphering the complex systems that caused the collapse seems nearly impossible. But knowledge is power, even as these shadowy banking practices continue. Jonathan Jarvis's animated video *The Crisis of Credit Visualized* demystifies terms such as the Glass-Steagall Act and subprime lending; the fraught relationships between the banking system's various stakeholders; and the casualties left in the wake of the system's collapse. His is design in the service of public good, one weapon among many in the arsenal sorely needed to combat the economic violence preoccupying us all.

Gillian Tett

Knowledge is power. Or so the old adage goes. And during recent decades, Wall Street has utilized that timeless principle to its benefit—and to its vast profit. For as finance has swelled in scale and complexity, the number of people who actually understand how this modern, shadowy behemoth works has shrunk.

Little wonder, then, that most politicians, journalists, pundits, and ordinary voters failed to see the size of the credit bubble last decade; or that most people were utterly shocked and baffled when that bubble burst, causing pain for millions of Americans. In our twenty-first-century society, finance has become akin to weather: something deeply capricious that affects all of our lives, but which few of us can understand or predict. Control has sat in the hands of a tiny, technocratic elite.

But this is what makes Jonathan Jarvis's animated video *The Crisis of Credit Visualized* so interesting and compelling, if not subversive. His art uses simple graphics, catchy images, striking messages—and a wonderfully irreverent shade of green. And by combining these everyday images, he makes the complexities of finance seem accessible. Breezy cartoons blow apart gravitas, undermining the aura of experts. This is pop banking as it affects us all.

By stripping finance of its pretension and complexity, his video makes two important points: Firstly, the madness of the credit bubble cannot be blamed on just one or two people; an entire system was at fault, interlinked through financial flows (or, in the case of his art, stick figures, boxes, and arrows). Secondly, when the aura of mystery is stripped away from this network of financial flows, it is clear just how unsustainable the entire system had become; the comic nature of the trading patterns shows us that a collapse was inevitable.

Indeed, in retrospect, the only thing that is more striking than the scale of last decade's credit bubble is the fact that the madness went unnoticed so long. Or to put it another way: if more people such as Jarvis had produced videos like this one a decade ago, with chirpy green screens and laughable stick-figure bankers, the public might never have turned such a blind eye to finance and allowed the bubble swell to such a monstrous size. And that would have been better for us all; even (or especially) those stick-figure bankers.

As assistant editor and columnist, Gillian Tett writes two weekly columns for the *Financial Times*, covering a range of economic, financial, political, and social issues throughout the globe.

Jonathan Jarvis (American, born 1984). Media Design Program (est. 2000). Art Center College of Design, Pasadena, California (est. 1930). *The Crisis of Credit Visualized*. 2009. Digital video (color, sound), 11:10 min.

Q: This project defines violence as a manifestation of the power to alter circumstances against the will of others and to their detriment. In light of this definition, can we regard the financial sector's actions that led to the credit bubble as overt violence?

COMMENT 1. B Comenius:
Ancient teachings equate the game of credit creation and erasure to violence. You can find that interest-bearing money was banned in Vedas, Buddhist, and Muslim teachings. It was banned in Christian teachings, too. There was a reason for this.

COMMENT 2. Steffi Duarte:
Like the interconnected web of motivations and systems that triggered the credit bubble itself, the classification of the financial sector's actions as overtly violent may seem complex. Yet, through actions and illustrations like those of Jonathan Jarvis—through design—we can come closer to an answer, and eliminate the information asymmetry that made so many people unwilling players.

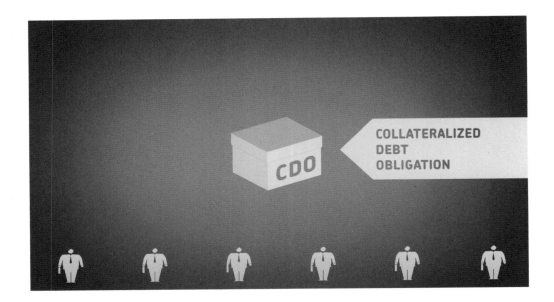

Left and opposite:
Jonathan Jarvis. Media Design Program.
Art Center College of Design, Pasadena,
California. *The Crisis of Credit Visualized.*
2009

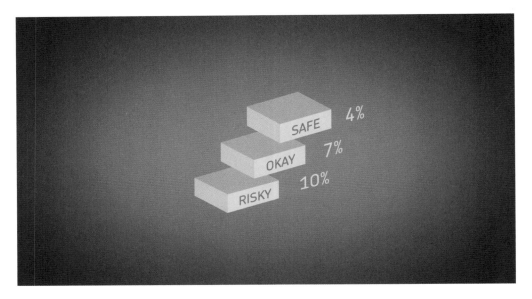

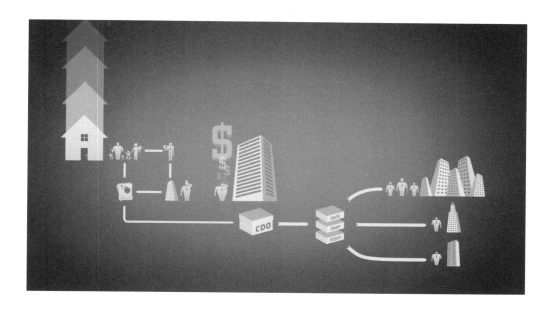

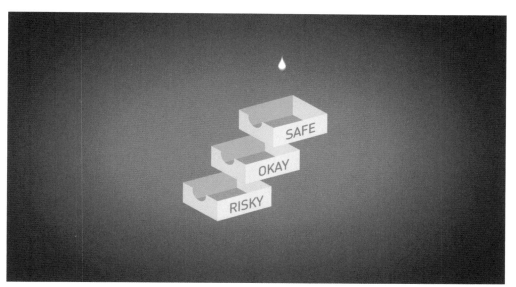

The Liberator
(Defense Distributed, 2013)

Defense Distributed, a Texas-based nonprofit group, was formed in 2012 with the goal of creating a firearm that anyone could fabricate using a 3-D printer. Invoking civil liberties, and challenging notions of gun control and perceived information censorship, the group created a block-like, .380-caliber polymer gun printed in sixteen pieces, now known as The Liberator. Their project trumpeted newly available 3-D-printing technologies as tools of political and social subversion. The 3-D weapon's fabrication files were immediately made available online where they were downloaded over one hundred thousand times before the State Department Office of Defense Trade Controls Compliance, adhering to arms-export control regulations, forced their removal from the web. On May 1, 2014, Defense Distributed released a Bitcoin application called Dark Wallet that allows the digital currency to change hands anonymously. Part of a larger umbrella strategy called Dark Market, this crypto-anarchist provocation highlights The Liberator as but one design in an arsenal of weapons built to disrupt regulatory systems and entrenched modes of governance.

Rob Walker

Cody Wilson first demonstrated The Liberator for the masses on May 5, 2013, by way of a YouTube video and a barrage of media coverage. It was a curious-looking pistol, cream colored and blocky, but it appeared to work. This was remarkable, because this deadly object was built almost entirely from plastic parts produced by a 3-D printer. ("Almost" because its design included a common nail that served as the firing pin.)

The implications were clear enough. We'd already been hearing, for years, how 3-D printers could enter our lives as an efficient, humane, and empowering alternative to mass manufacturing. Now Wilson's video suggested that the very same techno-magic that produced fun toys and handy housewares could also be used to whip up a functioning firearm. The design plans were made available online and downloaded one hundred thousand times before the government intervened (and the plans, of course, resurfaced via unofficial channels).

It's possible that, as an actual weapon, The Liberator is overrated. It still requires traditional ammunition, not to mention a rather expensive 3-D printer. And at least one set of police tests found it had a tendency to essentially blow up on discharge. But if we concede that it nevertheless appears capable of the core task of inflicting violent damage, then I think we can only conclude that it is a highly successful design.

That's because the real function of The Liberator has very little to do with making an excellent weapon and everything to do with making a point. Wilson, whose work on the gun competed with his law school studies, is a strident libertarian. He might choose a different label, but clearly his project means to express a point of view about the individual's relationship to the state in general and to gun regulation specifically. Thus The Liberator—consistent with its self-important name—has been promoted with bombastic, sometimes bellicose, and essentially propagandistic rhetoric and aesthetics. Wilson and his associates, for instance, operate under the name Defense Distributed. They are freedom-loving rebels, you see.

This is why it's almost more useful to think of The Liberator not as an object but as an example of "design fiction"—the practice of devising plans for or prototypes of objects and systems that, while impractical, express some critique

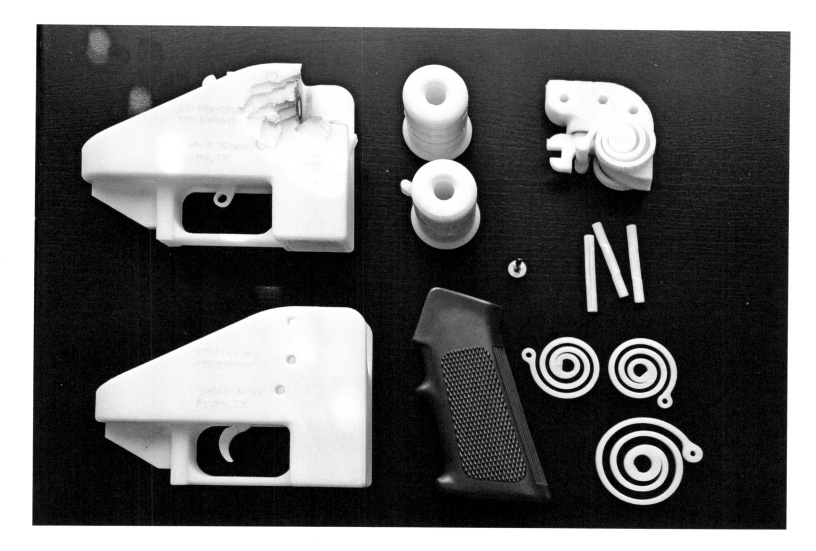

Partial components of The Liberator (clockwise from top left): ABSplus thermoplastic frame, barrel, hammer body, frame pins, springs, grip; aluminum nail (center)

Defense Distributed (USA, est. 2012). The Liberator. 2013. CAD files; ABSplus thermoplastic pistol and aluminum nail, 2 ½ x 8 ½" (6.4 x 21.6 cm)

of the present or vision of the future. It's a trendy strategy these days, but the politics behind it tend toward the progressive. Similarly, tech enthusiasts who have rhapsodized about the "disruptive" possibilities of 3-D printing and who frequently strike quasi-libertarian notes have largely recoiled from Wilson and his Liberator, preferring to focus on happy and optimistic scenarios involving home-made alternatives to mass consumer goods or the creation of clever art objects. To them, Wilson and the controversies he courts are mucking up their project, setting back their progress, spoiling their utopia.

But really, Wilson has done nothing more than call the enthusiasts' bluff. He didn't subvert the dream of a future where we can all manufacture whatever we want, whenever we like—he hijacked it. And in doing so, he made plain the full stakes of that dream, something that should probably happen more often in our global discourse about how to reckon with technology's powers.

I don't share Wilson's politics, so I'm somewhat sympathetic to the tech-nologists' frustration with his effect on 3-D printing as an idea. But I wish they would recognize that there's something more important going on here: Wilson is not out to thwart someone else's utopia; he is pursuing his own. And with The Liberator, he's made his vision so clear that it deserves—demands, even—a considered and reasoned response that accounts for the full implications of the system he has so cunningly exploited.

For a design provocation, there is no higher goal.

Rob Walker is a technology and culture columnist for *Yahoo Tech*.

Q: Is there such a thing as a right to violence?

COMMENT 1. Anne Burdick:
The real threat behind this gun—and behind all open systems—is to the governments, corporations, and institutions that have histori-cally controlled the means of production, distribution, and access. Regardless of whether the gun works right now, crowdsourcing has proven to be quite reliable, and a 3-D gun better than you can imagine will appear soon enough.

COMMENT 2. James Auger:
I have to admit that I am jealous—The Liberator is the perfect speculative-design piece, extrapolating the potential of a disruptive technology to suggest and communicate a plausible future use.

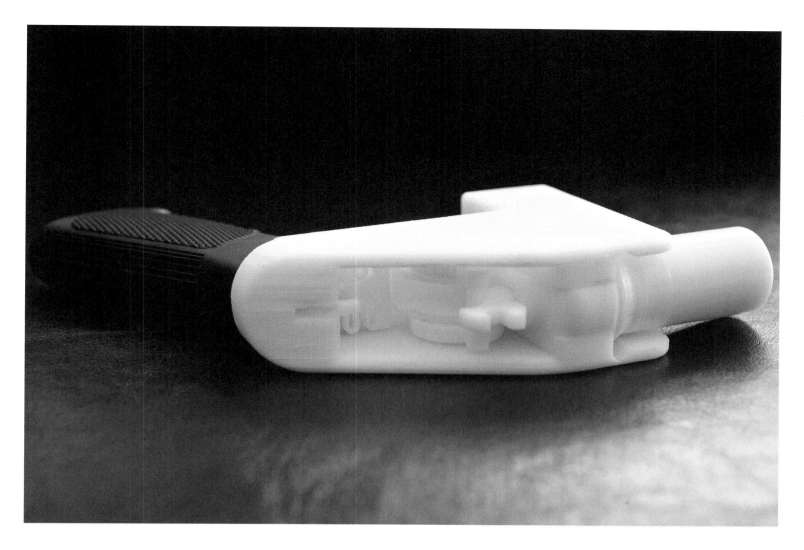

Defense Distributed. The Liberator
(barrel view). 2013

HonestAds
(Harriett Levin Balkind, 2014)

The connection between politics and truth is shaky at best and quite often nonexistent. Politicians and their strategists are masters of spin who contort everything from campaign promises to personal peccadilloes. Political lies are pernicious; they undermine public trust in government and in the perceived relevance of the democratic process. Their cost is literal, too. Around 75 percent of campaign funding in the United States is spent on political advertising, and those with the deepest pockets can shout the loudest. The ensuing cacophony often includes false statements and unwarranted smears that stick long enough to cause damage at the ballot boxes. Enter HonestAds, a nonpartisan web-based platform designed by brand and marketing consultant Harriett Levin Balkind. HonestAds intends to ignite conversation about disinformation across the political spectrum and to galvanize voters to demand from politicians more transparent and truthful publicity. Balkind reasons that if truth-in-advertising laws prevent us from lying to sell toilet paper, then we shouldn't be allowed to lie to sway votes.

Leslie Savan

Most ads lie. But there are Big Lies and Little Lies. A Big Lie is a claim so subjective or inherently unprovable—like, for instance, "This beer will make you a babe magnet"—that, no matter how ludicrous, is not legally actionable.

On the other hand, Little Lies are objective claims that can be proven true or not—like, "This beer will make you lose weight"—and they could land you in court.

But there's one kind of advertising where even Little Lies can be told with impunity, and that's in a candidate's political campaign. Under the First Amendment, candidates can tell the most deceptive whoppers—e.g. "My opponent dumped rat poison into the beer you're drinking"—and, while they may or may not receive public opprobrium, it's perfectly legal.

"Laws protecting consumers from false advertising of products are enforced pretty vigorously," journalist Brooks Jackson writes on FactCheck.org. But political candidates "can legally lie about almost anything they want. In fact, the Federal Communications Act even *requires* broadcasters who run candidate ads to show them uncensored, even if the broadcasters believe their content to be offensive or false."[1]

Political groups, as opposed to individual candidates, don't carry such a get-out-of-court-free card. But that may be changing. The Supreme Court recently ruled unanimously that the antiabortion group Susan B. Anthony List has standing to challenge a state law in Ohio prohibiting false statements about political candidates (a law Justice Antonin Scalia mocked as coming from the Orwellian "Ministry of Truth").

The usual ways to counter lying political ads help only around the edges. You can sue for defamation, for instance, but by the time a suit winds its way through the legal system, the lying candidate may have already won election and reelection.

Political fact-checking sites and newspaper blogs, like the aforementioned FactCheck.org and the *Washington Post*'s "Fact Checker," are proliferating and have been the prime way to call out the lies. The sites have mixed results. On occasion, if a lying ad generates enough bad publicity, it could be pulled; just as often, the fact-checked findings are quoted in the lied-about party's ads—where they may be used to further distort reality.

But a new group, HonestAds, is trying a completely different tack: it targets the political consultants, ad agencies, directors, actors, and writers who make

Harriett Levin Balkind (American, born 1945). HonestAds. 2014. HTML5, CSS3, and JavaScript

the truth-torturing ads in the first place.

"HonestAds is a group of pissed off, tuned in citizens who refuse to be lied to by politicians any longer," its website reads. "We're not out to change laws. We're out to take action and demand the truth."

HonestAds founder Harriett Levin Balkind, who has previously worked in brand strategy and communications, wrote to me in a July 2014 email that she hopes to "appeal to the advertising and media community in such a way that they will get on board with this. There are lots of reasons they should want to." For one, "It's becoming more difficult to attract young talent and one reason is because of their desire for truth, justice, and authenticity," she says, referring to findings from a McCann Worldgroup study.[2]

HonestAds' debut video makes that point. In *Candid Camera*–like fashion, they got a real actress to do the voiceover for a fake candidate; a fake political consultant instructs her to tweak the copy until it becomes outright false. The actress, clearly disgusted, tells him, "I know the studio time is very expensive . . . but I'm not OK with not telling the truth."

That is, she refused to lie even though it would have cost her a money-paying gig.

If—and it's a big if—HonestAds can gain momentum, it could trigger a refreshing rebellion among the more conscious descendants of *Mad Men*.

Leslie Savan is a writer and critic currently blogging about media and politics for the *Nation*.

1. Brooks Jackson, "False Ads: There Oughta Be a Law!—Or Maybe Not," FactCheck.org, http://www.factcheck.org/2004/06/false-ads-there-oughta-be-a-law-or-maybe-not.
2. McCann Worldgroup, *The Truth about Youth*, May 2011, http://www.scribd.com/doc/56263899/McCann-Worldgroup-Truth-About-Youth.

Q: Which is more violent—one Big Lie or one hundred Little Lies?

COMMENT 1. Simha Gulkarov:
. . . William Lutz wrote about "weasel words" [see Doublespeak (1990)]—words that hold no weight, but are used in the advertising world to sell things—all with little lies. For example, the word "help" can change the meaning of something. "Help" means to aid or assist, but consumers purchase things when advertisements use the word "help" because they imagine the immediate elimination of their problem. "Helps keep you looking young" is a phrase cosmetic ads use with the obvious intention of selling their products, but the people buying these products think they will get relief from their old age. . . . It seems the only solution is to open the eyes of consumers . . . it is we the consumers who need to become aware.

IR8
(International Rice Research Institute, 1962–63)

In the mid-twentieth century, as the world's rapidly growing population provoked concerns of imminent global famine, scientists of many nationalities united to redesign agricultural practices and increase crop productivity. The result was newly mechanized agricultural technologies used in tandem with grains genetically modified to be higher yielding and disease resistant (including those developed by American scientist Norman Borlaug who won a Nobel prize for his work). These efforts, which came to be known as the Green Revolution, were concentrated primarily in Asian and Latin American countries with developing infrastructures, and led to a massive boom in crop productivity from the late 1960s onward. In 1962, the International Rice Research Institute (IRRI), at the University of the Philippines's Los Baños site, produced a genetically modified high-yield rice dubbed "IR8." (Later the plant would be commonly referred to as "Miracle Rice.") But cultivating this rice requires an excess of nitrogen fertilizers, pesticides, and intensive irrigation; while IR8 and other Green Revolution technologies have greatly increased global food production, their use has not been without significant impact on local and global ecosystems and economic structures. The full effects of the Green Revolution are elusive, complex, and yet to be realized. Today, a second iteration of the Green Revolution continues to develop in China, and Green Revolution ideas are now being introduced in Africa.

Bruce Nussbaum

It haunts me still. I was twenty-one years old when I participated in a design research project that ultimately saved millions of people from starvation—but it did so by sacrificing the good of many along the way, and I've often wondered about the project's true cost.

I was in the Peace Corps in the Philippines in the late 1960s when the International Rice Research Institute (IRRI), an NGO established by the Ford and Rockefeller foundations, was designing new varieties of rice. One such cultivar, dubbed "IR8," or "Miracle Rice," basically tripled rice yields, and, together with versions of "Miracle Wheat" and other grains, significantly diminished the number of famines worldwide (the natural, climate-induced kind that happened with depressing regularity for nearly as long as humans have populated the earth). The design of the new rice was a massive breakthrough that we now take for granted.

At that time I was teaching third-grade science in Caloocan City, outside of Manila, and I traveled south to the institute's headquarters in Los Baños, where Miracle Rice was being tested. The scientists from Ford and Rockefeller, with support from the United States Agency for International Development (USAID) and large chemical companies, were in the last stages of analyzing the newly designed rice plant. I assisted with a study comparing the efficacy of using water buffalo versus small Japanese tractors to cultivate rice fields with the new seed. Water buffalo had long been used in Asia to plow and level land, puddle rice fields, and cultivate field crops, all while providing no-cost fertilizer. Japanese planting tractors, on the other hand, had been recently introduced to help farmers save on labor time, since mechanized tillage requires fewer field laborers for the same output. I still remember how wonderful the warm, deep mud felt on my legs as I moved across the paddy, and how scared I was of the venomous paddy snakes that were known for biting between the toes. I was happy to participate in the final testing.

In the end the Japanese tractors proved more efficient; but, as with Miracle Rice, their use had unforeseen outcomes. Soon it would become clear that, in designing new rice seeds, the scientists had also designed new growing requirements. Miracle Rice needs much more water, fertilizer, insecticide, and, in part

Field of IR8 rice plants, Los Baños, Philippines. 1966

because of its increased reliance on tractors, more fuel to grow than do other rice varieties. The Green Revolution, as this new method of high-yield agriculture came to be called, could triple production, but the new growing requirements also meant higher costs—financially, but also socially and environmentally.

In the months before Los Baños, I had begun going up into the mountains of Pampanga and Tarlac in the region of central Luzon. At that time, the country's handful of oligarchic families, who effectively dominated the political system and ran the country, presided over enormous feudal landholdings in the region. There were still many small peasant farms, however, and people were eager to own their own land. When the government began to roll out Miracle Rice, these small farmers could not compete against the oligarchs who had access to both the financing and water needed to sustain the new crop. Promises of special loan programs enabling small farmers to buy pesticides, fertilizer, and fuel for the new tractors never materialized on any significant scale. Water buffalo, one of the only sources of capital wealth, depreciated in value. Small farmers were squeezed and, in the end, lost their land to the oligarchs. The design of Miracle Rice was for these peasants a disaster.

Historically, Luzon had been a center of rebellion in the country, with peasants rising up against the country's dominant families to reclaim the land that was taken from them. The Hukbalahap insurgency in the 1950s, for instance, which nearly brought the Philippines government to collapse, was centered in this region. With the introduction of Miracle Rice, central Luzon exploded once again. The first article I ever wrote as a journalist was for the *Far Eastern Economic Review* and was titled "How the Green Revolution Turned Red."

It would be many years before I would again become involved in the field of design (I now consult, write, and teach on subjects in design, innovation, and creativity). Yet the violence that resulted from the invention of this new food crop has always tempered my view of the optimism that is so much a part of design culture. The profession proclaims good intentions; and we must be fully aware of what harm good intentions may sometimes bring.

Bruce Nussbaum is professor of innovation and design at Parsons The New School of Design.

Q: Does this kind of design actually lessen the threat of global famine or merely leave space for greater disaster?

COMMENT 1. Harry Rhoades:
I don't know if one can claim genetic modification is always violent, but this nudge to evolution doesn't allow time for adaptation the way "normal" evolution allows.

IRRI scientists Peter R. Jennings and
Henry "Hank" M. Beachell join IRRI director
Robert Chandler, Philippine president
Ferdinand E. Marcos, and U.S. president
Lyndon B. Johnson in a field of IR8 rice
plants (left to right), Los Baños, Philippines.
1966

Menstruation Machine
(Sputniko!, 2010)

With Menstruation Machine, Sputniko! explores the relationship between identity, biology, and choice, while also probing the meaning of gender-specific rituals. The metal device, which resembles a chastity belt, is equipped with a blood-dispensing system and electrodes that stimulate the lower abdomen, replicating the cramping and bleeding of the average five-day menstruation period. It is designed to be worn by men, children, postmenopausal women, and whoever else wants to experience menstruation. An accompanying video is about Takashi, a young man who wants to understand both physiologically and psychologically what it feels like to be a girl. Takashi builds the Menstruation Machine and wears it out on the town with a girlfriend, strutting around a shopping mall and occasionally doubling over in pain. Thus an internal, private process is transformed into a wearable display of identity. Since the 1960s, advances in hormone-based contraception that suppress ovulation have challenged the biological necessity of monthly periods. Sputniko! notes that the Menstruation Machine may be particularly desirable in a future in which menstruation becomes obsolete.

Elizabeth Grosz

The menstrual machine is the machine that produces all that is living. A body comes only from another body, or from several bodies. Every living thing has its own kind of blood, its own forms of circulation, nutrition, reproduction, sexuality, excess. Everything bleeds in its own way—even the earth itself as it creates new forms of land, new orders of sea. The earth's blood is volcanic blood. We can write and paint with blood, a congealing, tracing, supporting, oozing liquid. It may be, along with milk, what conditions all writing and makes possible all art, even as it dries up in its support for the emergence of these things. All of the universe is made of liquids moving at slower or faster speeds, at lower or higher temperatures, and with greater or lesser force. This is how new planets and universes are created, bleeding minerals and energies from a great leak in space and time.

Menstrual blood leaks from a uterus. This is true of developed primates and of bats. Females leak menstrual blood. Freud contentiously claimed that it was the cause of women's shame and the trigger for their art-making, especially weaving, a uniquely female art in his consideration. Women's "shame" constitutes their art-making potentiality. Their blood leaks everywhere, infecting everything, every living being, with the marks of birth, the ties of lineage that connect and infect generations, and that trace life. It is the blood that nourishes emerging life. We now have medications that can temporarily or permanently delay or prevent menstruation, a great boon to birth control; but menstrual blood is a fluid connection that is now threatened through its chemical regulation. We still bleed in other ways; we still require to be brought into being, to be nested, nurtured, developed. Even with machines that function as prosthetic augmentations of our bodies, as devices that permeate our bodies, we need to continue our blood-filled lives. Even machines bleed.

To hack is to infect—to overtake one program, purpose, trace, or path with another. Hacking existed long before there were codes, written programs, or even language, and long before there were humans: life is hacked, made as it is from infections, contagions, and crossings of unlike things that came somehow to inhabit or to be inhabited by one another. Life is chemistry infected with a temporary coherence and cohesion, which nevertheless leaks, sheds its insides

Sputniko! (British and Japanese, born Japan 1985). Design Interactions Department (est. 1989). Royal College of Art (UK, est. 1837). Menstruation Machine–Takashi's Take. 2010. Installation with video (color, sound), screens, and printed panels, 3:24 min., dimensions variable; device: aluminum, electronics, and acrylic, 13 3/8 x 13 13/16 x 13 3/8" (34 x 35 x 34 cm)

Sputniko!. Design Interactions Department. Royal College of Art. Menstruation Machine–Takashi's Take. 2010

and its surfaces now and then, and renews itself by exchanges sometimes (often) violent between what is inside it (whether it is a cell's inner structure or a complex being's organs) and what is outside it (a milieu or environment in which life and nonlife participate without reciprocity). In order to thrive, to enjoy, to expand, to make art, life must live both sides of the boundary (skin, cell wall, carapace) that enables it to exist. This is why leakage and hacking are possible and effective: the contamination of inside by outside, and vice versa, is creative, enhancing, estranging. It leads life beyond its boundaries to encounter objects, things, practices outside of itself, things that enhance or diminish it in particular ways. These encounters, infections, or hacks are the condition not only of life but of life living beyond itself; that is, a life capable of art—of feeling itself and sensing itself, not just acting on or regulating itself but expanding itself through its relations to a world.

Elizabeth Grosz is the Jean Fox O'Barr Women's Studies Professor in Trinity College of Arts and Sciences in the Women's Studies and Literature programs at Duke University.

Q: When we change our biological templates, are we doing violence to nature, or are we offering a path to mutual empathy?

COMMENT 1. Chris Bobel:
I think there are limits [to empathy]. My capacity to experience something outside myself is very limited, but I think we should strive to get as close to the experience of someone else as possible as long as we respect the boundary or fact that we can only experience a dimension, a partial reality. We have to carefully examine the intent behind that exploration. Am I trying to encounter you so that I can dismiss you? Is it a fetish? What is inspiring the exercise?

Control

To use power or violence in order to discipline, dominate, or restrict one's own or another's ability to act with free will.

Nirbheek Pistol
(Ordnance Factories Board, 2014)

On December 16, 2012, a brutal sexual assault occurred in Delhi, India. A young woman, traveling home on a bus after watching a movie with a friend, was beaten, gang-raped, and thrown naked into the street. The young woman, who later became known to the public as *Nirbhaya,* or "Fearless," died two weeks later as a result of her injuries; her male companion, who was also severely beaten, survived. The vicious attack drew widespread condemnation and quickly garnered media attention around the world. In response to the charged climate, the Ordnance Factories Board, a subbranch of the Indian government's Ministry of Defense, developed a lightweight revolver called *Nirbheek* (a synonym for Nirbhaya). The pistol was marketed specially to women, and its makers claimed the design would guard against sexual assaults. Since its release in January 2014, however, numerous objections have been raised in response to the design, not least over the inference that women must protect themselves from the status quo rather than change it, whether by agitating for legal protections, policy changes, or more progressive cultural attitudes. Sexual violence against women is endemic to cultures the world over, and it is estimated that the majority of such attacks remain either unreported or unprosecuted. (The trial that eventually brought Nirbhaya's rapists to justice was a rare case in India at the time.) Despite the controversial design intervention, more than two years after Nirbhaya's death the legacy of her ordeal remains uncertain.

Nivedita Menon

From the branches of a mango tree, in its spreading shade on a hot May morning in the north Indian village of Katra Shahadatganj, the bodies of two teenage women dangle. They have been abducted, raped, and hanged by their necks. The men arrested for their rape and murder, including two policemen, are from the women's own village, from a locally more dominant caste than theirs, although they all belong to a set of intermediate castes that in the alphabet soup of Indian bureaucratese is termed OBC—Other Backward Classes.

Meanwhile, routinely, Dalit women—lower than OBCs in the caste hierarchy and still treated as "untouchable," although untouchability has been abolished by the Indian constitution—are just touchable enough to be raped, often killed, in villages, largely by OBC men who are economically more powerful, though "backward" themselves. *Dalit* literally means "oppressed," but it's a political identity militantly taken on by the former untouchable castes.

Rape is a way of teaching Dalits their place—since they seem to be in danger of forgetting.

Women—whatever their class, whatever their caste—seem to be in danger. Of forgetting their place. Of facing sexual violence.

From men whose houses they clean, men they meet at parties, boyfriends, men who offer to help tourists, organized "rioters" during well-planned intercommunity violence, husbands, relatives. From strangers in gangs (a man doesn't have to be physically stronger than a woman if he is many and she is one). India reports on average over twenty-two thousand rapes a year. This figure doesn't include rapes by policemen of women and transgender people—*hijras*— in their custody; nor rapes by Indian armed forces with legal impunity in large parts of India under extraordinary laws, where democratic rights are suspended.

Almost as beautiful as that shade-giving generous tree on a summer morning in Katra Shahadatganj is the delicate gun designed especially for women—small, lightweight, fitting easily into a lady's purse, with a polished wooden handle. It nests in a maroon velvet case, not unlike the kind fit for an ornate necklace, because, as the manager of the factory that makes the gun said to a journalist, "Indian women love their ornaments."[1]

The gun is named after the young paramedic who was raped and brutalized in Delhi in December 2012, whose courageous but eventually fruitless struggle for life brought thousands out on the streets in protest.

Nirbhaya. Unafraid Woman. This was the pseudonym given to her by a leading national newspaper, the *Times of India*, since she could not be named under rape laws. The gun's name, *Nirbheek*, means Unafraid.

A sleek weapon appropriately feminized, named Unafraid, for use by the woman Afraid of rape from strangers. For would you pull that gun on your boyfriend, on a policeman, on your uncle as he creeps into your bed at night?

Its cost is higher than the annual income of most Indian households. Could you afford this gleaming sinister ornament if you were that young paramedic, your father a loader at the Delhi airport? Could you afford it if you were one of the teenagers hanged to death in Katra Shahadatganj?

(Speaking of gleaming sinister power: the U.S. Ambassador-at-Large for Global Women's Issues, Catherine M. Russell, stated in a congressional hearing that the United States was "horrified"[2] at recent incidents of violence against women in India, Pakistan, and Nigeria. Chairing the hearing was Senator Barbara Boxer who said that she wrote to India's then newly elected prime minister, Narendra Modi, urging him to take immediate action to combat violence and improve the safety and security of women and girls. Presumably in our perfectly equitable world, in which one in five women in the United States have experienced rape, a Nigerian politician can write to Barack Obama, asking him to take immediate action to ensure justice in Steubenville, Ohio, or in Torrington, Connecticut, where violent, victim-blaming reactions to rape accusations have horrified the rest of the world.)

Cheaper than the gun, not beautiful like the mango tree, but its design smart as a whip, is an app—the VithU app. At the touch of a button on her phone, a woman can send alerts to designated receivers: "I'm in danger. Please follow my location."

Endorsing the app on television, the intoxicating eyes of a leading Hindi film star seek out your deepest fears: "I'm an actress, celebrity. Encircled by security, but still afraid. The criminal may not be a stranger, it could be anyone. In hotels, in elevators, in washrooms, *you cannot take your safety for granted.*"

Design to enhance fear. The sharp awareness of that delicate bulk in your handbag; the sense of that smart program embedded in your smartphone.

To feel afraid always. So you can feel safe.

How about design to make you unafraid? Spaces, institutions, minds—unraveled and made over. Design that recognizes the intricate intimacy between life and risk, for to live is always to risk something valuable. Design to galvanize that thoughtless step into the unknown. Design that animates your careless laugh as you map the world with your stride.

Nivedita Menon is a professor at the Centre for Comparative Politics and Political Theory at Jawaharlal Nehru University, Delhi.

1. Geeta Pandey, "A Gun Designed for Indian Women," *BBC News Magazine*, January 17, 2014, http://www.bbc.com/news/magazine-25727080.
2. Senate Foreign Relations Committee Hearing, "Combating Violence and Discrimination Against Women: A Global Call to Action," June 2014. See "U.S. Negotiating MoU with India on Women's Issues," *Press Trust of India*, June 26, 2014, http://ibnlive.in.com/news/us-negotiating-mou-with-india-on-womens-issues/481904-2.html.

Ordnance Factories Board (India, est. 1775). Nirbheek Pistol. 2014. Titanium-alloy .32 caliber pistol, 7 x 3" (17.8 x 7.6 cm)

Q: What does "design to make you unafraid" look like?

COMMENT 1. Manak:
A really incisive post. I feel that the problem comes when we design objects as solutions to a larger problem. The design lens needs to be applied to social processes and systems. Once we examine design that creates violence, we may begin to think of design to enable freedom.

COMMENT 2. Rebecca Bell:
An incredible and moving piece that throws out questions that go to the core of crucial issues around relationships to gender inequality in our society. In terms of how design responds to these issues, obviously the fundamental political, economic, and class-related problems need to be addressed on a governmental and daily level. But if design is going to be incorporated into this conversation, which it inevitably should be, the philosophies and aims of organizations like Design against Crime (part of University of the Arts London) come to my mind. [Their ideas include] designing products and services that are "fit for purpose" and contextually appropriate; and developing "products, services and environments via an iterative process related to the problem-oriented approach in crime prevention and user-focused approaches in design, extended to encompass abusers and/or misuser" [see the DAC website]. Speaking with victims and abusers for understanding . . . rather than imposing unaffordable, high-risk design that isolates women yet again, would be one small (ideal and complex but possible) step design can take.

Republic of Salivation
(Michael Burton and Michiko Nitta, 2010)

Designers Michael Burton and Michiko Nitta (Burton Nitta) often work from a conceptual perspective, meaning they identify future problems and imagine possible outcomes. In the Republic of Salivation scenario, which is part of their larger After Agri project, they contemplate what could happen if our society were confronted with food shortages and famine. They envision a dystopian fallout in which the government is forced to implement a strict food-rationing policy that carefully tailors food allotment to the emotional, physical, and intellectual demands of an individual's employment. The example explored here is that of an industrial worker's diet: composed largely of starch, the diet allows the body to work for longer periods on fewer nutrients.

John Thackara

I'm with poet and environmental activist Wendell Berry on this one: "The cities have forgot the earth / and they will rot at heart / till they remember it again."[1]

In Republic of Salivation, part of the series After Agri, these oh-so-urban artists—Michael Burton and Michiko Nitta—ask us to imagine what the world will be like in the event of a global food shortage, but they exhibit no curiosity as to the causes of this imminent threat. They focus, instead, on ways to change the body so that it can be fed synthetically—a solution that contrives to be both downstream and fantastical at the same time.

With their knowing references to "the scientific study of nutrigenomics,"[2] and an airy promise that "new organisms will be tasked with erasing Man's destructive effects,"[3] this kind of work masquerades as radical. But in its steadfast refusal even to think about the roots of our alienation from living systems—among them, food—it belongs squarely within the neoliberal worldview that only Man is smart enough to correct the odd mistake that He may have made.

If the artists were to focus more on observable nutrient and energy flows, and less on infantile science fictions, they would discover that the roots of our food crisis lie in a bad idea that can rather easily be fixed. The bad idea involved pumping nutrients out of distant ecosystems and feeding them to cities in a one-way process. This misstep dates back a long way, to the beginnings of agriculture, but its malignant effects have accelerated under thermo-industrial capitalism (a term which captures precisely the relationship between energy and the industrial revolution).

For a long time, we did not realize that the benefits brought by the plough and its successors would be time limited. Now we do know. We are also beginning to understand how living soils function and how plants grow. In this new light, the idea of feeding ourselves by force, rather than by artful husbandry, is absurd.

The good news is that we are on our way to "remembering the earth" once again. We are discovering—thanks, in part to science—that when left to do so, soil organisms support flora and food webs in mind-bogglingly complex but self-renewing interactions. These processes are interconnected, too, in a most modern way. Regarding mycorrhiza, a symbiotic association between a fungus and the roots of a plant, mycologist and author Paul Stamets, in his book *Mycelium Running: How Mushrooms Can Help Save the World* (2005), makes the analogy that nature has evolved its own Internet over billions of years.

Knowing what we do now, the ecocidal impacts of industrial agriculture can be eliminated by a transition to methods still used by hundreds of millions of poor farmers to this day. Yes, of course these practices can be improved. But the proper role of science is to help us work mindfully with living systems—not, by violent means, to subjugate them.

John Thackara is a British writer, philosopher, and event producer.

1. Wendell Berry, "A Letter to Ed McLanahan and Gurney Norman in California," *Farming: A Hand Book* (Berkeley, Calif.: Counterpoint Press, 2011), p. 103.
2. "Republic of Salivation," on Burton Nitta's official website, accessed January 8, 2015, http://www.burtonnitta.co.uk/repubicofsalivation.html.
3. "Shadow Biosphere," on Burton Nitta's official website, accessed January 8, 2015, http://www.burtonnitta.co.uk/shadowbiosphere.html.

Q: Do violent, dystopian visions ever lead to positive, substantive change?

COMMENT 1. Tim Parsons:
. . . This project comes from the realm known as speculative or critical design, which does not work from the problem-solution paradigm but from the position of raising awareness and debate of issues through the creation of fictional scenarios that the creators do not necessarily advocate. This work does not therefore hinge upon its scientific accuracy, its moral relationship to our own values, or even its plausibility to become reality. It rests on its ability to get its audience to discuss and react to the central subject matter—here, food shortages and famine. . . .

COMMENT 2. Matt:
Thackara is spot on. Critical design isn't just a waste of time, it actually does damage to how people understand design. The critique of critical design has nothing to do with its departure from instrumentalism. The problem is that it does so without committing to anything other than noncommittal aesthetic play. This is precisely why it is a form of liberalism and the reason it is so at home within a fine-art milieu. The appeal to "raising awareness and debate" should be categorically refused. . . .

COMMENT 3. Anon:
As a brown, lower-middle class, radical leftist designer living in one of the most dangerous cities in Asia, all I can say is that, while I can sympathize with the fact that the intentions of most speculative fictions lie in provoking thoughtful debate, critical design is a) largely speaking to the small community of people interested in avant-garde solutions to design problems, and b) a huge funnel for money into solutions that are largely not feasible. It's a classic "design-as-persuasive-rhetoric" vs. "design-as-problem-solving" debate. Rarely have I seen a design fiction lead to something that can be implemented to solve real problems, and my third-world sensibilities are often shocked at the large amounts of money spent on creating and then exhibiting these pieces. . . .

COMMENT 4. James Auger:
. . . I appreciate that the post was initiated by an analysis of a specific project (After Agri) but it is unfair and unhelpful, both to Burton Nitta and to SCD [speculative and critical design], to examine a whole approach by basing the critique on one project. . . . One of the strengths of SCD is that it operates (entirely from my experience) on minute budgets. . . . The purpose of many SCD projects is similar to that of philosophers of technology, such as Langdon Winner and Neil Postman; but through using a product language, [SCD] aims to make this discussion accessible to a much broader audience. SCD does not solve problems but attempts to understand better what the problems are—both today and in the near future. As Anon [above] points out, design works when it fully understands the phenomena, but phenomena today and in the future are becoming increasingly complex. For example, how might disruptive technologies such as synthetic biology and informatics impact our future lives? . . . How many other practicing designers actually solve real problems? The majority of products shaped by designers are on a fast track to landfill sites through making ephemeral (and in many cases pointless) objects desirable. Design itself can be the problem. By moving away from markets and their constraints, SCD is free to explore related issues, expose problems, and imagine new possibilities. . . .

COMMENT 5. Tobie:
I identify my practice with what's being described here as SCD, and, like other commenters here, it's the topic of my PhD thesis. My sense is that descriptions of SCD are often restricted to texts that go in exhibitions and on blogs. Often our claims to bring about debate are conflated with aims for the dissemination of the work. So it's probably a good thing that practitioners are writing scholarly accounts, and vital that the approaches are extended and challenged, otherwise there is a danger that the practice will become repetitive and irrelevant.

Michael Burton (British, born 1977) and
Michiko Nitta (Japanese, born 1978).
Republic of Salivation from the series
After Agri. 2010

Plastic Handcuffs and Anti-Bite/Spit Masks
(Various designers, c. 1970s)

Designs for use in the criminal-justice system, despite being highly specialized, are often produced en masse and retail at low cost. Since the 1970s, the use of plastic handcuffs, sometimes called "flexicuffs," has grown increasingly prevalent among law-enforcement and military personnel, especially during demonstrations and riot scenarios, when large numbers of arrests are expected. The increased use of plastic handcuffs has become a source of controversy, particularly in the wake of the recent Occupy movement, when these disposable and easily deployed restraints were used to conduct mass arrests (on one occasion, more than seven hundred protesters were arrested and cuffed while crossing the Brooklyn Bridge). Arrestees later complained the cuffs were used to deliberately inflict pain; if fastened too tightly, the cuffs may cut off circulation, abrade the skin, and, at worst, inflict nerve damage. Plastic cuffs are preferred in part due to their disposability, thus eliminating sanitation concerns associated with the reuse of metal restraints. Preventing transmission of infectious disease has similarly prompted the rising use of anti-spit or anti-bite masks, which, when worn by hostile detainees, create a protective buffer for supervising law-enforcement officers or medical professionals. Like plastic handcuffs, these masks can be used as a way to control noncompliant inmates. They also require careful and proper application to be truly safe, and human-rights activists have criticized their (mis)use. More generally, the mass production of plastic handcuffs and anti-bite masks is in many ways symptomatic of the rising tide of overcriminalization and mass incarceration in the United States.

Shira A. Scheindlin

Violence begets violence. In the name of preventing violence, we have become accustomed to its use. This accommodation desensitizes us as a society and leaves many of us—particularly those in positions of power—remarkably unaware of the pain often inflicted on innocent people. Inarguably, law-enforcement officers must have legitimate means to protect themselves from danger, and physical restraints are sometimes a necessary tool. But fear, anger, disdain, stereotyping, and the desire for control can each distort the legitimate need for self-protection and incite dangerous abuses of power that escalate fairly ordinary events into violent ones. It has become all too common for those in positions of authority to employ restraints unnecessarily, when safety is not a concern.

Let us take, for example, police overuse of flexicuffs. Oftentimes, officers will slap these disposable plastic handcuffs on suspects who present no immediate danger so that they might perform the "perp walk," a public shaming orchestrated for the benefit of media photographers and videographers. Similarly, they might use flexicuffs to restrain peaceful protesters, as they did at demonstrations outside the Republican National Convention in 2004 and in support of Occupy Wall Street in 2011. Or, as frequently happens with suspected prostitutes, police will use cuffs for needlessly long periods of time, keeping the accused restrained in a police van for hours while they pick up other suspected prostitutes. (As an aside, prostitutes are repeatedly victimized—first by their pimps, then by their customers, and then by the criminal-justice system, which not only forces them to wear painful handcuffs, but also to watch fellow prostitutes suffering the same discomfort and humiliation.) In each of these examples, cuffing the accused in no way protects the arresting officers; instead it merely inflicts violence as punishment.

Another example of the nebulous ground between disciplining and punishing is the use of anti-spit or anti-bite masks (sometimes called "spit shields," "biter masks," or "protection masks"). These ugly devices can serve a legitimate function: to protect officers from communicable diseases like hepatitis C and tuberculosis that

Opposite, above and below:
Designer unknown. Purchased in 2014. Polyurethane, 7 ⅝ x 6 ¾ x 6" (19.4 x 17.2 x 15.2 cm)

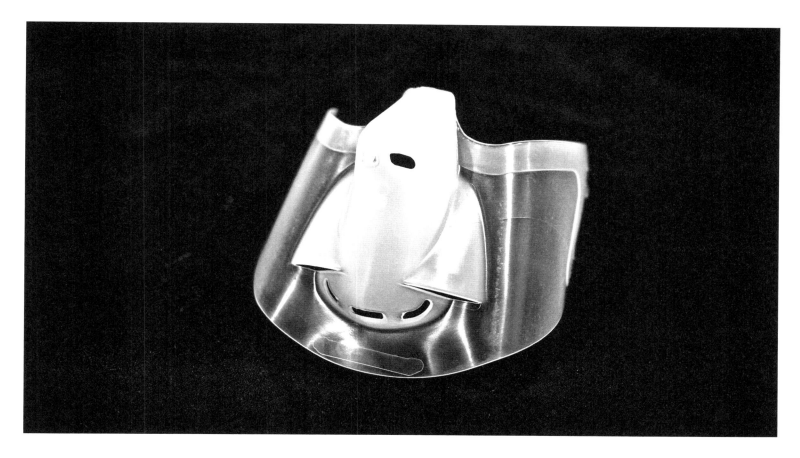

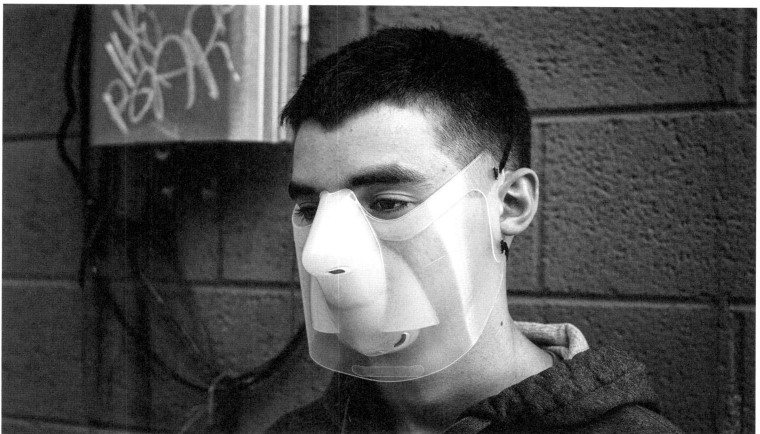

Left: Plastic handcuffs deployed

Right: A policeman carrying several pairs of plastic handcuffs, New York City. 2009

can be transmitted by spitting and biting prisoners. But what about the use of such devices to silence defendants who verbally abuse or demean their restraining officers or who shout obscenities at the court? Does this not merely reproduce and intensify violence when a less brutal response would accomplish the necessary goal?

A civilized society would encourage the use of the least restrictive restraint necessary to provide safety. Once a society tolerates the use of more force than is required, bad things inevitably happen. Guns are drawn when they needn't be. Shots are fired when they needn't be. Innocent bystanders are injured when shots go astray. Flexicuffs and anti-bite masks are not guns. But we should appreciate that justifying the misuse or overuse of one tool may license the same for others.

Bearing witness to raw abuses of power, such as the videotaped 1991 beating of Rodney King in Los Angeles, or the well-publicized 1999 murder of Amadou Diallo, an unarmed African American man who was shot by four plainclothes New York City police officers outside his home, is always heartbreaking—but it's *never* surprising. American culture accepts and even glamorizes violence; just look at the number of movies with shoot-outs or slashings or explosions, often instigated by government agents as necessary means to noble ends. (Is it any wonder that so many wannabes kill their classmates in school shootings?!) In the name of preventing violence, our culture has enshrined it. Would that our officers carried only billy clubs, as in England, or that we eliminated the death penalty, as with most of the civilized world. However, we cannot expect to see a decline in violence so long as we continue to accept its unnecessary, if legal, infliction by law-enforcement officers, prison guards, and yes, even judges (of which I am one). Instead we must forcefully oppose its misuse and overuse. As Walt Kelly, creator of the Pogo cartoon, has said, "We have met the enemy and he is us."[1]

Shira A. Scheindlin is a United States District Judge for the Southern District of New York.

1. Quotation first appeared as "We shall meet the enemy, and not only may he be ours, he may be us," in Walt Kelly, "Foreword," *The Pogo Papers* (New York: Simon and Schuster, 1953), ii.

Q: Protection, humiliation, or both?

COMMENT 1. Raphael Sperry:
As compared to the older metal handcuffs, plastic cuffs are far less expensive to purchase and much quicker to put on. They are a tool for mass arrests rather than for responding to individualized threats. Like the LRAD [Long Range Acoustic Device], they empower police over civilians, but through the economics of mass production rather than through high-tech innovation. . . . Designers can do our best to help shape these forces not only in our role as citizens and voters, but also through design of the public realm.

Designer unknown. Plastic Handcuffs
(also known as Plasticuffs or Flexicuffs).
Purchased in 2014. Injection-molded nylon,
34 ⅝ x ⅜ x ½" (88 x 1.9 x 1.3 cm)

Thomson Correctional Center
(Illinois Department of Corrections, building completed 2001)

From Jeremy Bentham's seminal investigation *Panopticon; or, The Inspection-House* (1791) to Michel Foucault's *Discipline and Punish* (1975) to, more recently, the specter of the Guantánamo Bay detention center, prisons and their design have long ignited public discussion. The relationship between prison design and violence is central to this fascination: prisons are meant to protect us from those who violate the law, but we know they are overcrowded spaces where criminality may become even more ingrained. Thomson Correctional Center (TCC) is a super-maximum-security prison, or "supermax," located just north of the village of Thomson, Illinois. (Thomson is otherwise known by its quaint nickname, "Melon Capital of the World," for the prodigious amount of watermelons grown there.) Its approximately 590 villagers live in the shadow of TCC's fifteen-foot-high electric fence, rolled razor wire, and 1,600 prison cells. The facility was built between May 1999 and November 2001 at a cost of $140 million. Due to political and public controversy over its high operating costs, it lay inactive until 2006 and has never operated at intended capacity. Its future is uncertain.

Raphael Sperry

Violence swirls around Thomson Correctional Center in all its iterations. Built between 1999 and 2001 to house prisoners deemed most dangerous by the state of Illinois, the facility fell victim to a budget crisis and sat empty. In 2009, it was notoriously offered to the federal government to house terrorism detainees from Guantánamo Bay, a plan that also fell through (due in part to political posturing over housing suspected terrorists on American soil). The current plan, which may be implemented as soon as 2015, is to redesign the facility to hold federal "administrative maximum security" prisoners (ADX—the highest security classification) in long-term isolation, a plan moving forward over the strenuous objections of human-rights advocates who identify prolonged isolation as a form of torture. Thomson is an exemplar of the double-edged nature of American incarceration: punishment and rehabilitation defeat each other at every turn, reflecting a society scared of violence but unsure of how to protect itself except through further retribution. Its concretization of violence denies the possibility of any other outcome.

The available satellite imagery and press photographs of Thomson's site planning and architecture demonstrate the intentional barrenness of prison life (requests to view prison design documentation are routinely denied). Vegetation might be used to conceal contraband or to fashion weapons and so is removed from the landscape. Recreation is reduced to one basketball hoop per fifty men in an otherwise vacant, concrete-walled yard. The library, central chow hall, and what appear to be classroom buildings are accessed by uncovered walkways in all seasons. The maximization of surveillance is the immediately apparent design principle in the geometry of Thomson's hallways, yards, and guard towers; small apertures in otherwise completely hardened building facades and fence lines convert lines of sight into potential lines of fire from specified control points. Despite the prominence of violence in prison life, however, guards do not carry weapons in prisoner areas to prevent the possibility of a hostile takeover.

One of the ironies of "tough on crime" policies best understood by prison guards is that more restrictive prisons are harder to manage. Prisoners engaged with jobs and classes have less time to make trouble and more incentive to cooperate. Thomson manages the potential for prisoner violence not through engagement but through segregation: its 1,600 beds are divided among eight housing blocks, and each block is subdivided into four wings. Within each wing, prisoners will be housed in individual cells, a modicum of privacy ironically denied at lower security levels (more compliant prisoners are housed in dormitories to reduce construction costs). This design means that violent individuals

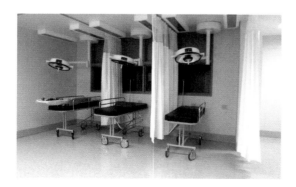

may be locked down inside their cells, often for days or weeks at a time. It also means that group riots can never exceed two hundred prisoners per block—losses are limited to a company's worth, but not an entire brigade.

Thomson's planned conversion into a federal super-maximum-security prison raises the prospect of extended solitary confinement for hundreds of men, as at the infamous

Opposite: Interior of a cell block, Thomson Correctional Center, Thomson, Illinois. 2004

Right: Interior of a medical bay. 2004

Overleaf: Prison exterior. 2004

ADX Florence U.S. Penitentiary in Fremont County, Colorado, the only federal facility to currently hold this security classification. There, some four hundred of the nation's putatively most violent prisoners—"putatively" because often they are not the most dangerous but merely the most despised—are punished using sensory deprivation and twenty-three-hour-per-day solitary confinement. The twenty-fourth hour (granted only five days per week despite seven-day-a-week full-time staff) is spent alone in a chain-link outdoor cage only slightly bigger than the cells. Other supermax prisons use concrete-walled individual exercise yards (or "dog-runs," as prisoners often call them) open only to the sky.

To reach the level of isolation at other supermax prisons, Thomson's already small, barren yards would be subdivided to provide the legal minimum of five hours out-of-cell time per week per person: roughly eight outdoor spaces per fifty-man wing, each no more than 10 feet by 30 feet. Showers built to vandal-resistant specifications could be added to the cells, as at ADX, to eliminate the twice-weekly possibility of momentary hallway interactions. People placed in prolonged isolation frequently experience serious mental illness, including paranoia, psychosis, and depression so severe that it leads to suicide. The ability to withstand isolation varies among individuals, but the effects are ultimately just as violent as other internationally condemned human-rights violations: about 4 percent of prisoners are held in isolation (itself an unacceptably high fraction), but almost half of prison suicides occur there.

Thomson Correctional Center, like Pelican Bay State Prison in California, Upstate Correctional Facility in New York, and the nation's other supermax prisons, is located in a remote, rural area. The legal limbo of Thomson's never-arrived Guantànamo prisoners—many of whom are still detained despite having been deemed innocent and cleared for release—echoes the broader status of prisoners in state and federal prisons, where remoteness and other mechanisms of invisibility cloak the basic inhumanity of prolonged solitary confinement and the injustice of decades-long sentences for those who pose no public safety risk. Americans who fear defiling the homeland—the same fear exemplified by those who protested the transfer of foreign "enemy combatants" to Illinois—would be better off directing their concern toward the use of isolation in domestic prisons and jails like Thomson Correctional Center. Statisticians have shown that mass incarceration does little to reduce crime and that people released from solitary confinement are among the most likely to reoffend given their acquired maladjustment to social life. Thomson prison and other facilities like it may contain and subdivide violence, but ultimately they fail to end the cycles of crime in our most troubled neighborhoods, mirroring a broader social failure to rehabilitate communities terrorized by the drug war, starved by a lack of investment, and hobbled by decaying physical and social infrastructure. We may push this violence to the perimeter, but we will never bring an end to it there.

Raphael Sperry, AIA, LEED AP, is president of Architects/Designers/Planners for Social Responsibility (ADPSR), and the first architect to receive a Soros Justice Fellowship from the Open Society Foundations.

Q: What are the goals of prison design, and (how) are they achieved? Are prisons meant to perpetuate, contain, or resolve violence?

COMMENT 1. Paul B. Jaskot:
I would add one more question to this provocative list: Are prisons designed to be aspirational? Architects inevitably approach their problem from functional, aesthetic, economic, etc., terms that are also meant to solve problems and make things, apparently, better. We need to acknowledge that these structures do indeed make society better, but only for specific controlling interests and for the short term. . . . Why do most architects refuse to challenge these clearly dominant interests more frequently through their work?

Magnasanti
(Vincent Ocasla, 2007–09)

After three years performing extensive calculations and modeling experiments, Filipino architecture student Vincent Ocasla used the urban-simulation video game *SimCity 3000* to create Magnasanti, an ideal virtual city optimized to an overall residential population of six million inhabitants—no small feat within the game's parameters. (According to Ocasla, six million is *SimCity*'s maximal population size.) But living in Magnasanti comes with a significant price: high unemployment rates, air pollution, below-average life expectancies, strict regimentation, and a stifling police state. With Magansanti, Ocasla wished to explore the slippage between the city's illusion of perfect order and the dystopian virtual community it necessarily produced. As the debates surrounding the legacy of architects such as Le Corbusier attest, separating the benevolent from the coercive when planning an ideal community is never as straightforward as we may expect.

Ayssar Arida

Vincent Ocasla's radical experiment with the video game *SimCity 3000* inspired me to reflect on the inherent violence in designing any preconceived community, in spite of all the goodwill an architect can have. I once designed the perfect non-gated gated community in Saudi Arabia. It was commissioned by an enlightened developer who wanted a mold-breaking project: a new prototype for middle-to-high-income Muslim-family residences. It needed to distinguish itself from the high-walled private villas and paranoid expatriate ghetto compounds that make up the bulk of the country's real-estate market, while still offering some of their more familiar "quirks": socializing, for instance, was to remain a purely domestic and secluded matter.

The resulting complex was inspired by traditional Arab, Mediterranean, and Islamic urbanism, where clusters of private rooms and protected terraces

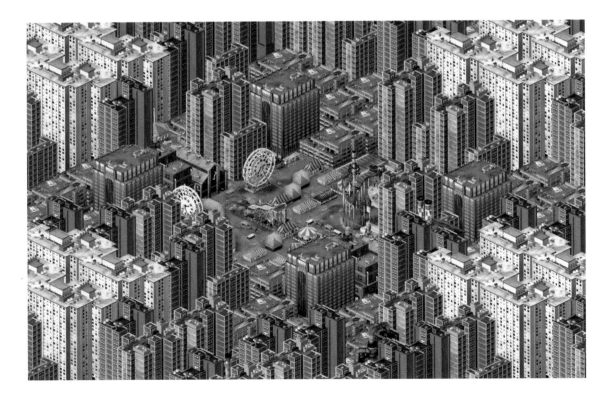

Left and overleaf: Vincent Ocasla (Filipino, born 1987). Magnasanti. 2007–09. City simulation using *SimCity 3000* video-game software

form buildings with blurred boundaries that wrap around lush courtyards and gardens. The project, which I'll call "Saudisanti," has unique features and statistics, presented here without the bombastic music that usually accompanies the promotional videos of real-estate developers (the same kind that backs the video Ocasla made for Magnasanti). Saudisanti features

Socially engineered design:

Only 5% of apartments share an elevator lobby on their entrance floor; the other 95% are single-unit entrances, so residents can *consistently* avoid greeting neighbors. Each apartment meets the requirements of the contemporary Islamic family, with two separate entrances designated "family" and "men only" respectively. Internally, sliding partitions easily reconfigure the space from "family-time" to "men only" modes of socializing. Each unit also has at least one large patio, an outdoor reprieve from the air-conditioned utopia. The patios are protected from both the elements and the neighbor's gaze by wooden screens inspired by *mashrabiyas* (wood latticework that encloses oriel windows in traditional Arabic cities).

Fractal efficiency:

188 families are housed in 47 buildings using just 31 elevators (33% more efficient than a typical development). Apartment plans have front-to-back, side-to-side, and rotational symmetries, thanks to independence from any natural orientation (the sun is almost always vertical here, and air-conditioning renders wind directions irrelevant). This Rubik's Cube–like system allows an impressive number of possible four-story building configurations using only four different apartment types (8^4 or 4,096 to be exact).

Invisible movements:

Just like in Magnasanti, there are no streets. Continuous underground parking limits the necessity for aboveground vehicular circulation and pedestrian-priority landscaped piazzas replace local streets. Families move from car to apartment through direct elevators without ever crossing an open space.

Utopian score sheet:

100% modular construction and development system! 100% domestic lifestyle adaptability! 100% respect for its social and cultural context! 100% flexibility for developers! 100% privacy!

100% privacy? Just like the doomed Pruitt-Igoe housing project in St. Louis, Missouri, half a century before, Saudisanti received some of the industry's highest awards. As my final atonement for the violence inherent in this socially deterministic complex, I used immersive 3-D simulations to disrupt its insularity. Without the developer's knowledge, and probably against his will—and that of the residents (although not necessarily to their detriment)—I built in perfectly positioned gaps between the walls and *mashrabiyas* of each unit to allow voyeuristic sight lines between neighbors.

Ayssar Arida is a practicing "urbatect," writer, educator, and entrepreneur.

Q: What makes a community great, and how much of this greatness derives from top-down design and regulation?

COMMENT 1. Nara Hohensee:
. . . The complex relationships between designers and institutions, politicians, developers, and the economic realities of any society (even a totalitarian one) mean that architects have only the slightest say in how a community looks or operates. It seems to me that the best kind of community is one that balances these various forces, while allowing opportunities for all kinds of "voyeurism," planned or not.

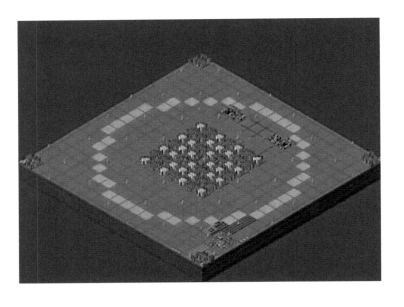
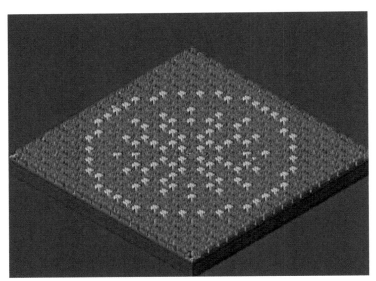
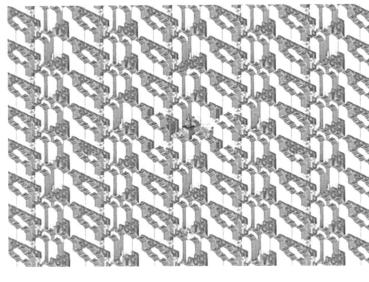

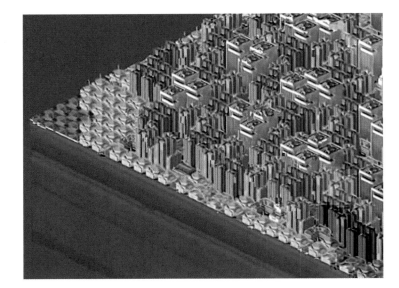

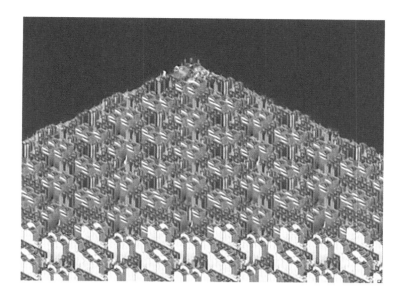
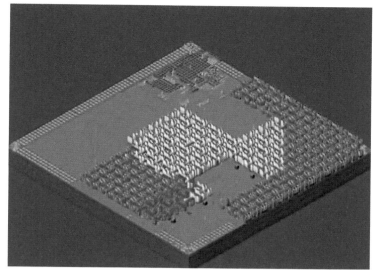

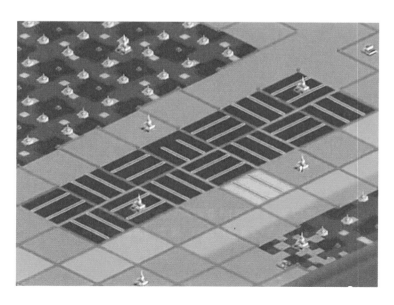
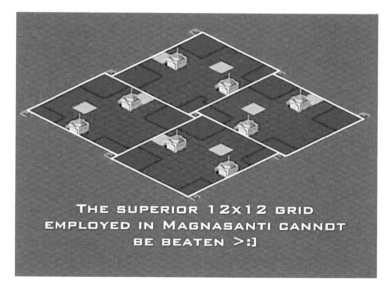

THE SUPERIOR 12x12 GRID EMPLOYED IN MAGNASANTI CANNOT BE BEATEN >:]

Borderwall as Architecture
(Ronald Rael and Virginia San Fratello, 2009–ongoing)

Ronald Rael and Virginia San Fratello, practicing architects as well as professors at the University of California, Berkeley, and San Jose State University respectively, created Borderwall as Architecture to reimagine the design, function, and use of the controversial dividing wall between the United States and Mexico. The current border wall is not one monolithic fortification, but rather several distinct physical barriers that stretch across parts of Texas, New Mexico, Arizona, and California. Rael and San Fratello's multilayered proposal, which includes new infrastructure designed to benefit both countries economically, socially, and environmentally, is at once serious and deliberately satirical. Their speculative designs include a divider made of solar-energy panels that would enforce the border while capturing the fierce sunlight native to the region; adjacent water collection and purification points that would provide respite to anyone in proximity; a binational and bilingual library that would foster reciprocal cultural understanding; and a cross-border teeter-totter that highlights the absurdity of a barrier that is both imposing and porous. While the Mexico-U.S. border as we know it today was set in 1848, construction of the physical barrier began in 2006, when then-President George W. Bush signed the Secure Fence Act. A desire to mitigate the flow of illegal border crossings and to protect U.S. citizens from drug-cartel violence formed the official rationale. Over six hundred miles of fencing and concrete were installed before the project was halted in 2010 due to excessive costs. As Rael and San Fratello's provocation highlights, the Mexico-U.S. border wall remains hotly contested, as do the politics and policies that surround its design.

Judith Torrea

When in 2006 former Mexican president Felipe Calderón waged the country's so-called war on drugs, Ciudad Juárez became the most dangerous city in the world. As a journalist residing in Ciudad Juárez, and covering Mexican-U.S. border relations, I began asking myself how it was that the same drugs that caused such brutal destruction in Mexico could become, once transported to U.S. soil, objects of (outwardly peaceful) commerce.

Some days in Ciudad Juárez seven people were killed; other days it was fifteen or twenty. Occasionally it was more. On too many evenings, I returned home unable to remember the exact number of corpses I had seen. Nearly every-day, the same scenes of murder, of mothers trying to find out if the most recent victims were their sons or daughters. Maybe to shield my mind from the atrocities, or so that I might continue reporting, I would return to my house, review my notes, write up the latest story, and post it to my blog. By then my reports were no longer accepted by conventional media, and my blog was the only outlet available to me. Despite the risk, I found a way to fulfill my mission as a journalist: to tell the stories that must be told in order not to serve, through silence, as an accomplice to corruption, violence, and injustice.

In my beloved Ciudad Juárez, one survives the horror by transforming adversity into strength: a timid smile, a guarded thought, a token of irony—each becomes a shield against desperation. I recognize in Ronald Rael and Virginia San Fratello's Borderwall as Architecture a similar message. With Borderwall, Rael and San Fratello, professors at the University of California, Berkeley, and San Jose State University respectively, redesign the fence separating Mexico from the United States with fanciful, albeit not altogether impracticable, modifications. Where today we observe coiled barbed wire, hovering drones, guard towers, and laser beams, Rael and San Fratello envision solar farms, binational libraries, food carts, and water-treatment systems. Using humor and irony, they foresee better possibilities—much as the people in Juárez do—and call into

question a senseless wall that fails to fulfill its stated function: to stop the
emigration of those who flee horror in search of a better life, of those who
long for a peaceful and productive future for themselves and their families.
(This latter goal, it should be said, is shared by even the most conservative
American politicians.)

Inevitably, Rael and San Fratello's redesign asks the observer to consider
parody as a form of postmodern artistic communication. Much contemporary art
asks this of its viewers, although as a literary device it began centuries ago in an
obscure corner of Spain: Cervantes's *Don Quixote* exaggerates epic discourses
in order to expose the conventions of the chivalric romance, with its grandiose
tales of heroic knights, loyal squires, and virtuous ladies, and move instead
toward a literary realism that more accurately encompasses lived experience.
Don Quixote pushed the development of the novel by establishing a continuous
dialogue with other literary genres. And he accomplished this by framing irony
and humor, of which he takes full advantage, with a strong component of realism. Rael and San Fratello's wall operates in much the same way: their use of
irony helps us to understand humanity as it truly is, not as those who build walls
and false paradises might wish it to be.

Rael and San Fratello know that the empty violence around these cruel
borders must be put to rest. They dream not of the romantic utopias common to
the Arthurian legends, but of something much simpler—ending the absurdity of
a selectively porous border that produces only death and suffering. Converted
into a place of light and transparency, and without the shadow of hate, Borderwall
reveals that another world is possible and invites us to fight for change.

In the meantime, the border's cocktail of indifference and impunity, supported
by the politics of silence, continues. Mexico endlessly attempts to clean up its
image, but without ever addressing the causes of economic and political violence.
Ciudad Juárez is the locus of this living hell. Attesting to this: twenty-two years

of missing women and femicide; more than eleven thousand murders and ten thousand orphaned children since 2006, all in a city of just over 1.3 million inhabitants. Political decisions on the part of the United States to support the war on drugs promote the further destabilization of Mexico and other Latin American countries, and in turn prompt more violence and more emigration.

On those days when there are so many dead I cannot remember their names, I wonder: How many deaths in Juárez (or elsewhere in Mexico, Central or South America) are necessary so that a well-off partygoer in the United States can consume a gram of cocaine? When I cross one of the three bridges separating Ciudad Juárez from El Paso, Texas—one of the most guarded regions in the United States—I ask myself: Have all these deaths been in vain? Heroin, cocaine, and methamphetamine are smuggled into the United States just the same as they were before all the violence. Are these deaths but a symbol of the failures of the Mexican government? And what of those American politicians who should by now understand that what happens on U.S. soil stems from murder on mine?

With Borderwall, Rael and San Fratello bring to light the absurdity of a wall that arrests the movement of people but not drugs. They express hope for the future—the possibility that the wall will affirm our shared humanity.

Judith Torrea is an award-winning investigative blogger, journalist, and author who has covered the Mexico-U.S. border for sixteen years.

Q: What is the most apt metaphor for national borders? Walls? Open wounds? Filters? Please comment or add your own.

COMMENT 1. Tim:
National borders are abominations to humanity and nature. The first time I heard the phrase "Doctors without Borders" I thought "WOW! What a profound statement on the proper priorities for a species that calls itself humanity." National borders are arbitrary lines on the ground where someone has declared, "We are good, compassionate people, but be it known to the world that HERE is the place where our priorities change and compassion becomes less important than greed and fear!" Economically, of course, national borders are simply benign tools for bureaucratic organization, but to the extent that humanity is defined by our capacity for compassion, they may be seen as seams along which the substance of humanity cracks, where the compassion leaks out and the poisons of prejudice and intolerance and selfishness and hatred seep in, and most appalling of all, where that defect in the substance of humanity has been officially declared to be righteous.

National borders also serve as constant reminders that our governments have declared themselves above nature. Even though it's hard to imagine a more inalienable natural right than moving from one place to another on the land, national borders serve as a declaration that, inalienable and natural or not, exercise of such a right will not be tolerated and that intolerance will be upheld under threat of force.

COMMENT 2. Bruce Sterling:
Twenty-first-century border fortifications—they're a kind of orange-juice strainer that separates flesh from flows of money.

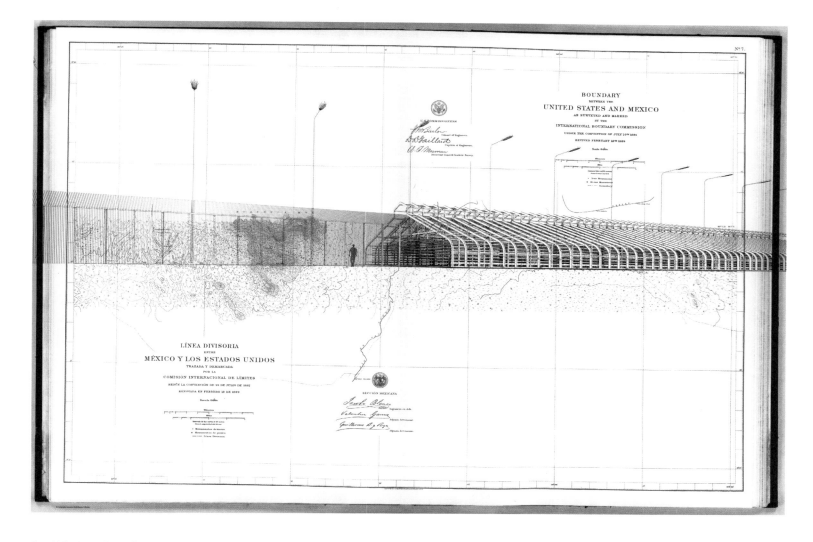

Ronald Rael and Virginia San Fratello.
Greenhouse Alternative Border
Solution from the series Borderwall as
Architecture. 2014

Ronald Rael and Virginia San Fratello.
Teeter-Totter Alternative Border
Solution from the series Borderwall as
Architecture. 2014

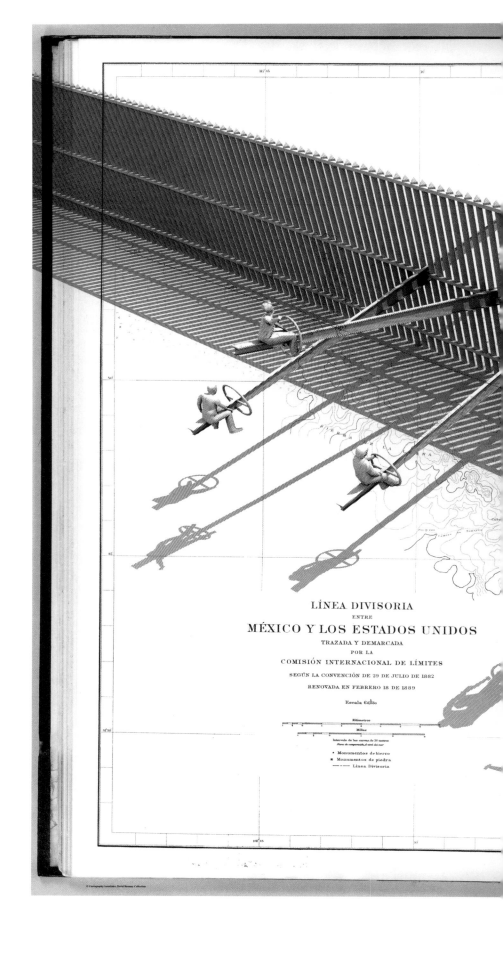

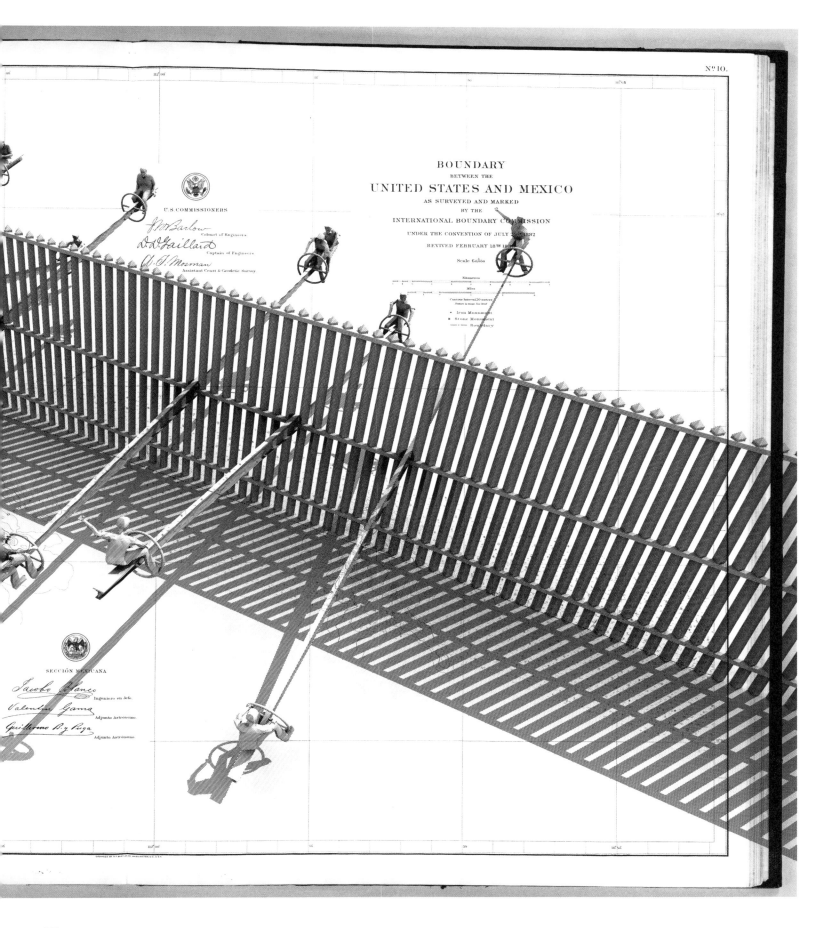

BOUNDARY
BETWEEN THE
UNITED STATES AND MEXICO
AS SURVEYED AND MARKED
BY THE
INTERNATIONAL BOUNDARY COMMISSION
UNDER THE CONVENTION OF JULY 29, 1882
REVIVED FEBRUARY 18TH 1889

Scale 6/10000

U.S. COMMISSIONERS

SECCIÓN MEXICANA

Technicals
(Various designers, early twentieth century)

For as long as automobiles have existed, so have vehicles modified for use in conflict zones. Even earlier, horse-drawn carts adapted to fit machine-gun platforms, known by their Russian name, *tachanka*, were prevalent in Eastern Europe. During World War II, the British Special Air Service used unarmored vehicles outfitted with machine guns and other weaponry. Only in the early 1990s, however, did these improvised vehicles earn their current name: "technicals." During the Somali civil war, the United Nations hired on-the-ground guards and drivers, dubbed "technical assistants." Over time, the term "technicals" evolved to mean any vehicle with heavy weaponry mounted on the back. Now used in war- and guerrilla-torn areas worldwide, including by Taliban and Al Qaeda leaders, technicals symbolize power, moving men and weapons with speed and efficiency. From Sierra Leone's civil war to Iraq's ISIS conflict, these vehicles remain integral to modern-day asymmetric warfare.

Aminatta Forna

In 2000, two years before the end of the war in Sierra Leone, I returned to the country of my father, where I had spent part of my childhood. Like many returnees, I had come to help members of my family caught up in the fighting, which by then had lasted more than a decade. The village where my family lived had been behind enemy lines. To reach them I needed to rent a car, preferably a four-wheel drive, but available vehicles were scarce. Eventually I secured one: a black Toyota 4×4 with tinted windows. I was with a driver, my husband, a cousin who acted as a guide. We departed Freetown at dawn, drove along and around roads cratered by shellfire. In the late afternoon, we had reached the dirt track to the village. What struck me most was the emptiness, the absence of people. Occasionally in the distance we saw men repairing damaged roofs, but along roads where I was used to seeing schoolchildren, women toting loads, men on bicycles—we did not pass a soul. Then, rounding a corner: a small group of women carrying firewood. We slowed for them, but instead of waving and greeting us, they dropped their loads and ran into the bush. We laughed. We thought we had merely surprised them. Then the same thing happened again. And then again. Women saw our approaching vehicle and fled in silence. We looked at ourselves through their eyes: deep-throated engine, darkened windows, alloy wheels. The kind of vehicle a rap artist might drive. The kind of vehicle the rebel militia might drive.

The women had been running for their lives.

When I was a kid we were driven to school every day in a Land Rover. A decade out of British rule, we maintained a high regard for the possessions of the overlord. The Sierra Leone army inherited British army vehicles: the stripped-down Defender, light, rugged, possessed of almost rigid suspension, made for fighting men—and we schoolchildren, who bounced on our arses on the bare benches in the back. Over the years the Land Rover was replaced with new objects of desire: the Nissan Pathfinder, the Nissan Patrol, the Toyota 4Runner, the ever-popular Hilux, flatbeds and pickups in all their forms. The Peugeot 504 pickup, King of the African Road throughout the 1970s. The saloon cars became the continent's most popular bush taxi. Defender. Patrol. These names invoke violence, force. Protection, the manufacturers would doubtless say. Discovery, 4Runner, Pathfinder: adventure, boldness, machismo. Landcruiser: the big beast of Third World wars. The Landcruiser would become the status symbol of the top brass, of Osama bin Laden, the U.N., the world's NGOs.

U.S. Marine Corps soldier firing a missile from a Ford M151 Military Utility Tactical Truck (MUTT), Camp LeJeune, North Carolina. Date unknown

By contrast the name of by far the most widely used technical vehicle seems less of a fit. Hilux. Hi-Lux. High as in "high riding." "Lux" meaning luxury. "The vehicular equivalent of the AK-47," a former U.S. Army ranger told *Newsweek* magazine.[1] A rigid steel-frame construction with a cab and body fitted on the top. Beloved of farmers, construction crews, rebel armies, warlords, Somali pirates, and Afghan insurgents. Good for moving workers, good for moving contingents of men. Mount a machine gun on a tripod on the back and you have a gunship. The design of the Hilux on the battlefield has proved a perfect and unintended synthesis of form and function. Fast. Maneuverable. High ground clearance. Light enough to cross minefields without detonating mines, it's said. So popular they even named a war after it: the Libya-Chad "Toyota War" of the 1980s was fought with cavalries of Hiluxes.

In 2012, when I was writing about Croatia, a friend—a war correspondent who had reported the conflict in the former Yugoslavia—pointed out something that later seemed so obvious I wondered how I could have missed it. "The reason that war kicked off so fast," he said, "was because they were a nation of hunters. Every man had a gun and knew how to use it." When people go to war they fight with whatever comes to hand. In Sierra Leone every man was a farmer, every man owned a cutlass or a machete. In Sierra Leone before the war if you saw a gang of men in the back of a Toyota Hilux carrying machetes, you'd think they were farm workers on their way to clear the bush.

A few years later, you'd be running for your life.

Aminatta Forna is the award-winning author of three novels, including *The Hired Man* (London, Bloomsbury Publishing, 2013).

1. Ravi Somaiya, "Why Rebel Groups Love the Toyota Hilux," *Newsweek*, October 14, 2010, http://www.newsweek.com/why-rebel-groups-love-toyota-hilux-74195.

Q: Does the "technical" suggest that no design is inherently benign?

COMMENT 1. Sam Haddix:
There is a . . . narcissism to the framing. Are we asking the right question? Should an interrogation of the Libya-Chad violence . . . center around the design of the Hilux or the political and cultural implications borne from the "design" of colonial rule?

Technical on coastal road B13, west of
Marsá al Burayqah, Libya. 2011

Operation Sovereign Borders Graphic Storyboard (Australian Customs and Border Protection Service, 2013)

Operation Sovereign Borders is Australia's multipronged initiative to prevent people without visas, often refugees fleeing persecution, from entering the country by boat. Implemented by Prime Minister Tony Abbott's center-right coalition government—though groundwork was laid by the preceding ministerial cabinet—the military-led campaign diverts boats full of asylum seekers to Indonesia before they can reach Australian shores. The campaign went into effect September 18, 2013, the day Abbott and his ministry were sworn into office. In November of the same year, the Australian Customs and Border Protection website published a short graphic storyboard, aimed at deterring asylum seekers, or "Illegal Maritime Arrivals" (later changed to "Irregular Maritime Arrivals"), from making the journey to Australia. Over eighteen pages, the controversial storyboard illustrates the intense suffering and peril faced by those who voyage from southern Asia to Australia (usually landing on Christmas Island) in boats operated by people smugglers. Text in Farsi and Pashto on the front and back covers warns that "if you go to Australia by ship without a visa you will not settle down there." The graphic novel was produced by STATT, a Hong Kong–based consulting firm. Immigration, the act of coming to live permanently in another country, is as old as history—as is the urge to demarcate and police geopolitical territory, the desire to circumvent such restrictions, and the propensity to exploit the misfortune of others for political or financial self-aggrandizement.

Ahmed Ansari

In translations of the annals of the Assyrian king Ashurbanipal (ca. 668–627 BCE), we find descriptions of the practice of gibbeting prisoners of war as an effective deterrent to would-be invaders and rebels: "Afterward those kings, as many as I had appointed, violated their covenants with me . . . they (i.e., my generals) destroyed them with weapons, both small and great, and left not a man in them. They hung their corpses on gibbets, stripped off their skins, and therewith covered the wall of the city." Similar tactics, according to the ancient Roman senator and historian Tacitus, were employed by the British queen Boudica as a warning to Roman occupying forces in the first century CE. We find history littered with similar examples of corpses used as grisly signposts to tell people to stay away.

Today the word "invade" or "invasion" is commonly used in rhetoric around not only military and occupying forces but also the subject of illegal immigration, collapsing two otherwise distinct categories. For example, quickly googling the words "invasion," "immigration," and "asylum" together gave me 1,270,000 results scattered across article headlines and copy, as well as forum discussions and debates. While governments today rarely use the gibbet, public institutions have found other, more creative ways to discourage would-be invaders. One such example is a recently published graphic storyboard commissioned by the Australian Customs and Border Protection Service (CBPS) addressing itself to Afghani émigrés trying to enter the country by sea.

As journalists Luke Mogelson and Joel van Houdt described in painstaking detail in their 2013 feature, "The Dream Boat," published in the *New York Times Magazine,* the journey is not an easy one. Afghani refugees risk capture, internment, and deportation when crossing into Pakistan, and as they wait for passports in Karachi. Once at sea, refugees risk drowning, malnutrition, dehydration, heat, and sickness. At the end of it all lies the prospect of detainment by the Australian authorities.

Much of the Australian CBPS's storyboard presents a wholly illustrated portrayal of the journey from departure to arrival at Australia's Christmas Island. That the novel assumes its target audience is unaware of the risks involved is absurd;

Front cover of the Australian government's Operation Sovereign Borders graphic storyboard. Text in Farsi and Pashto warns, "If you go to Australia by ship without a visa you will not settle down there."

Pages 91–95: Interior pages from the Operation Sovereign Borders graphic storyboard

on the contrary, many asylum seekers have described being acutely aware of the journey's hazards before setting out. Also at odds with what the storyboard shows is the fact that the majority of asylum seekers are not fleeing their home countries to escape poverty, much less with the blessings of their parents; more likely they are escaping religious or ethnic persecution, oppressive regimes, or the perils of war. Since 2010 the majority of Afghan and Pakistani Illegal Maritime Arrivals, as they are referred to by the Australian government (called "Irregular Maritime Arrivals" until 2013), are Hazara, an ethnic and religious minority that has been the consistent target of extermination by Sunni Muslim radical groups. Many who choose to undertake these journeys do so out of a profound feeling of hopelessness—a sense that no other options remain.

The effectiveness of the gibbet as a deterrent stems from its stark and excessive corporeal brutality. The instrumentalization of the body exacts obedience through the spectacle of terror. It gives the unwanted invader, the foreign other, a clear and direct message that pierces even the most urgent or desperate reasons to set roots in foreign soil, to forge a new order on the ashes of the old: try, and your corpse too will adorn the borders of this land. Thus, the gibbet counters the wish for vitality and life with the threat of savage death. Its opposition to life is absolute and uncompromising.

As an instrument, the graphic novel lacks this persuasive power. The gibbet did away with abstraction in favor of unadulterated realism. The storyboard, on the other hand, abstracts too much and misunderstands the psychology of the perceived "invader." Given a choice between the risk of persecution, torture, or death and that of temporary internment, it is not hard to imagine which anyone would choose. Nothing these émigrés face could be worse than what they have already experienced.

Ahmed Ansari teaches courses in design and in science and technology studies in Karachi, Pakistan.

Q: How far can the state go to "protect" its borders from immigration before doing so becomes an act of violence?

COMMENT 1. Cameron Tonkinwise:
. . . Why choose an expressionistically illustrative form? A first answer is because the Australian government thinks that refugees are child-like semiliterates. The [government is] speaking loudly the way bigots do when speaking paternalistically to foreigners, mistaking translation difficulties for hearing impediments. . . .

COMMENT 2. Matt Kiem:
1. It must always be remembered that Australia is a settler colonial state. The very foundations of its political-economic infrastructures are invasion and genocide, and, particularly in the lead-up to and [following] the event of its federation, a liberal-nationalist form of ethnic cleansing. As many authors have noted, the invasion anxiety that characterizes the political constitution of (white) Australia is animated by the logics of its initial act invasion. What (white) Australians seem to fear most is that some other group will do to them what they have done to others. The violent acting out is the mark of a profound sense of insecurity.

2. If I recall correctly, the comic under discussion was commissioned during the period of the previous Labor government administration. While the Liberal-National coalition currently in power has successfully branded itself as the more hard-line party, it is worth remembering that mandatory detention was initially introduced by a Labor government in 1992. This is to say that, despite the spectacle of parliamentary politics, Australia's border violence is a bipartisan project. It is also highly lucrative, with detention-center contracts worth billions. The politics to end this violence will emerge in spite of, not from, the Australian parliament.

3. The problem is international. . . . As far away as Australia may seem, its experiments in the production of despair represent the honing of techniques within a global border-industrial complex.

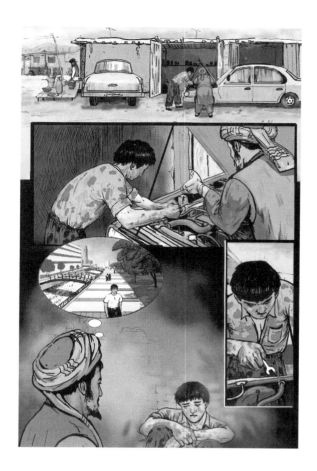

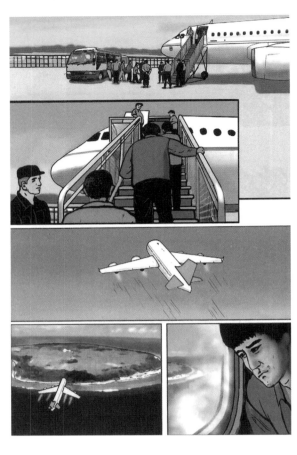

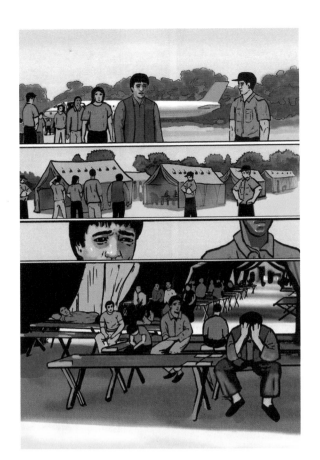

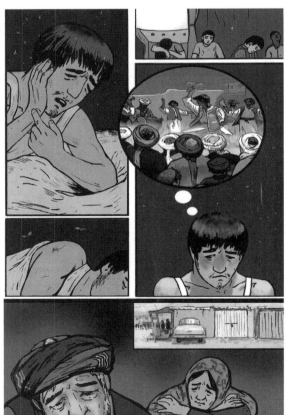

Female Genital Mutilation Awareness Poster Campaign (Volontaire for Amnesty International, 2009)

Female genital mutilation (FGM), also known as female circumcision or cutting, is a term that encompasses all procedures involving partial or total removal of the external female genitalia. The physical and emotional harm inflicted on the girls and women who experience FGM is unarguable. However, the practice is rooted in a mixture of social, cultural, and religious factors, and is therefore a complex and controversial issue. The poster design by the Swedish agency Volontaire for Amnesty International illustrates the stitches and closures used in three of the four different categories of FGM—clitoridectomy, excision, and infibulation—as outlined in a joint statement by the World Health Organization (WHO), the United Nations Children's Fund (UNICEF), and the United Nations Population Fund (UNFPA). (The fourth category is a catchall for any other harmful non-medical procedure not covered by the other three categories.) WHO estimates that in the twenty-nine mostly African and Middle Eastern countries where the practice of FGM is concentrated, more than 125 million girls and women alive today have undergone FGM. Recognizing the practice as a contravention of human rights, UNICEF, UNFPA, WHO, and Amnesty International are leading the charge to end FGM as part of a larger campaign to eliminate violence against women.

Angélique Kidjo

So much artistry and money is devoted to the design of advertisements. Campaigns are everywhere and their purpose is simple: they want us first to desire a product and then to buy it. Often they are most successful when they make us want to be part of the brand's glamorous image.

There is at least one exception: when an advertising agency creates a campaign for a charity. What does the ad sell? There is no car or perfume to buy, no glamour to affect. Instead the ad aims to mobilize us—to make us aware of an unbearable reality that exists elsewhere in the world; and to make us think that we have the ability to change it.

This is not an easy task. As a UNICEF Goodwill Ambassador, I've traveled to the poorest parts of Africa. There I've witnessed people living in dire circumstances, their basic needs left unfulfilled. When it is time to come back to the Western world and to speak to the media, I sometimes feel powerless to express my outrage. If I'm too angry, I'll turn people away; if I'm too soft, nobody will care. The traditional singers from my native country, Benin, provide an excellent precedent for how best to express outrage. Listening to their music, which is simultaneously uplifting and profound, has taught me that the way the message is delivered—its tone and tenor, for instance—is as important as the message itself. Don't make people feel guilty if you want to have a lasting effect on their conscience.

When glamour and desire aren't available as lures, advertising agencies may sometimes manipulate our emotions with shocking or violent images. Is the use of such images fair game for charities and nonprofit organizations whose missions are to promote the well-being of humanity? The answer seems obvious: a graphic ad will provoke an immediate reaction. It will tap into our predisposition for compassion and pity and push us to donate right away. By donating, we will assuage our guilty consciences and soon enough we will feel good again.

But this manipulative strategy comes at a cost: not only does it border on voyeurism but it also perpetuates preconceptions of Africa as a continent defined wholly by poverty and disease. More important, however, pity prevents us from connecting meaningfully with the people we're trying to help. Ads that do nothing but put misery on display strip these "suffering victims" of their dignity.

Right and overleaf: Volontaire (est. 2009) for Amnesty International (est. 1961). Female Genital Mutilation Awareness Poster Campaign. 2009. Various materials, dimensions variable

Help us stop Female Genital Mutilation, stop violence against women. Support our work for human rights at www.amnesty.se

amnesty

For the viewers targeted by these ads, the sufferers seem to exist in a radically different world, one that bears no relation to our own, and cease altogether to be human.

With their campaign denouncing excision, or female genital mutilation, Amnesty International manages to avoid these pitfalls. Excision is a complex and tragic issue. The tradition is harmful, but it's also a rite of passage, one in which the perpetuator—the older woman who performs the procedure—is also a victim. Passing laws isn't enough; rather, smart advocacy and education over the long term are what's required.

Creating an awareness campaign on this subject was undoubtedly a great challenge for the designers. The campaign might have exploited the issue by trading on graphic images. Or it might have diluted the issue by deploying the beautiful faces of young, impoverished girls with forlorn expressions. Instead the designers chose a powerful solution that in my view expresses outrage without degrading the viewer or the victim. The posters call on strong symbolism, evocative (and provocative) similitude (the practice of infibulation is depicted with near-realism), and the power of imagination to ensure we won't stay indifferent. And we should not.

Angélique Kidjo is a Grammy Award–winning Beninoise singer-songwriter, activist, and UNICEF Goodwill Ambassador.

Q: Kidjio writes, "Don't make people feel guilty if you want to have a lasting effect on their conscience." Is outrage counterproductive when fighting for human rights?

COMMENT 1. EMM:
I struggle with how to productively express my outrage, too. I just want to press my understanding into other people, but blunt-force instruments do not work effectively. When I think of the stories that have moved me, they have told me a story, gently opening me. I think this poster has the capacity to touch hearts in a way screaming never will. Make good art.

COMMENT 2. Nuria Benítez:
I am astonished by the graphic coherence of the posters' design, both powerful and beautiful, so accurately illustrating feminine genital mutilation, and yet effectively making us aware and sensitive toward approaching this topic. I hope they can awaken our conscience and appease violence as we look at each stitch.

Help us stop Female Genital Mutilation, stop violence against women. Support our work for human rights at www.amnesty.se

amnesty

Prospectus for a Future Body
(Choy Ka Fai, 2011)

The work of Choy Ka Fai is part of a growing field of speculative design practice, a provocative probing of future possibilities that eschews more traditional design processes characterized by a concrete final product. Choy's performances, including his four-part series Prospectus for a Future Body, explore the potential of technology to remember, recreate, and store movement, and then to translate these memories back to the body via wired, electrical impulses. With these performances, he redefines traditional relationships between choreographer, dancer, and audience. Choy breaks down his investigation into several strands that include creating a library of movements, each movement digitally designed and triggered; examining muscle memory and programming; and analyzing the possibilities for choreography and movement mapping when they are digitally controlled by forces external to the body. Prospectus for a Future Body takes the body as a site of access—to which movement and action are relayed by an external choreographer—and asks whether we can design future memories for it.

André Lepecki

Ten Notes for Choy Ka Fai's Prospectus for a Future Body

1. Were we to find a principle of violence in choreography—the latter understood as the design and execution of predetermined movements and gestures—it would be the following: a subject will be formed, created, designed, trained, physically as well as mentally, to receive someone else's movements and then to execute them perfectly, upon command.

2. It's as if violence in choreography functions according to the principles of abduction: first one captures (young) bodies, bends them, trains them to be ideal receptors of movement; then one captures minds and makes them yield to commands, while demanding also perfect memory. Not surprisingly, the modern notion of discipline is a product of the era that also brings choreography (the word and the practice) into the world.

3. In this scheme, choreography also functions according to military principles, or according to a technology predicated on structures of command and obedience. This is why choreographer William Forsythe once referred to ballet as being a "system of command."[1] Regarding the transmission of movement, such a system requires the ideological fantasy of the dancer as tabula rasa, as ideal receptor who will move according to someone else's will and corporeal attributes.

4. Choreography then can be seen as a body snatcher, and the dancer as a host for spectral possession.

5. Under this violent formation, the dancer's body is ideally conceived as an open body on at least three levels: telepathically, telekinetically, and teletemporally. It is triply available for all sorts of spectral intrusions, manipulations, receptions: telepathically, to receive the choreographer's intentions without a glitch; telekinetically, to incorporate and then excorporate muscular and nervous expressions from this virtual transmission; teletemporally, to be an ephemeral station, a precarious, momentary receptacle for movement that must continue, into the future, beyond any individual dancer's life.

6. But there is more to this violence than the ideal of endless and flawless transmission. There is what we may call (after Michel Serres) the "parasitical principles of communication": inevitable deviation, unavoidable disturbance, permanent noise.[2] These are the inherent conditions of the world. Choreographic violence

starts when choreography cannot stand deviation, cannot accommodate the dancer's agency, cannot accept that the nervous system has its autonomy, and that sometimes it takes over, that it has to take over, that sometimes bodies do break apart, are always breaking apart, that all dancing is break-dancing, and that all minds forget, and that forgetting is the precondition for the unexpected, the crack through which irresistible wishes and improper desires creep in, inflecting choreography away into unforeseen becomings, making it align with *something else*.

7. Violence meets choreography thanks to the mystery of animation, the omnipotent theocratic dream of infusing movement into the inert, of wanting to control matter and its futures by controlling the life and sense of its movements. Freud saw in the sudden eruption of movement, in what is supposed to be inert, the perfect example of the uncanny. But it is precisely in the uncanny that choreography pokes its fingers—a fatal attraction. Choreography's violence is to always go about pushing and plucking some mass of bone and meat to see if it can make it dance: *Dance!* It's the ultimate colonial sadism over the bare life of the barely living, nearly dead slave.

8. Choreography's violence feeds off an omnipotent belief that everything must move according to its wishes. Call it Dr. Frankenstein's paradigm: animation at all costs.

9. Choreography's violence lies in its belief that life is only movement; and, moreover, that living movement is the oriented circulation of electrons shooting through inert matter. It hallucinates that as long as an electrical connection is secured, the rotten shall move, regardless of costs.

10. And yet, despite all this potential for violence, there is a profound irony in Choy Ka Fai's project. A choreographic laughter emerges as potential for freedom within the machinations of commanding transmissions and obedient bodies. In Choy's project we find buzzing noises all the time, and movement happens in and as noise. In this racket, in this commotion, the sonic and the kinetic fuse as one and the same. Leibniz understood the soul (in Latin, *animus*, that is to say, animation) as a permanent buzzing, and Choy links this buzzing animation directly to the ghostly video image of a dancer who is now a corpse (Tatsumi Hijikata) in his own body. And, of course, despite the supposedly direct electric link, the resulting movement is always erratic and *never* the same. This is Choy's revelation—deep, profound, uncannily real: choreography is a dance macabre, and the dancer's softest gestures are but a tamed spasm.

André Lepecki is an associate professor in the Department of Performance Studies at New York University and artistic professor at Stockholm University of the Arts.

1. William Forsythe, lecture at BAM Dialogue (Brooklyn Academy of Music, Brooklyn, New York, October 2, 2003). Quoted in Mark Franko, "Dance and the Political: States of Exception," in *Dance Discourses: Keywords in Dance Research*, ed. Susanne Franco and Marina Nordera (London and New York: Routledge, 2007), p. 16.
2. Michel Serres, *The Parasite* (Minneapolis: University of Minnesota Press, 2007), see especially part two.

Q: Electricity flowing through the human body has a heavy legacy of violence and control, from the execution chamber to electroshock therapy. Can we find levity in Choy Ka Fai's appropriation?

COMMENT 1. Saisha Grayson:
I really appreciate the way artworks can often critique social norms by overperforming them, taking them to their absurd, extreme, blackly humorous ends. In feminist and postcolonial thinking, the fantasy of total control is one of the most dangerous, while the pressure to embody or perform kinds of identity has been something to resist. Here you see the violence of enacting those fantasies upon a body, with jerks and spasms that are both funny and frightening.

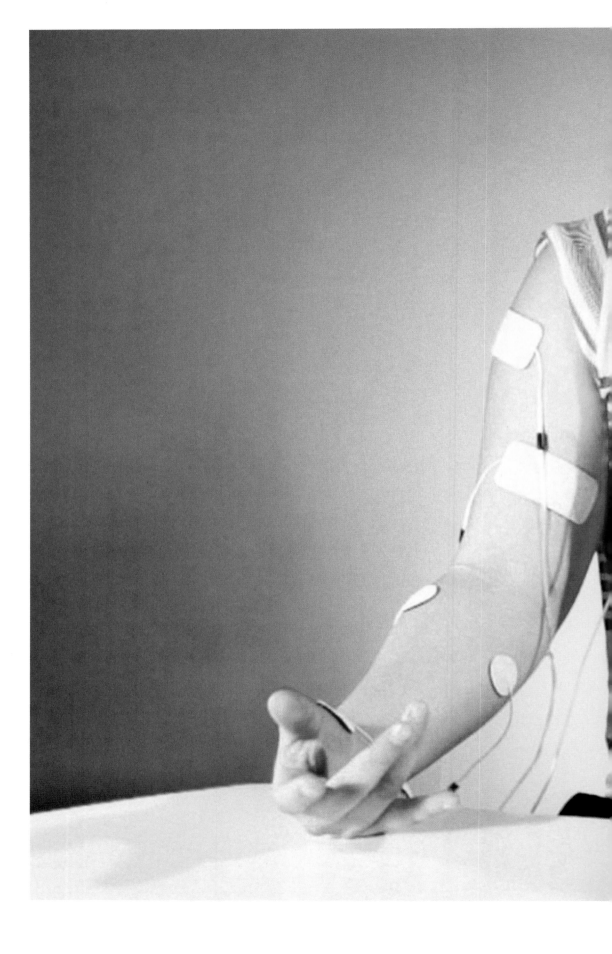

Choy Ka Fai (Singaporean, born 1979).
Bionic Movement Research from the
series Prospectus for a Future Body.
2011. Video (color, sound)

Above and opposite: Choy Ka Fai.
SynchroMetrics from the series
Prospectus for a Future Body. 2011.
Video (color, sound)

Overleaf: Poster image for Choy Ka Fai's
Prospectus for a Future Body. 2011

Scary Beautiful
(Leanie van der Vyver, 2012)

The history of reshaping our feet in the name of aesthetics or as a tool for social control is as old as the practice of foot-binding. The stiletto heel first emerged in the 1930s and was popularized by fashion designer Roger Vivier's work for Christian Dior in the 1950s. This innovation has fomented an obsession with re-forming and deforming the female silhouette using fashionable footwear. Leanie van der Vyver's Scary Beautiful, a pair of "front-heeled" leather shoes, push this vertiginous quest to its limit, exploring the friction between pain and pleasure experienced by the wearer and in some respects the viewer. Scary Beautiful requires the wearer to insert pointed toes into the shoe openings; her shins rest on extensions that tower upward from the heels, forcing the body forward into a taxing semi-squat position. The traditional position of the heel is effectively reversed, moving from the back of the shoe to the front, and the wearer can perform no more than an awkward shuffle forward. Van der Vyver's design critiques our often harsh and sometimes violent standards of beauty by asking how far we will go to meet these standards. How much pain and discomfort are we willing to endure before we begin to reassess what beauty looks like?

Alison Bancroft

Received wisdom tells us that the purpose of fashion is to make women beautiful so that they will be attractive to men. When women are attractive to men, men will then want to have sex with them and/or marry them and/or buy them nice things, and any or all of these will validate the woman in the eyes of the world.

This is what underpins the design philosophy of the formerly disgraced but now seemingly rehabilitated John Galliano. Galliano—fired from his role as creative director at Christian Dior in 2011 for making anti-Semitic and racist remarks, and appointed head of Maison Martin Margiela in 2014—went on record to say, "I want men to look at a woman wearing one of my dresses and to think 'I have to fuck her.'"[1] Whether the woman wants to be fucked, by this mythical gentleman or anyone else, is neither here nor there. A man sticking his penis in you is to be welcomed as the highest accolade you can get as a woman.

As with most received wisdom, the really interesting stuff happens when people reject it, question it, or interpret it in different ways. The same is true of fashion: the most compelling design happens when the necessity of heterosexual penetrative sex is jettisoned in favor of an entirely different endgame. We see this in particular in the work of the late Alexander McQueen, who was often accused of misogyny, but whose stated aim was to make a woman "so fabulous you wouldn't dare lay a hand on her."[2] We see it in Rei Kawakubo's famous distortions of the female form. We see it in Iris van Herpen's sci-fi-esque, shrink-wrapped models suspended in bags above the runway. And we see it in Scary Beautiful. These shoes, conceived by the South African designer Leanie van der Vyver and fabricated by the Dutch shoe designer René van den Berg, reverse the usual relationship between foot and footwear, and the high heel becomes an elevated toe that tilts the wearer to an inhuman angle.

With conventionally attractive body modifications—stiletto-heeled shoes, for instance, or corsets—it is anticipated that the wearer will adapt to the discomfort and restricted movement and will learn to function relatively normally, while still looking as fabulous as the modification intends. No one could ever adapt to the requirements of Scary Beautiful. Instead, the wearer becomes monstrous— another kind of fabulous entirely to the one usually associated with fashion. The elegance associated with high-heeled shoes is replaced with awkward lumbering.

Leanie van der Vyver (South African, 1980). Fabricated in collaboration with René van den Berg (Dutch, 1964). Scary Beautiful. 2012. Leather, carbon fiber, 3 ^{15}⁄₁₆ x 31 ½ x 15 ¾" (10 x 80 x 40 cm)

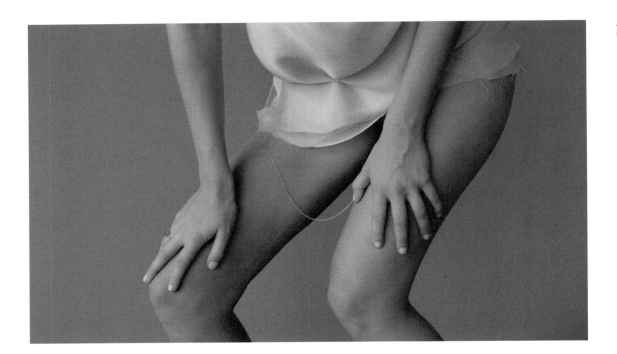

The quality of movement the shoes engender in the model is like something from a *Pan's Labyrinth* monster, not a Fashion Week sashay. Although the model is, as van der Vyver says, "raring to go with her butt crudely sticking out," there is nothing conventionally erotic about her posture. Quite the contrary, in fact. The model looks awkward, distended, misshapen, deformed. Galliano's mythical man would most certainly not want to "fuck her." He'd run a mile at the very idea.

We live in a world where women are expected to be compliant and acquiescent, and are rewarded for providing men with beauty and the type of sex they require. What makes Scary Beautiful so radical is that it rejects these expectations and declines their reward. It suggests instead that the distortions women perform to fulfill the expectations placed on them, when taken to their logical conclusion, are deformations of the self. Body and soul become twisted and contorted beyond recognition.

Scary Beautiful crosses the imaginary line between what is acceptable and what is unacceptable in terms of fashion and feminine sexuality, and in doing so shows how arbitrary the very existence of that line actually is. Beautiful and ugly, sexy and scary, are creations of our own imagining, but there is still the tendency to assume that these things are natural, inevitable, and unchanging. Scary Beautiful is a timely and helpful reminder that they're not.

Alison Bancroft is a writer and cultural critic, specializing in interdisciplinary approaches to modern culture and media.

1. John Galliano, interview by Michael Specter, "Le Freak, C'est Chic," *Observer Magazine*, November 30, 2003, p. 17.
2. Alexander McQueen, interview by Marion Hume, "Scissorhands," *Harpers and Queen*, August 1996, p. 82.

Q: No pain, no gain? Can painfully restrictive clothing ever be beneficial aesthetically, culturally, personally?

COMMENT 1. Lizzie Lincoln:
. . . We need to remind women . . . [that] comfortable is sexy. . . . Unfortunately, there's probably more money in shoes than in women's empowerment so it's unlikely we'll get much help from the marketplace. We'll have to demand the change ourselves.

Trace

To make visible, before or after the fact, the immaterial legacy of violence upon our mental and physical landscapes.

Vice/Virtue Water Glass Series: Dispensary, Exhaust & Fountain (Diller + Scofidio, 1997)

Diller + Scofidio (and Renfro, as of 2004) is a New York–based architecture firm whose practice relies on a lively dialogue with the visual arts, performance, and technology. The Vice/Virtue glass series was produced for the 1997 exhibition *Glassmanifest*, in Leerdam, the Netherlands. In this installation, Diller + Scofidio use drinking glasses along with a measure of subtle humor to explore our often contradictory cultural attitudes toward addiction and health. Their interventions in the design of these glasses—for example, a syringe that forms the stem of a wine glass, suggesting an ambiguous relationship between drinking alcohol and pharmaceutical drugs; are the drugs remedy for alcohol's aftereffects or additional "vice"?—"accommodate the dual pursuits of health and hedonism," explain the architects on their website, one always the ghostly backdrop to the other.

Susan Yelavich

One of my earliest childhood memories lives in a photograph. I was probably five years old, at the beach with my family in Point Pleasant, New Jersey. That was "our" shore town because my grandparents built, owned, and ran a motel there called Ocean View Courts, which, being eight blocks from the beach, actually looked out on Broadway, not the Atlantic. On this particular day, in this particular picture, my parents and I had left our blanket, and on it my younger sister Christine, all alone, just long enough for her to find an illicit prize.

In the 1950s, it was not considered neglectful to turn your back on a small child for a moment or two at the beach. The shore insulated you from the vices of the everyday. (Now, the opposite is apparently true.) Your small, square, plaid cotton badge of admission, pinked around the edges—purchased on the boardwalk and pinned on your bathing suit—was the insurance policy that this was a domestic space, a family haven. (My dad worked for Prudential in Newark, so we knew all about insurance.) Even today, it's common to leave a wallet or purse on your blanket while you take a dip; and when you leave the sand and cross over the boardwalk to the parking lot, you are acutely aware that you've left a peaceful vacuum for a world just waiting to insert you back into its timeline.

On the day in question—and "day" is inaccurate, it was a moment suspended in time just like the photograph that documents it—I remember coming back to our blanket and seeing my sister, who couldn't have been more than three, trying to light one of my father's Winstons. There she sat crouched under the umbrella, her small fingers trying to cup a flame around the cigarette in her mouth. We howled at her dogged determination to light the match, much less the cigarette, and her defeat by the ocean breeze.

Today, when I look at the photograph—and it was always one of our favorites in the family scrapbook—I see a knowing, gleeful parody of an adult. A towheaded blond in a child-size Brown University sweatshirt (my father's alma mater, of course), Chris ignored the camera, daring it to contradict her version of adulthood populated with wisecracking fathers proud of any signs of street-smarts in their offspring, just in case an Ivy League education didn't cover all the bases.

Maybe another family would have simply been horrified at the sight of the child smoker and wouldn't have commemorated it the way we did. (The camera must have been grabbed from the blanket quickly to catch her in the act.) But then that family wouldn't have had a father who was a teenage pilot in World

War II, who kept that romance alive with the angle of his cigarette; a father who was the first in his family to go to college (much to their chagrin—his penance was managing the motel for a year), and who masked his insecurities in smoke.

We children of the 1950s had no idea of the mythology we were imbibing, nor did our parents fully realize that they were perpetuating myths. My father, at eighteen, was told in flight training that he was one of the golden boys—substitute "gods" for "boys" and you get the picture. Even after the counterculture years of the late 1960s (and my parents' own embrace of civil rights and feminism, and their rejection of the Vietnam War), the lingering glow of the 1940s still hovered over our family's sense of itself. Time and memory have no respect for chronology.

War and romance, death and cigarettes, the pleasures and pains of family, beginning with the excruciating act of birth when a new person enters the room and love takes over—we are not hardwired to separate them fully, as anyone's family photo album will prove. If we could only know the future, we might be able to dodge the bullets of addiction, but this is the folly and the tragedy of youth. We wouldn't believe it if they told us.

***

So my father thought. And I do, too, but only to a point. For he also passed on the gene for skepticism, tacitly giving me permission to take exception with his fatalism. Since his death in 1996, an insistent staccato of acronyms—IED, WMD, PTSD—has shot through our veil of ignorance, shredding the glamorous dress uniforms that marched off to war once and for all. My father's grandchildren and their children can no longer maintain the illusion that they don't know the future. They can only choose to believe it will not be their future.

Susan Yelavich is an associate professor and director of the MA Design Studies program in the School of Art and Design History and Theory at Parsons The New School for Design.

Q: Is addiction a form of violence?

COMMENT 1. Aline:
Addiction may be considered violence only in as much as any other disease is also considered violence. Violence, as defined in this project, "is a manifestation of the power to alter circumstances, against the will of others and to their detriment." Although diseases are by nature harmful to our bodies and to our cells, rarely are they inflicted on an individual deliberately and against his or her will. According to the World Health Organization, addiction is a chronic disease. If we accept that addiction is a disease, then to consider addiction violence would be very arbitrary.

The real violence, I believe, emerges when addiction is publicized as something desirable. When ads promote cigarettes, for instance, associating smoking with adventurous or glamorous lifestyles, they mask the real consequences of cigarette addiction, and, in so doing, glamorize a harmful disease.

Elizabeth Diller (American, born Poland 1954) and Ricardo Scofidio (American, born 1935) of Diller + Scofidio (USA, est. 1979). Dispensary from the Vice/Virtue series. 1997. Blown glass with Prozac capsules, 4 x 2 ⅞ x 2 ⅞" (10 x 7 x 7 cm)

Opposite: Elizabeth Diller and Ricardo
Scofidio of Diller + Scofidio. Exhaust.
1997. Blown glass with cigarette,
4 5/16 x 3 3/16 x 3 3/16" (11 x 8 x 8 cm)

Right: Elizabeth Diller and Ricardo Scofidio
of Diller + Scofidio. Fountain. 1997.
Blown glass with hypodermic needle,
variable x 2 7/8 x 2 7/8" (variable x 7 x 7 cm)

Violence
(Sissel Tolaas and Nick Knight, 2013)

From the skunk's capacity to fend off attack using odorous musk to the great white shark's ability to detect even the smallest trace of blood in water, scent has long been yoked to violence in the animal kingdom. Scent designer Sissel Tolaas and photographer Nick Knight teamed up to create a fragrance that charts the emotional landscape of violence in the human world. The scent was created by collecting sweat samples at cage-fighting matches and analyzing the chemicals by means of gas chromatography. The result—an unpleasantly pungent perfume—evokes a provocative mixture of aggressive dominance and sexual behavior captured in the throes of violent action.

Anne-Marie Slaughter

After reading about the production of Violence, a perfume designed by Sissel Tolaas, and looking at the accompanying photographs by Nick Knight, I did not want to open the vial. The thought of a smell wrung from the sweat-soaked T-shirts of cage fighters creates a ripple of distaste and even fear at the imminent prospect of inhaling it, a sensory reaction before the sense in question is even engaged. I shy away, imagining the dankness and rankness of gyms and locker rooms, the nose-wrinkling assault of a packed summer subway or a urine-soaked stairwell.

The vial is incongruously clear and white and sterile; I had imagined a bloodred glass rose with twisted petals and a black heart. The smell seems to hit me even before I remove the cap—old socks? No, the scent is far, far stronger—too strong to hold to my nose for more than a second or two. It is rank, but rank like musk; held at a distance it summons images of stags or musk ox or elk fighting—horns locking, hoofs pawing, the raw pushing of strength against strength. The violence of sex.

Would those images come to mind without the context of cage fighting? I cannot know. But once my initial disgust at the scent wears off, and I smell it again and again, a transformation takes place. The smell itself separates from its context, becoming a spectrum of different scents as if flattening and elongating under my nose. I think, for an instant, that I catch a whiff of rose, surely suggested by Knight's pictures of torn petals. It reminds me that the scent of rose is actually many different scents blending into one. Again and again I smell, until it begins to become denatured—an essence, yes, but of what?

Surely not of man. As I kiss my sons goodnight and press myself against my husband's back in bed, I think about how we know each other by scent just as we do by voice—instantly and individually. Lovers know each other years later by the deep smell of skin; parents inhale their children's hair and neck and chubby folds. So perhaps the violence here is the transformation of the individuality of all men into the hormones that define them as male; the testosterone that creates the characteristics we identify with men rather than women. It is the transformation of design, the claimed search for an essence that is in fact a brute reduction of infinite variation: the distinctive features and feelings even of two men fighting in a particular cage on a particular night with a particular set of instructions, much less of all the men who fight and love and work and care and create.

But by distilling something to an essence—not *the* essence but *an* essence—we also create building blocks for something new. We reduce complexity to simplicity to build a different complexity. If that is the violence of creative destruction, it feels far gentler than grappling for a death grip in a cage. But I may never again look at a vial of perfume without thinking of torn petals and crushed calyces, a violence at the heart of beauty.

Anne-Marie Slaughter is the president and CEO of New America and the Bert G. Kerstetter '66 University Professor Emerita of Politics and International Affairs at Princeton University.

Q: Is violence "male"?

COMMENT 1. Paul:
We should clarify that the scent in question is of physical violence. Don't forget its pernicious sibling—psychological violence. Let's swab some mean girls' underarms after they cyberbully someone and compare, yes?

COMMENT 2. Lisa:
First I just laughed at Paul's comment about the mean girls and cyberbullying. But then I thought how lucky I am that my experiences of physical violence are all detached and scripted: domestic scenes buried within novels, blurred graphic violence on cable news, the flying fists of a rugby game, or the choreographed fighting of Hollywood. And yet I would not think to say I did not know violence or had not experienced the hostility of visible aggression. So I find myself grappling, like other posters, with what the companion pieces to a cage-fighting scent might be? The sheer physicality of cage fighting seems so appropriate to reduce to a scent . . . because I can visualize the sweat. Yet if I think of the hostility that comes with a menacing glare, the hostility that is cast without touch or words, I find myself reflecting not on the scent of the cool aggressor but on the scent of fear emanating from the receiver. Gender aside, for we unfortunately know there are mothers (grown-up mean girls?) capable of psychological violence, it is interesting for me to reflect on how violence structured as sport, entertainment, or even foreign affairs surely has a different scent than the aggressor and victim of a domestic or civilian situation. Or perhaps the scent of fear always goes hand in hand with violence?

COMMENT 3. Diala:
I was born in violence. The true kind, the ruthless, evil, and truly rotten kind; the violence of a civil war. But I still feel lucky, especially compared to the life my mom and dad had to lead. They met under the bombs, got married under siege, and had three daughters in the midst of corruption. And yes, we all made it safe and sound, fifteen years later.

The bomb exploded in our faces, ripping all our senses apart. The smell of violence was not condensed in a jar; it was the air we breathed and the oxygen that made our bodies go. Sadly, it still is today as we reap the aftermath of a wicked bomb exploding inside our guts.

I do not tell you this story to make you feel bad about my family or me. We are not the only country to have suffered from war. I tell you this story because you seem to be looking for violence, and I thought this would be a good time to meet.

I am violence. Or maybe I have become it. Either way; nice to meet you.

In French "violence" is female and in Arabic "violence" is male. I say violence has no gender. Violence is just human, and it is inside each and every one of us.

Where I grew up violence was embraced and almost necessary, so I grew up feeling that it was normal to express loudly my rage. Violence is in our traits, it is benign among us. And it is only when I moved out of the violence (like physically moved continents) that I truly began to see it, distinguish it from the mass.

But violence, in a weird and twisted way, is good. It is good for the soul. When one is not afraid to inhale it in every day, and smell the rank musk, they can begin to move past the violence and can begin to "reduce complexity to simplicity to build a different complexity"—so, basically, reduce the complexity of violence to the simplicity that it is us, inside us. And then the different complexity becomes the intricate relationship between us humans and the violence inside us. We cannot live apart, and it is only by acknowledging that we are violence that we can begin to distill the world around us and maybe even see hope.

And then, and only then, maybe the bomb that exploded in our faces can begin to melt and transform into the cement that holds us together.

Sissel Tolaas (Norwegian, born 1965) and Nick Knight (British, born 1958). Violence. 2013. Scent simulation and glass

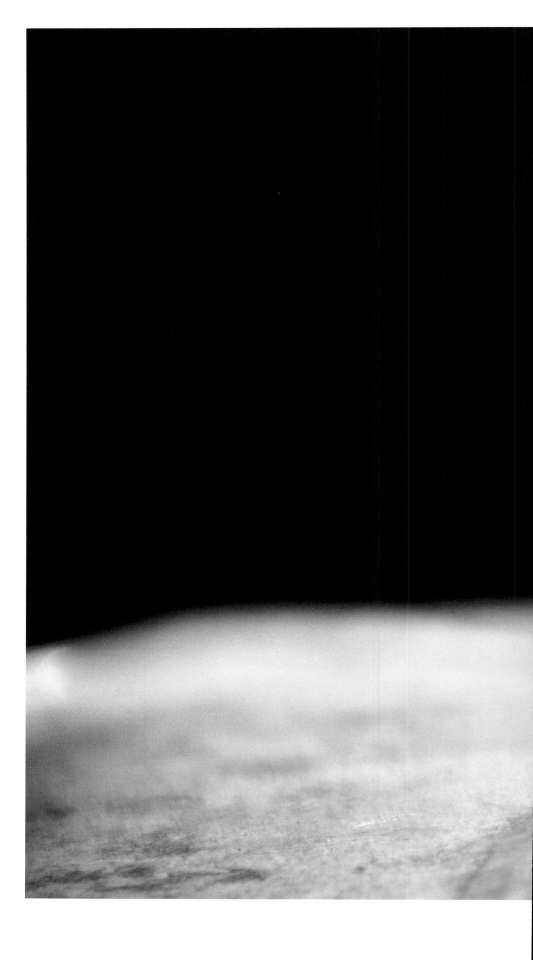

The Stiletto Heel
(Various designers, 1930s)

The stiletto heel, named after the slender Italian dagger of the Renaissance, first appeared in the 1930s. The inventor of this long, often steel-spiked, thin heel remains in dispute, but today many attribute its rise to fame to the work of designer Roger Vivier for Christian Dior in the early 1950s. The stiletto has woven its way in and out of fashion history, but remains a highly charged symbol of sexuality, aggressiveness, and fetishism.

Camille Paglia

The stiletto high heel is modern woman's most lethal social weapon. First imagined in the 1930s, but not realized until postwar technology made it possible in the early 1950s, the stiletto is a visual slash born to puncture and pierce.

While platform shoes increased stature for both men and women, from Greco-Roman actors to Venetian sophisticates on flooded walkways, the slanted structure of current high heels descends from the boots of early medieval horsemen seeking traction in the stirrup. Hence high heels have a masculine lineage, latent in their use by emancipated women eager to rise to men's level.

But this quest for equality, dominance, or merely assertive presence at work and play is contradicted by a crippling construction: no item of female dress since the tight-laced Victorian corset is so mutilating. Pain and deformation are the price of high-heeled beauty. The high heel creates the illusion of a lengthened leg by shortening the calf muscle, arching the foot, and crushing the toes, forcing breasts and buttocks out in a classic hominid posture of sexual invitation.

The eroticization of high heels (still at medium height) was sped along in the 1920s by the rising hemlines of flappers showing off their legs in scandalously hyperkinetic dances like the Charleston. Alfred Hitchcock's fetishistic focus on high heels can be seen throughout his murder mysteries, from his early silent films in London to his Technicolor Hollywood classics like *Vertigo* and *The Birds*, where Tippi Hedren (a former fashion model) demonstrates the exquisite artifice of high-heel wearing as well as its masochistic vulnerability, chronicled in a thousand low-budget horror movies. A woman in high heels, unable to run, is a titillating target for attack.

But the high heel as an instrument of sex war can be witnessed in action in a stunning face-off in *Butterfield 8* (1960), where Elizabeth Taylor as a glossy call girl, her wrist painfully gripped by Laurence Harvey at a chic Manhattan bar, implacably grinds her phallic spike heel into his finely leathered foot. This was at a time when stiletto heels, which concentrate enormous pressure in a tiny space, were banned from buildings with susceptible linoleum or hardwood floors.

It was already being rumored in those pre-Stonewall days that drag queens, harassed on the street, would whip off their high heels and ferociously wield them against assailants. In 2006, noted New York drag queen Flotilla DeBarge was jailed after a barroom fracas where she swung her black high heels (impounded by the police as evidence) to inflict wounds requiring stitches upon an insulting straight man and his date. (One online headline: "Meatpacking District Drag Queen High-Heel Beatdown."[1])

Reports of high-heeled crime were on the increase in 2013. In Washington, D.C., a man complained to the police that a petite woman had hit him in the head with her shoe outside the Ibiza nightclub. After a fight at a Washington 7-Eleven, three women were arrested for stabbing their opponents; one wielded a knife, but the other two used their shoes, leading to the charge "assault with a dangerous weapon." In Houston, Texas, a forty-four-year-old woman was charged with murder after a bloody clash in a condominium tower during which her professor boyfriend died after being struck in the head, face, and neck by thirty blows from her stiletto heels.

The dagger later called a stiletto began as a needle-like medieval tool to finish off a fallen knight by a thrust through chain mail or between plate armor. During the Renaissance, the stiletto became the favorite weapon of Italian

Roger Vivier (French, 1913–1998) for Christian Dior (France, 1946). Evening Shoe. 1954. Silk satin and tulle

assassins, jabbing from behind through heavy fabric or leather and killing invisibly while barely leaving a drop of blood. The stiletto's historic association with deception and treachery thus gives an aura of sadistic glamor to the modern high heel, whose stem contains a concealed shaft of steel. Woman as seducer or seduced can also lance and castrate.

Helmut Newton, whose superb fashion photography was suffused with the perverse worldview of his native Weimar Berlin, captured the disturbing complexities of the high heel in *Shoe*, a picture taken in Monte Carlo in 1983. Here we see the fashionable shoe in all its florid delicacy and dynamic aggression. The stance, with shifted ankle, seems mannish. Is this a dominatrix poised to trample her delirious victim? Or is it a streetwalker defiantly defending her turf? Or a drag queen scornfully pissing in an alley? The shoe, shot from the ground, seems colossal, a pitiless totem of pagan sex cult.

The luxury high heel as status marker is directed not toward men but toward other women—both intimate confidantes and bitter rivals. The high heel in its dazzlingly heraldic permutations (as dramatized in *Sex and the City*) is beyond the comprehension of most men: only women and gay men can tell the difference between a Manolo Blahnik and a Jimmy Choo. In full disclosure, I never wear these shoes and indeed deplore their horrifying cost at a time of urgent social needs. Nevertheless, I acknowledge and admire the high heel as a contemporary icon and perhaps our canonical objet d'art.

At the Neiman Marcus department store at the King of Prussia Mall in suburban Philadelphia, a visitor ascending the escalator to the second floor is greeted by a vast horizon of welcoming tables, laden with designer shoes of ravishing allure but staggering price tags (now hovering between $500 and $900 a pair but soaring to $6,000 for candy-colored, crystal-studded Daffodile pumps by Christian Louboutin). Despite my detestation of its decadence, this theatrical shoe array has for years provided me with far more intense aesthetic surprise and pleasure than any gallery of contemporary art, with its derivative gestures, rote ironies, and exhausted ideologies.

Designer shoes represent the slow but steady triumph of the crafts over the fine arts during the past century. They are streamlined works of modern sculpture, wasteful and frivolous yet elegantly expressive of pure form, a geometric reshaping of soft and yielding nature. An upscale shoe department is a gun show for urban fashionistas, a site of ritual display where danger lurks beneath the mask of beauty.

Camille Paglia is the University Professor of Humanities and Media Studies at the University of the Arts in Philadelphia and the author of six books.

1. Chris Mohney, "Meatpacking District Drag Queen High-Heel Beatdown," *Gawker*, October 3, 2006, http://gawker.com/204921/meatpacking-district-drag-queen-high-heel-beatdown.

Q: Is the stiletto heel "modern woman's most lethal social weapon"?

COMMENT 1. Burcu:
. . . The sound of a stiletto heel hitting the ground violates silence around the wearer in many ways, and surely signifies the presence of a woman without the appearance. In a silent library, a hospital corridor, or a conference room, the stiletto wearer manifests her presence: an imposing, abstract weapon that approaches to others without permission. Sound, however, also makes this weapon's bearer quite vulnerable. As much as we can detect self-confidence, seduction or flirtation, and determination through rhythm, frequency, and volume, we can also detect impatience, hurry, fear, and anger. . . .

COMMENT 2. Juan Pablo Pemberty:
For me, the stiletto heel functions within a social realm. Their use is not wholly explained by their function. They do not work as a form of self-protection as Paglia suggests. Neither are they strictly communicative, nor do they conform to the kind of feminist discourses that say that the stiletto heel is an object of women's subordination. Rather their form lets women transform their body image and get an intense sense of corporeality, as the body elongates and reaches upwards. Lee Wright, in "Objectifying Gender," [published in *Fashion Theory: A Reader*, ed. Malcolm Barnard, 2008] writes, "The stiletto heel points out that clothes were meant to be an extension of the female figure to emphasize it rather than distract from it."

The stiletto heel changes the gait of women, the measure at which they normally walk, and, more fundamentally, their posture. Far from being an actual weapon, they are a prosthesis, an extension of the body, a symbol of status that gives woman a sense of power and control.

COMMENT 3. Shenyangzi Wang:
In response to Burcu's post, I think her recognition of sound as a part of the design of stiletto heel is brilliant. Sound is a feminine signal. The clear and striking noise cannot be ignored since it is making a ringing statement about its existence. It is interesting because the sound has various rhythms and beats, which depend on the wearer. [Stilettos] show their owners' characteristics by making different types of noises. Therefore, sometimes we can recognize the female just by judging the sound of her heels without actually seeing her. The sound and the person have somehow merged into a new being, which owns its unique power and strength.

However, not everyone likes the click of the heels; the beat of the shoes sometimes affects the speed of heartbeat, especially when the sound is approaching. The real terror of a weapon is not its physical power but the uncertainty it creates. When sound is perceived before we see where it comes from or from whom it comes, we do not know what is going to happen next; all we can do is to wait until the sound passes and fades away. Maybe that is the real weapon of women: mysterious uncertainty.

COMMENT 4. Katherine Moyer:
The stiletto heel's association with a weapon should be separated into two notions: on and off the foot. When off the foot, this pointy-heeled shoe is simply another dagger-like object useful for self-defense and the infliction of pain on an attacking enemy, as in the Washington, D.C., crime discussed above. This use of the stiletto comes as no surprise considering it derives its name from the small Italian dagger its heel brings to mind. Sharp and dangerous, yet elegant and powerful, the stiletto shoe, when placed upon a female foot, becomes a psychological weapon within the society in which it walks.

This brings me to the second notion: its use as a weapon once on the foot. This shoe immediately enhances its wearer, making her not only physically taller, but also socially more powerful. The most immediate shift is upward, as the heel is raised several inches off the floor. Through height, one is given power and presence, making the stiletto a weapon of personal ambition and pursuit. The authority embedded in the shoe is translated directly to its occupier, creating supremacy over others when in social situations. The feeling of mastery and accomplishment that comes from wearing the shoe trumps the pain and aggravation caused by its wearing. The shoe is also rooted with historical agency—the notion that powerful women over the years have worn these shoes. This intensifies the appeal and creates a consistent demand for this elegant yet powerful shoe style. The stereotype of the heel wearer is one that endures a life of desire, poise, and injury. The stiletto is inherently paradoxical in its form and function. Camille's statement cautions this. It is "a site of ritual display where danger lurks beneath the mask of beauty." In the literal sense, it is a pointy object; in the figurative sense, it is a symbol of ambition and power. The stiletto shoe is a double-entendre form of a weapon.

Head Hand Bag
(Yael Mer, 2006)

The Head Hand Bag translates the violence of decapitation into an object of practical use. Designer Yael Mer's practice focuses on turning two-dimensional sheet materials into shaped forms. Here, flat felt is molded around the foam template of a human head to create a shadowy but recognizably male facial mask in the shape of a bag. The bag is part of a series inspired by the biblical story of Judith and Holofernes, a favorite subject of seventeenth-century Baroque painters such as Caravaggio and Artemisia Gentileschi. In a story that is now presumed to be parable rather than history, brave Judith, having first gained the trust of Assyrian general Holofernes, approaches him in his tent. She then decapitates him in his drunken stupor in order to save her people, the Israelites. The bag, as Mer explained in an email, isn't unisex; it is designed for women to channel Judith's glory at her moment of victory. "Even if the wearer doesn't know the backstory," Mer writes, "there is still something very clear, powerful, and primitive about the meaning of holding a man's head in this way." Mer studied at the Royal College of Art in London, graduating in 2006. She is part of Raw-Edges Design Studio, a collaboration with designer Shay Alkalay.

Cintra Wilson

Yael Mer's drawstring Head Hand Bags are the MUST "It bag" for this or any other fashion season. While a Louis Vuitton doctor bag, an oversize Goyard tote, or the ever-prohibitive Hermès Birkin is each equally capable of toting a human head from the boardroom to the beach to the speakeasy and straight to Perdition afterward (the discotheque under the speakeasy), only Mer's Head Hand Bag also contains the Judith-and-Holofernes subtext that insouciant, in-the-know Renaissance artists like Donatello liked to employ as an allegory of the commune rising up against the tyranny of the ruling class.

It's a handbag that asks today's rebel fashionista: What's the point of going through all the trouble of seducing and decapitating your oppressor if you're just going to conceal your victory in a Coach weekender? Let everyone know what's really going in your overhead rack on Hampton Jitney. Flaunt that trophy, Girl—and hang it from the tallest wooden stake outside your bedroom as a warning to unwanted invaders.

Even decades before that cross-dressing silver fox with the homespun toga and trendsetting lumberjack beard brought the first stone tablets of Fashion Law down from Mount Bergdorf, ladies have endured numberless tortures at the hands of sartorial sadists: forehead flattening, foot binding, whalebone corsets, chemical peels, the Hervé Léger bandage dress (ad nauseam and an extra fifteen pounds).

Head Hand Bags are Yael Mer's bloodlusty howl toward a brave new psycho-sexual-cum-socioeconomic battlefield (which, like the ever-recurring themes in fashion itself, is pretty much exactly the same psychosexual-cum-socioeconomic battlefield that it has always been, recut for today's nonstop lifestyle, without references to outré standby silhouettes like the cast-iron chastity belt or the monochromatic Gloria Steinem pantsuit).

Don't let your inner witch burn with unfulfilled handbag desire, ladies. This is a killer investment piece (particularly if you've taken out a healthy life-insurance policy on your prospective victim, wink-wink).

Whether you're a seasoned snuff-drunk murderess or just beginning to assemble your new look for crime, cry, "Have It!" And let's swipe Head Hand Bags of war!

Author, performer, and disgraced *New York Times* fashion critic Cintra Wilson is the author of three books denouncing the hypocrisies of our age, including *A Massive Swelling: Celebrity Re-Examined as a Grotesque, Crippling Disease* (New York: Viking Penguin, 2000).

Yael Mer (Israeli, 1976). Royal College of Art, London (est. 1837). Head Hand Bag. 2006. Woolen felt, 8 ⅝ x 7 ⅟₁₆" (22 x 18 cm); circumference 22" (56 cm)

Q: Can fashion ever productively or seriously engage with violence?

COMMENT 1. JW:

I am sure that, from the point of view of any artist, there can be a want/will to productively engage with any subject that weighs on her mind or stimulates her creatively. However, authorship is not limited to the artist and in this day, when exposure is at an all-time extreme, eliciting the reaction for which the artist might have hoped seems as likely as finding the needle in the haystack, particularly in the arena of fashion.

By now, we've seen fashion filter just about everything for every different reason and we are inured to the impact of that which once would have been "shocking." Kitsch, fetishism, irony, cultural expression, and self-expression are the standard of the day and one could, through any of those lenses, note this bag and react without real regard. That isn't to say that there isn't merit in the expression of the artist, but I do presume that its ability to make a greater/more serious impact is markedly limited. The ability for interpretation in a world that is habituated/fascinated by violence is too broad. My initial thought might have been "maybe the designer just likes the drama of Greek tragedy and wishes there was more in our daily life . . . " A severed head can be silly just as easily as it can be severe in 2014.

If fashion wanted to productively engage with violence, I would imagine that it could not effectively do so via the gimmick (i.e., the image), but rather it would need to take a stand about how and where and from what and in what way its products are made. The end result of design, no matter how graphic, can mean nothing if we all remain complicit in the atrocious things that happen in order to fill our stores and our closets.

Drone Shadows
(James Bridle, 2012–ongoing)

James Bridle is a writer, publisher, artist, and technologist based in London. Drone Shadows, a series born in collaboration with product designer Einar Sneve Martinussen, forms but one part of Bridle's wide-ranging visual and textual activism tackling issues germane to the post-privacy era: secret surveillance, extraordinary rendition, and the systems that permit and encourage such violence against and among citizen subjects. He has written and lectured extensively on what he terms the "New Aesthetic"—the visual and social systems produced by the increasing interconnectedness of virtual and physical worlds. Drone Shadows makes the impact of unmanned aerial vehicles (UAVs) visible at a one-to-one scale. Drones are effectively invisible, leaving the operators completely unaccountable for their actions. For Bridle, the drone also represents the now ubiquitous network of technologies that makes observation and action possible at a distance. As Bridle writes on his blog Booktwo, "Those who cannot perceive the network cannot act effectively within it, and are powerless. The job, then, is to make such things visible."

Arianna Huffington

James Bridle's Drone Shadows, a series of one-to-one renderings of military drone aircraft outlined in chalk, does what all great art does: it makes us see what was already there in a new way. His work spotlights a contemporary fact of existence all too easy to forget when we are not ourselves directly threatened. We now live in a world of drones—but most of us don't see them or experience the terror they provoke.

The invisibility of the U.S. drone program in countries like Pakistan and Afghanistan is, of course, by design. And that's what's so dangerous about this new world. Drones are operated covertly, as they surveil and target flickering, shadowy "suspects." The idea that they perform with surgical accuracy is a fallacy; these hi-tech machines cannot ensure zero civilian casualties or clean consciences. The drone was first introduced to the U.S. military arsenal with very little political discussion; even as its uses proliferate, the degree of dialogue remains unchanged. This is one of the effects of drones—to take what should be part of our national discourse and make it unseen, hidden, secret. (Except, of course, for the increasing number of those living under drones twenty-four hours a day.) And that is why it is so valuable when artists bring this dialogue back to the open where it belongs, as Bridle does with a work that's both powerful and provocative.

Bridle's series at once evokes past crimes (by echoing the chalk outline at a crime scene) and foreshadows possible crimes to come. It acts as public memorial to the thousands of nameless and faceless drone victims. He makes us see—or, more important, unable *not* to see—the fact that for many, drones are a persistent presence both in the air and on the ground.

His work augments our vision; events ordinarily on the periphery are brought into focus. By moving the world of drones out of the shadows, Bridle forces us to confront what's being done in our name.

Arianna Huffington is the chair, president, and editor in chief of the Huffington Post Media Group; a nationally syndicated columnist; and the author of thirteen books.

Q: What other secretive acts carried out on behalf of the public need to be made more visible?

COMMENT 1. Hussain Salahuddin:
Although this post just described James Bridle's [Drone Shadows] through an observer's perspective, it failed to analyze or acknowledge the lack of connection between the artist and the subject. Bridle made life-sized chalk outlines of drones in different areas. After reading the essay by Ian Hargreaves and Nassim Jafarinaimi about human-centered design and its different forms of implementation, I think that this is another example of design labeling itself as human centered just for validity and purpose. Arianna Huffington talks about how this design reiterates and reinforces the presence of something that already exists. This post spoke about how we forget things when they do not physically threaten us because we do not encounter them daily. "The invisibility of the U.S. drone program in countries like Pakistan and Afghanistan is by design." However, coming from Pakistan, it is something that is definitely instilled in our minds. The drone serves as a MacGuffin in a movie: we know of their presence, and there is constant fear instilled in our minds, even though there might not even be a real threat. This project spoke to me in its content, but failed when it came to its context and setting. Had Bridle visited countries that were frequently affected by U.S. drone attacks, and done the same thing, it would be more of a design statement, and would fuel support against fear instilled through this device. Through that, the design would be more meaningful because not only will it set a problem, but it will make a statement about how to solve the problem. It can make people more aware, by getting people's support against such protocol because as the post stated, "The idea that they perform with surgical accuracy is a fallacy; these hi-tech machines cannot ensure zero civilian casualties or clean consciences." He brings the "world of drones out of the shadows," but making that in Washington, D.C., is hardly making a statement.

I think the post poses a very interesting question in the end: "What other secretive acts carried out on behalf of the public need to be made more visible?" I think this could evolve a project like this to a larger scale. Thinking about companies like Google and their recent case over the Google Street View car stealing computer history and passwords from the locations it crossed. Hidden cameras everywhere, devices recording conversations, the FBI having the ability to activate anyone's MacBook camera and viewing them without their knowledge. All of these actions, although we might personally think are invading our privacy, are justified by the cause of the greater good and safety of our community.

James Bridle (British, born 1980). Drone Shadow 004, Washington, D.C., USA, from the series Drone Shadows. 2013. Spray paint, 66 x 36' (2,000 x 1,100 cm)

Overleaf: James Bridle. Drone Shadow 003, Brighton, U.K., from the series Drone Shadows. 2013. Road-marking paint, 66 x 36' (2,000 x 1,100 cm)

James Bridle (British, born 1980). Drone Shadow 002, Istanbul, Turkey, from the series Drone Shadows. 2012. Road-marking paint, 49 x 30' (1,500 x 900 cm)

Digital Attack Map
(Google Ideas, 2013)

Since the late 1990s, hackers, cyberactivists, and other denizens of the Internet have deployed distributed-denial-of-service (DDoS) attacks to slow or crash the websites of multinational corporations, political administrations, and, less often, individuals: by overwhelming a site's servers with hundreds of thousands of requests, the attacks render the site temporarily unavailable, disrupting service to legitimate users. Motives include anything from vandalism to censorship to causing financial loss. Google Ideas, Google's Big Picture Group, and security experts Arbor Networks teamed up to create the Digital Attack Map, a way to visualize in real time these elusive offensives as they are carried out across the globe. This interactive map documents daily DDoS attacks using data from Arbor Networks customers who have agreed to share anonymous network traffic and attack statistics. This process of data visualization reveals trends and patterns over time. The controversial nature of these online threats is perhaps more difficult to parse. Are we witnessing anticapitalist hacktivism? State-sponsored terrorism? Corporate espionage? In our post–Edward Snowden reality, there are no ready answers.

Gabriella Coleman

The early era of the Internet was all glowing-green, text-only VT100 console displays in computer labs on xterms, connected over dial-up modems, Unix-to-Unix Copy Protocol (UUCP), and Usenet; a small set of people, mostly engineers and academics using as well as designing its protocols; people playing multiuser-domain roleplaying games (MUDs) or arguing over newsgroup hierarchies; unbounded and breathless enthusiasm for its future possibilities and potential impact on humanity; delight and wonder imagined and experienced in this once-safe space, before trolls, "clueless" users, spam, viruses, and hacks invaded.

Clearly, so much has changed.

Today, large swaths of the population are plugged into the web, and it encompasses every sphere of human activity: trite and tiring work; entertainment, business, and moneymaking; informal and formal education; love, romance, and pornography; wily protest and civic endeavors; crime, intrigue, and conflict. Despite these transformations, and barring small moments of breakdown or annoyance, most Internet users, at least those with decent access, still experience the web as smooth and frictionless. They are blissfully unaware of its knotted and turbulent underworlds, or the worlds from which it grew.

But technologists, like the systems administrators who tend to the software and hardware that make the digital world come alive, work around the clock to contain the fires, mishaps, breakdowns, and conflicts that constantly bedevil the Internet. A computer, upon connection, is immediately at risk. The wilds of the Internet are constantly bombarding a system, either erroneously, maliciously, or experimentally. The deluge of problems, an exhaustive list that cannot possibly be enumerated, includes everything from spam, software compromises, and malware to distributed-denial-of-service (DDoS) attacks. The last of these, an online assault to either slow or crash a website by flooding it with traffic from multiple sources, now lands regularly in the news, thanks in part to its prolific use as a protest tactic. No longer residing in the realm of technical expertise alone, DDoS attacks have become a topic of careful contemplation and heated debate. Early Internet denizens are awed when they hear news reports of DDoS attacks. For them, worlds formerly discrete are colliding: not long ago these early

Fernanda Viégas (Brazilian, born 1971), Martin Wattenberg (American, born 1970), Colin McMillen (American, born 1981), and CJ Adams (American, born 1985). Google Ideas (est. 2010). Google Big Picture Team (est. 2010). Arbor Networks (est. 2000). Digital Attack Map. 2013. Custom Javascript, HTML, and D3

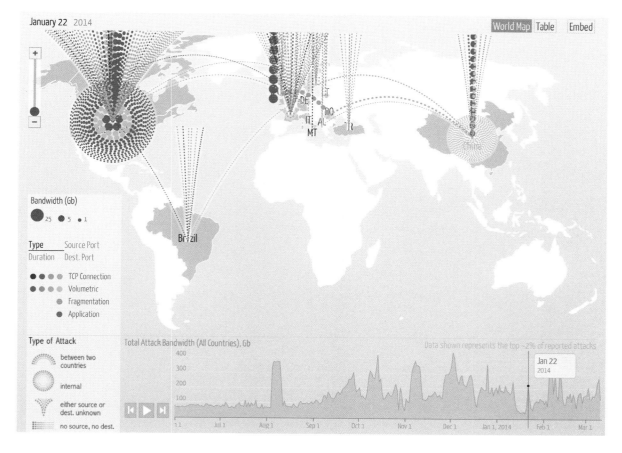

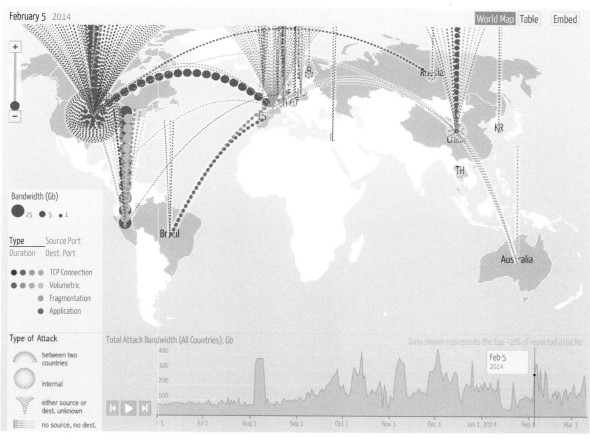

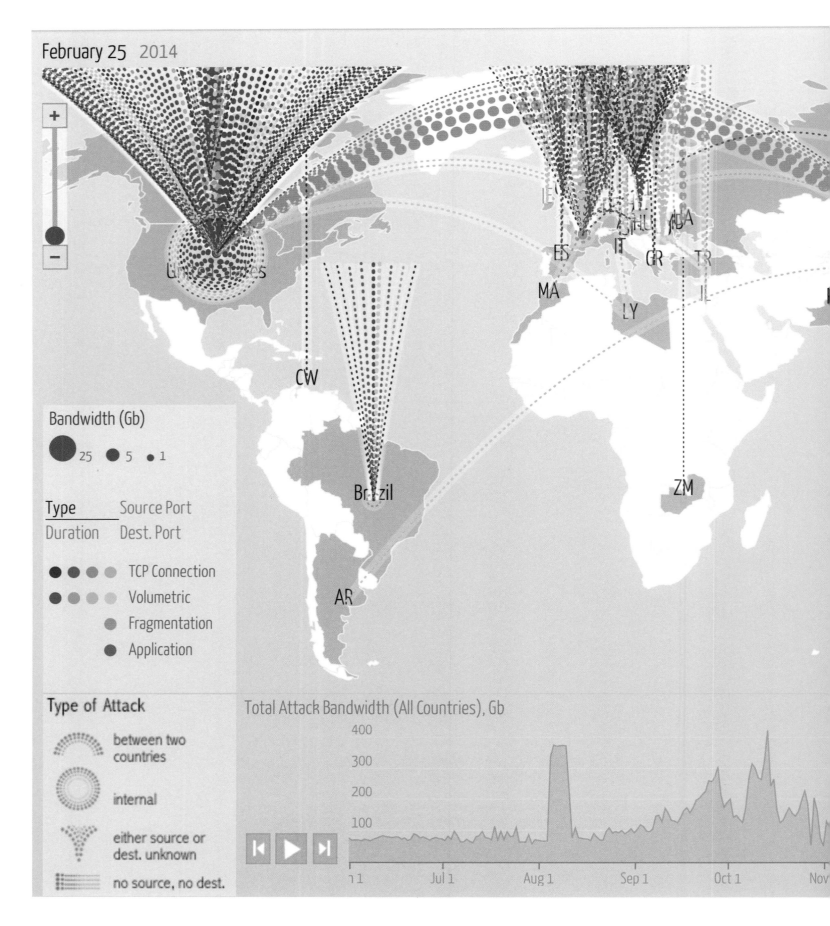

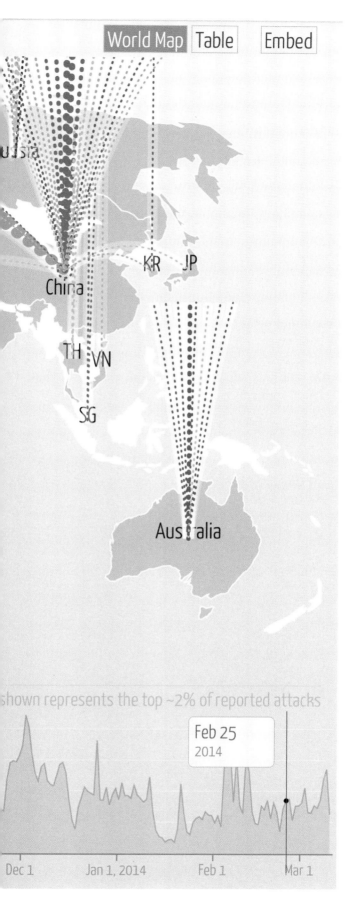

Fernanda Viégas, Martin Wattenberg,
Colin McMillen, and CJ Adams. Google
Ideas. Google Big Picture Team. Arbor
Networks. Digital Attack Map. 2013

World Map | Table | Embed

...shown represents the top ~2% of reported attacks

Feb 25
2014

Dec 1   Jan 1, 2014   Feb 1   Mar 1

adopters lived in a futuristic bubble, where the mere prospect of explaining email, even, was dismissed as an impossible endeavor.

If the DDoS attack has percolated into public consciousness, it has done so in fits and starts, spread by purposive offensives meant to send a political message or by those of incidentally massive scale. Many are unaware of the tactic's omnipresence—multiple attacks are happening at this very instant. Yet, despite its ubiquity, like so many conflicts online, the DDoS attack remains submerged, impossible for the public to see, gauge, or even sense. There is no photograph of a DDoS to tweet, no place to stand to witness the phenomenon firsthand, no object to hold up to the light and examine.

The Digital Attack Map swoops in to fill this void, rendering the invisible and arcane into the visible and legible. Its most important achievement is the simple fact of revealing presence. It shows not only that DDoS attacks are ongoing but also where they are happening and at what intensity. You can see the entire globe in one frame and watch the geyser of activity represented through so many streams of candy-colored bubbles.

The difficult task of showcasing a world's worth of complicated information in a visually beautiful, streamlined, and uncluttered presentation is stunningly accomplished but necessarily limited. The data animating the map is massive, yet partial. The map can only offer glimpses into what is happening and can never reveal what has motivated the different attacks. The source is almost always hidden through misdirection and cloaking. Still, in the face of necessary incompleteness, the design shrewdly offers more than a simple representation of the technical data on which the map is built, nudging the project toward the messy realm of social life. The map connects us to news reports that offer scraps of clues as to motivation and to source.

The patterns and flows might reveal broad geopolitical realities. At this point in time, Africa is rarely the target destination for DDoS attacks. A net positive, one might think—until considering that this happy state of affairs is predicated on the continent's digital desolation, an entrenched artifact of colonial underdevelopment. Russia, North America, much of Western Europe, and China, on the other hand, are constantly assailed. We can observe that geopolitical power is a magnet for conflict.

We can also see, nearly every day, an attack or two that demands individual scrutiny. In mid-March, Peru was one of the lone South American nations on the receiving end of a DDoS attack. Might it be in retaliation for the government's crackdown against nude streakers in Machu Pichu? Or did something far less conspicuous provoke the offensive? A war between drug lords over failed shipments, a political effort to stifle speech, or simply some misconfigured technology going haywire might have triggered the automated attempt to access a server ad infinitum, until some human took note and made it stop.

The map provides no answers to these questions. But the fact that it prompts us to ask them at all makes this design compelling. Even if the map cannot fully capture the architectonics and emotional valences of the DDoS attack, it allows us to see the Internet on slightly different terms—to grasp its dynamism, see its supports, and imagine it as a contested space. To examine the web's infrastructure, and the labor required to maintain it, is to step away from the false idol of "immateriality" that has plagued Internet studies for so long. The Digital Attack Map places the Internet squarely in the plane of its messy and conflicting actualities.

Gabriella Coleman is an author and professor. Trained as an anthropologist, she holds the Wolfe Chair in Scientific and Technological Literacy at McGill University, Montreal.

Q: Are DDoS attacks the most violent online threat, or does something even more threatening exist?

COMMENT 1. Tom Holt:

The attack map is an excellent demonstration of how to visualize complex big data to understand cybercrime on a global scale. DDoS attacks may not, however, be the greatest act of violence occurring online today. Some of the first groups to engage in this sort of attack, like the Electronic Disturbance Theater (EDT) in the 1990s, argued that [DDoS] constituted a form of nonviolent protest. In essence, they compared denial-of-service attacks to blocking the staircases or doors of a building and refusing individuals access without destroying or damaging services. Certainly the economic harm that results from long-term DDoS attacks against financial institutions and government resources are real and substantial, but the loss of actual information or damage to systems is hard to quantify relative to attacks like CryptoLocker or Stuxnet (though an extreme example). The author is absolutely correct that we need to understand the motivation of attackers as well. Since DDoS attacks have become easy to scale through botnets and other standalone attack platforms like the Low Orbit Ion Cannon, low-skill hackers (or script kiddies) and interested citizens may see this as a way to express their opinion about a person, a business, or a government. In addition, the capabilities of hackers and attackers varies by the access to technology and infrastructure within their nation. Thus, nations like Peru that have a very small hacker community may see DDoS attacks as a mechanism to gain notoriety in the short term, while developing greater sophistication over the long term. . . .

Million Dollar Blocks
(Spatial Information Design Lab, 2006)

Of the more than two million people in jails and prisons in the United States, a disproportionate number come from a few neighborhoods—typically low-income communities of color—in the country's largest cities. In some areas, the concentration is so dense that states are spending in excess of a million dollars a year to incarcerate the residents of single city blocks. Using rarely accessible data from the criminal-justice system, the Spatial Information Design Lab and the Justice Mapping Center have created maps of these "million dollar blocks" and the city-prison-city-prison migration flow in five of the nation's cities. Shown here is the map of Brooklyn, New York. Zeroing in on the Brownsville neighborhood, the data visualization bears witness to the fact that, as the project statement outlines, "on a financial scale, prisons can be said to be the predominant governing institution" in these million-dollar neighborhoods.

Steven Pinker

Information graphics have been given a bad name by *USA Today*. Many people think of them as ways of tarting up a trend of the day, as a bit of frivolous eye candy. Nothing could be further from the truth. Our ability to understand the world depends on grasping complicated relationships among variables—how people, money, actions, power, things, and qualities are distributed in space, how they vary in time, and how they affect one another. The human brain did not evolve to do such complex calculations. But we are primates, with almost a third of our brain devoted to vision and visual cognition. Translating complicated relationships into visual formats is a way to co-opt our primate neural circuitry to meet the demands of understanding our world. And it is a challenge in which the creativity of artists, graphic designers, and other visual thinkers is essential. We have made do with standard graphical formats—pie charts, line graphs, organizational charts, and so on since the eighteenth century, if not earlier. We need to figure out how to use the resources of the page and the screen—shape, contour, color, shading, motion, texture, and depth—not only to channel data into brains, but also to reveal subtle relationships as visual patterns.

Nowhere is this need more apparent than in the understanding of violence. Murder, rape, assault, and robbery all shot up in the 1960s, then came crashing down again in the 1990s, and no one really understands why. Most analysts believe the American imprisonment boom had something to do with it, since people behind bars cannot commit crimes on the street. But it's clear that long ago we reached diminishing or even reversing returns: we throw far too many people in jail for far too long. Knowing the right amount of criminal punishment—enough to keep rapists off the streets, but not so much that it ruins lives and communities and diverts resources from more productive uses—is the kind of multidimensional challenge that common sense is ill-equipped to handle. Million Dollar Blocks (a collaboration between the Justice Mapping Center and the Spatial Information Design Lab that maps the flow of prisoners in five major cities and highlights the blocks in which the annual cost of imprisoning its residents is higher than a million dollars) forces us to grasp the social and economic costs of overimprisonment in a way that no list of sentences or table of numbers could do.

Steven Pinker is the Johnstone Family Professor in the Department of Psychology at Harvard University and the author of seven books.

Laura Kurgan (South African, born 1961), Eric Cadora (American, born 1962), David Reinfurt (American, born 1971), and Sarah Williams (American, born 1974). Spatial Information Design Lab (est. 2004), Graduate School of Architecture, Planning and Preservation, Columbia University (USA, est. 1881). Architecture and Justice from the Million Dollar Blocks project. 2006. ESRI ArcGIS software

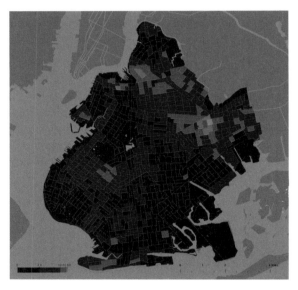

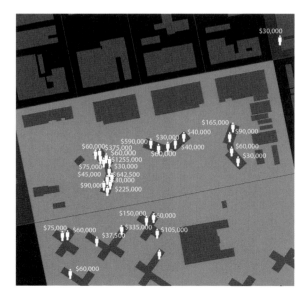

Laura Kurgan, Eric Cadora, David Reinfurt, and Sarah Williams. Spatial Information Design Lab, Graduate School of Architecture, Planning and Preservation, Columbia University. Architecture and Justice from the Million Dollar Blocks project. 2006

Q: Seeing is believing. Can information graphics alone clarify reality and influence policy?

COMMENT 1. Farai Chideya:
As someone who lives in Crown Heights, a rapidly gentrifying Brooklyn neighborhood that has gone from crack vials to eleven-dollar organic juice in the supermarket, I see how policing is affected by gentrification. . . . An important part of the neighborhood-to-prison-to-neighborhood pipeline is the paradox that violence and crime are seen as less problematic when the neighborhood is less wealthy. And of course, much of the crack cocaine sold in the old Crown Heights was sold to wealthier and whiter people who came to get their supply, and then left to smoke at home.

COMMENT 2. Shana Agid:
. . . Whose violence are we seeing here? In my own design work with an organization working in a midsize West Coast U.S. city on issues of policing, I've been wondering what happens to designers' practices when we allow ourselves to question the construction of some basic ideas that bring order and structure to our capacity to identify "problems" and "stakeholders." The group with which I work does not take "crime" for granted as a static category, but rather as one that is constructed to produce particular—and limited—ideas of both "violence" and "safety." If we, as designers, are willing to read across the grain, to not take for granted, for example, the idea that police are the primary experts on "crime" or that "violence" can be traced through arrest rates, then it has the capacity to greatly shift our practice, acknowledging that design (and designers) are one more contingent and moving part in complex design processes. This mapping project by the Spatial Information Design Lab and the Justice Mapping Center helps to reveal not only patterns of confinement and removal, but assumptions about what is worth seeing and how we learn to interpret what we see in relationship to hotly contested issues regarding policing, imprisonment, racism, and space. These questions are, and must be made, central to any designing around issues of imprisonment, violence, or "crime."

COMMENT 3. Cameron Tonkinwise:
"Eye-opening." And then? . . . The assumption is that the (designed) graphic does more than (undesigned) prose about the same issue. (Is the catchy title part of the design or the discourse? What about the concept that drove the research that the graphic merely illustrates?) If the graphic gains something in speed and force, it seems to lose other things with respect to complexity and context. The proposals to layer graphics onto each other would be difficult to design without re-prosifying the graphic. So there is a violence to the graphic in its reductivism and formalism.

And it is of course very beautiful in the modernist, clean-lines, silhouette-with-political-red, sophisticated-i.e.-expensive-data-tech way that my class and cultural upbringing have made me value. Is there even more violence to the graphic-as-violent-to-context detail (see above) when it conceals that violence beneath beauty? Or does it become even more beautiful precisely because it manages to make state- and capital-based violence beautiful? . . .

COMMENT 4. Susan Yelavich:
What is the value of this kind of navel gazing on design and violence? Of the value of commentary (through things and words) in an admittedly elite context, in the context of nowhere and everywhere—the web? What is the value of ideas without action? Hannah Arendt would, I think, have argued that political action flows from places that enable public speech. We are in one of those places here. What matters is the quality of speech it engenders. The objects seem less consequential than the comments they provoke or do not.

To return the legitimate and provocative critique offered by Cameron—that cultural institutions neuter violence by their distance from it—I would say that this is the paradox of design writ large. We can only hope that conversations, no matter how small, no matter whether conducted through words or things, will lead us to more thoughtful action.

The Refugee Project
(Hyperakt & Ekene Ijeoma, 2014)

People who flee across international borders seeking asylum, and thus refugee status, leave their homes and lives behind. The devastation wrought by such forced migrations due to conflict, famine, persecution, and other life-threatening circumstances has been chronicled historically through oral testimony, journalism, and photographs such as those made by Walker Evans and Dorothea Lange during the Great Depression. More recently, the advent of mass and social media has fostered a newly global awareness. Refugee crises are documented and disseminated through both television and the Internet, enabling the world to bear witness to the multilayered violence that displaces and uproots people. The Refugee Project synthesizes data gathered by the Office of the United Nations High Commissioner for Refugees (UNHCR) to visually narrate the forced migrations of refugees around the world since 1975. Although the United Nations is required under the 1951 Refugee Convention to provide protection to those seeking asylum "owing to a well-founded fear of being persecuted for reasons of race, religion, nationality, membership of a particular social group or political opinion," many refugees fall outside this categorization. The UNHCR tries to assist all stateless and displaced people, not just "refugees" as defined under international law, but data for The Refugee Project is limited to only those legal, registered refugees under the protection of the UNHCR. The data therefore excludes, for example, those who have been internally displaced; those who have become refugees due to natural disaster; and those who are economic migrants. In 1975, there were approximately 3.5 million documented refugees worldwide; by late 2013, the number had risen to almost 13 million. In the wake of continuing conflicts in Syria, Gaza, the Ukraine, and beyond, the number only continues to swell.

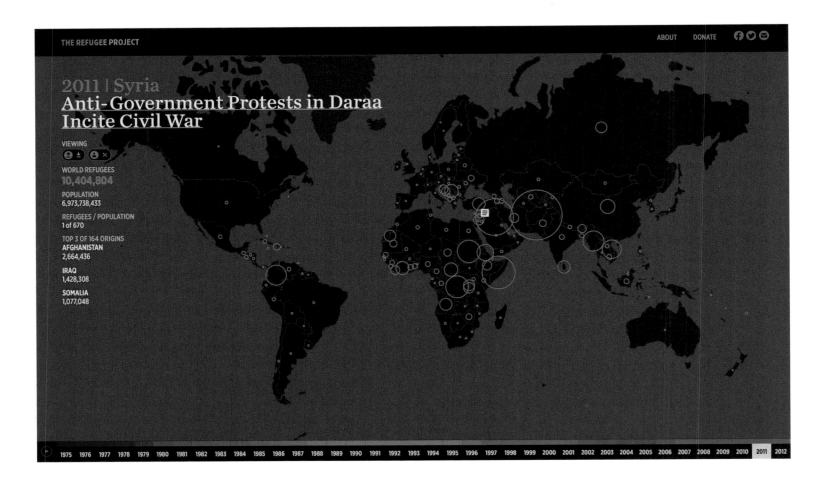

Hyperakt (est. 2001) and Ekene Ijeoma (American, born 1984). The Refugee Project. 2014. D3, HTML5, JavaScript, Adobe Illustrator, Adobe Photoshop

Overleaf: Hyperakt and Ekene Ijeoma. The Refugee Project. 2014

António Guterres

Every three seconds, somewhere on this planet, a person is forced to flee his or her home. Those who flee may be escaping war, conflict, violence, persecution, or human-rights abuses. Some will find a safe place inside their own country, while others will cross international borders and become refugees. Millions of people are in flight at any time, having left behind their homes, often suddenly, only taking with them what they could carry.

And yet, as the U.N. High Commissioner for Refugees, I spend a lot of time with refugees; and, whether in Pakistan, Jordan, Kenya, Iraq, Mauritania, or Ecuador, I am always deeply impressed by their resilience. Despite nightmares of past events and the challenges of living in exile, people find the courage and strength to rebuild their lives. As shown clearly by The Refugee Project, an inter-active website that uses data gathered by the U.N. since 1975 to illustrate forced-migration patterns worldwide, most of the world's refugees flee to neighboring countries and stay in their home region, contrary to popular belief. Today, 86 percent of refugees live in the developing world, compared to some 70 percent a decade ago. At the onset of an emergency, refugees initially find safety and help in neighboring communities, who share the little they have with the new arrivals while national and international aid is being mobilized.

On average, however, a refugee spends more than a decade in exile before he or she can go back home, or find an alternate one. For many communities, the long-term presence of large numbers of refugees places an enormous strain on their limited services and resources. Refugees are often confined to camps and not allowed to work. A refugee camp is a dire place, where life stands still. My organization, the Office of the United Nations High Commissioner for Refugees (UNHCR), and its partners strive to provide primary education to all refugee children, but the sad reality is that funding is barely sufficient to cover even the most basic of human necessities. Secondary and tertiary education, including trade-skills training, remain a distant dream for many refugee children.

In 2013 alone, 2.5 million people became refugees, the highest number in a single year since the Rwandan genocide. During that same year, only 414,000 refugees were able to return home. New conflicts erupt and humanitarian crises multiply, while existing wars remain unresolved. Peace is dangerously in deficit these days and human suffering is immense. It is crucial for the world to over-come its differences and to find political solutions that can halt conflict, if not prevent it altogether. Without this, the human cost of war will continue to grow.

António Guterres became the tenth U.N. High Commissioner for Refugees on June 15, 2005.

Q: While the origins of the sentiment are contested, it's true that the death of one person is a tragedy while the deaths of millions risk becoming a statistic. Does the visualization of big data regarding forced displacement help us to comprehend this particular type of violence, or does it merely increase our apathy?

COMMENT 1. Ala:
We must not perceive this type of representation (i.e., data visualization) as a full and comprehensive report on . . . the lives of refugees around the world. Nor does it go as far as increasing our apathy. It rather plays a role as a mere quantitative visual—a trigger to the curious mind. It is crucial to ask wheth-er design—the socially engaged type, of course—can achieve what data visualization [cannot] in representing this type of social and humanitarian injustice. Is it able to pose questions beyond those photography and journalism are already covering?

THE REFUGEE PROJECT

2012 | United States

VIEWING

RESIDING IN
UNITED STATES
262,023

POPULATION
315,960,562

REFUGEES / POPULATION
1 of 1,206

TOP 3 OF 184 ORIGINS
CHINA
60,615

HAITI
26,849

COLOMBIA
17,766

262,023
refugees reside in United States
(11st of 150 asylums)

1975 1976 1977 1978 1979 1980 1981 1982 1983 1984 1985 1986 1987 1988 1989 1990 1991 1992 1993 19

996   1997   1998   1999   2000   2001   2002   2003   2004   2005   2006   2007   2008   2009   2010   2011   **2012**

Blue Bra Graffiti
(Bahia Shehab, 2012)

Using sexual violence to intimidate protesters, crack down on dissent, or brutalize objectors is nothing new. Neither is graffiti—illicit drawings in public spaces are older than Pompeii. However, such designs have of late taken on new life, paralleling an increased public and political focus on female sexuality. During the wave of disparate yet interconnected protests that began in late 2010 and were labeled the "Arab Spring," graffiti emerged as an untamable form of grassroots resistance. The graffiti art sprayed in the streets of Cairo during and after the 2011 revolution attempted to raise awareness about injustices in Egypt, from the personal and gender-based to the economic and political, giving a voice to the oppressed. Witness, for instance, the stenciled images of artist and historian Bahia Shehab, the most recognizable of which was perhaps a bright blue bra. The tag refers to the young woman who was publicly dragged and beaten by members of the Egyptian military in Tahrir Square in December 2011. During the attack, the woman was half divested of her abaya, exposing her body and blue undergarments. Images of the attack rapidly became a symbol of the rampant abuse of power by Egyptian officials. As Shehab explains in her 2012 TED Talk, the stenciled blue bra and accompanying Arabic script mean "no to stripping the people": "The blue bra," she says, "is to remind us of our shame as a nation when we allow a veiled woman to be stripped and beaten on the street." Shehab's blue bra graffiti has since been covered and no longer exists on the streets of Cairo.

Nama Khalil

I look at the photograph, and at first I do not see the blue bra. The bold, black Arabic script spelling *la* ("no") and the text beneath it that reads, "No to stripping the people," are what catch my attention. Only then do I notice the bra, a private object made public, and a phrase stenciled in the shape of a foot: "Long live the revolution," it says. The photograph documents street art on a wall in Cairo. I see the outline of a woman's body. I pause to remember the young woman donning the *abaya* who, on December 16, 2011, was dragged and beaten by Egyptian policemen, her shirt pulled up over her head.

The blue bra is of course the bra worn by this young woman and exposed to the world in videos and photographs that captured the beating. There is one image in particular that testifies to the trauma of the event. The woman is on her back, chest exposed, face covered; two soldiers tug at her shirt while a third prepares to stomp on her abdomen, his foot suspended in midair. The image is a record of the blatant, state-sanctioned violence used to physically coerce and terrorize protesters and serves as an authoritative witness to the incident it captures. The act of violence itself was not unusual—the Egyptian police are notorious for their forceful handling of citizens—but that it took place in public, and involved an ordinary female citizen, reified the possibility of its happening to anyone.

Literature scholars Nancy K. Miller and Jason Tougaw write that testimony records an incident as it moves from "personal trauma to public memory" and from an individual experience to a collective one.[1] In Egypt's public memory, the woman was referred to as *Set el Banat*, or "honorable lady"; she was understood to be neither weak nor vulnerable. Nor was she objectified. On the contrary, she was highly regarded—and nearly instantaneously so. She represented the struggle for life, freedom, and social justice. She spoke for an entire nation, prompting its citizens to respond in outrage. She symbolized the Egyptian revolution.

Seeing the blue bra graffiti once again, I am newly enraged by the act of violence it signifies, and I am reminded of our nation's suffering. During the

Bahia Shehab (Lebanese and Egyptian, born 1977). Blue Bra Graffiti (No to Stripping). 2012. Stencil, spray-paint, 17 11/16 x 7 7/8" (45 x 20 cm)

Bahia Shehab. Thousand No Wall. 2012

revolution, the painted bra was not alone in provoking this response. All over Cairo, the word "no" was stenciled across building walls and city infrastructure, highlighting Egypt's social problems and the people's demands: "No to military rule," "No to a new pharaoh," "No to violence," "No to blinding heroes," "No to barrier walls." Each of these statements—including the blue bra, of course—belonged to artist Bahia Shehab and was made in direct response to events that occurred during the revolution. For instance, "No to blinding heroes" referred to a protester named Ahmed Harara, who lost his right eye, and then, six months later, his left—both to sniper bullets.

The ongoing use of graffiti and street art by Egyptians protesting the country's social and political conditions points to a wave of sharp and witty creativity. Street art gained momentum because as a form of expression it is fast, transitory, and interactive; once photographed and circulated online, it is also wide reaching. These stencils, murals, spray-paintings, and posters are designed to comment, sometimes mockingly, on the country's political turmoil; to educate the citizenry; and to communicate demands. That many of the images have their own backstory means they cannot be recycled or reused in another context.

Shehab's stencils stand apart in that they elicit from me a greater emotional response than any other work of street art so far, and, I suspect, than any will in the future. With Egypt having succumbed to a military coup—as I write this, the former military general, Abdel Fattah el-Sisi, is on his way to becoming Egypt's president—the country's political turmoil is ongoing. Although Shehab's stencils have since been erased from the city's walls, the state-sanctioned violence they highlight is ongoing, and the demands they make are still viable. Once again people are chanting "No to military rule" and "No to violence."

Nama Khalil is an artist and academic. She received her master of arts in Middle East studies from the University of Michigan, where she is currently pursuing a doctorate in sociocultural anthropology.

1. Nancy K. Miller and Jason Tougaw, "Introduction: Extremities," in *Extremities: Trauma, Testimony, and Community*, ed. Nancy K. Miller and Jason Tougaw (Champaign, Ill.: University of Illinois Press, 2002), p. 13.

Q: Can public art alter violent or oppressive behavior?

COMMENT 1. Meredith Brown:
Public art, like any form of public speech, can serve as a strong impetus for change (positive or negative) not least because it can provoke public discussion around issues both private and public in unexpected ways. Graffiti, in particular, when used as protest, has the advantage of surprise; it appears, illicit, in primarily urban locations not intended for visual art, and it is this aspect that can catch a person off her guard. A blue bra stenciled on the side of a wall functions as an unexpected reminder of ongoing social oppression and state-sanctioned violence. It evokes a particular incident, a violence committed publicly against an individual woman by the state, yet when stenciled on a wall next to a litany of "Nos," it becomes a generalized demand for justice and change.

Bahia Shehab. Thousand No Wall (detail).
2012. Stencil, spray-paint, dimensions
unknown

Five Classified Aircraft
(Trevor Paglen, 2007)

Military culture traditionally uses a visual language composed of intricate symbols and insignias to signify affiliation and association with a range of services and programs. Traditional military uniforms, typically adorned with embroidered patches flaunting these affiliations, act as markers of an individual's identity and position in hierarchy. Trevor Paglen, an artist and geographer, collected unofficial embroidered patches from the "black world" of classified intelligence and military units. Paglen uses these designs as a locus from which to probe both closely guarded, secret extramilitary operations and the esoteric visual language that accompanies them.

William Gibson

The symbolism of military insignias has traditionally been noncovert. These badges or patches, worn on military uniforms, associate the represented unit with patriotism and bravery; with a specialty in war fighting; and perhaps with campaigns or engagements key to its history. Insignias honor the branch or unit they identify, announce the unit's presence in the field, symbolically remind of its past prowess and fortitude.

The three most significant developments in such insignias in the late twentieth century are Velcro-backed uniform patches, "suppressed" patches, and "black patches" of the type on display in artist Trevor Paglen's *Five Classified Aircraft*.

Traditional uniform patches were relatively difficult to remove quickly. Sewn on, they left permanent evidence of the patch when removed, often in the form of a distinctive shape. The wearer demonstrated a formal and open commitment to membership in a particular group, as well as a certain trust in the rules of war. Captured, a soldier openly remained a member of that service, regiment, or unit. The advent of Velcro patches (uniforms may now have factory-applied "loop" fabric on which "hook"-backed insignia are placed) suggests a profound metasymbolic disjunction, a new fluidity, a previously uncharacteristic ambiguity. The patch as disguise. Or no patch at all.

Suppressed patches are those whose traditional symbolic colors are replaced in the service of camouflage—the U.S. flag or the Red Cross symbol rendered in two slightly different tones of whatever Pantone chip the U.S. Army currently favors. This practice is imminently practical, advisable, yet quite new, indicating the strength of a prior reluctance to alter these primary symbols. Until very recently, it evidently mattered symbolically that the U.S. flag was red, white, and blue, not coyote brown (or black). Another disjunction.

The crypto-patches of Paglen's *Five Classified Aircraft* are covert in-house advertisements. They are best viewed as industry marketing tools, each patch representing the occluded, unmentionable, quiveringly secret craft or product of a given contractor. As deliciously sinister as they are, and as redolent of our military-industrial hybridism, they are not as broadly ominous as the anonymity and evidential ambiguity afforded by either Velcro-backed or suppressed patches.

William Gibson's first novel, *Neuromancer* (New York: Ace Books, 1984), won the Hugo Award, the Philip K. Dick Memorial Award, and the Nebula Award in 1984.

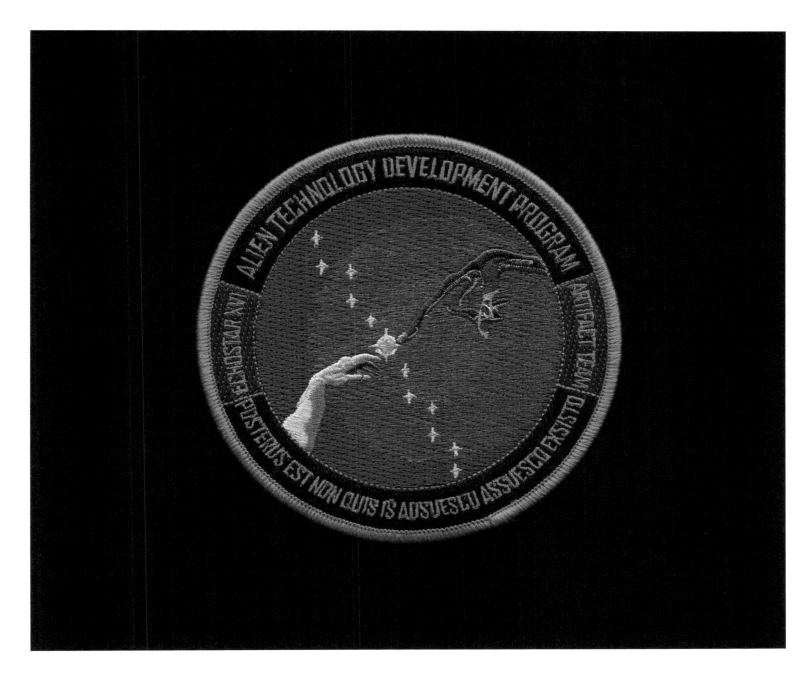

Trevor Paglen (American, born 1974).
*The Last Pictures (Development, Launch,
and Deployment Patched)* (detail).
2012. Three fabric patches, each patch
4 ⅜ x 4 ⅜" (11.1 x 11.1 cm); overall
12 ⅝ x 25 ½" (32.1 x 64.8 cm)

Q: Is covert violence more fatal than what you can see coming?

COMMENT 1. J P McMahon:
. . . An interesting thing about the patches
featured here is that there isn't some DoD
[Department of Defense] office that creates
these; it is the members of the units themselves, who either draw it out and send it to
an embroiderer, or have an artist create it to
their specifications. The Pentagon isn't really
involved in the process. . . .

COMMENT 2. Patrick:
. . . Once an object is stamped "violent" by MoMA,
does that make it so?
   The inherent problem with showing symbols
and pictures of violent design [outside of their]
context is an extreme fetishization of those symbols.
It's like gratuitous, sexed-up violence without the
"story" (insert unchallenging content). One wonders
if "chicks with guns" is around the corner.

Trevor Paglen. *Five Classified Aircraft.*
2007. Five fabric patches, overall
15 ¼ x 32 ¾ x 2 ¼" (38.74 x 83.19 x 5.72 cm)

Trevor Paglen. *Symbology Vol. IV.* 2013.
Twenty fabric patches, overall 12 x 10"
(30.5 x 305 cm)

Army Field Manual 5-0: The Operations Process (Department of the Army, 2010)

The U.S. military's Army Publishing Directorate has been producing field manuals, how-to books for men and women in military service, since 1905. Many hundreds are in use at any one time, providing guidance on everything from ordnance to operations for military personnel serving in the field. Army Field Manual 5-0, *The Operations Process,* or FM 5-0, was approved by the Training and Doctrine Command, the branch of the military that oversees recruitment and leadership, and published in March 2010. It is a set of guidelines for military commanders to adhere to when planning for the battlefield. FM 5-0 is unique insofar as it is the first army field manual to introduce design—and specifically "design thinking," the iterative process of problem solving that is considered by some typical of design—into its vocabulary. FM 5-0 devotes an entire chapter to design methodologies, suggesting they be used to frame, engage with, and provide solutions for "operational environments" like Iraq. As *Design Observer* noted in its May 2010 issue, the Army's co-option of design thinking was foreshadowed by a series of articles that suggested design thinking could enhance military strategy. (The series appeared between 2008 and 2010 in the academic journal *Military Review*.) As FM 5-0 notes in chapter three, "Design Defined," design "enables commanders to view a situation from multiple perspectives" and "requires agile, versatile leaders who foster continuous organizational learning while actively engaging in iterative collaboration and dialog to enhance decisionmaking." FM 5-0 was updated and replaced by Army Doctrine Reference Publication 5-0 in May 2012, but the references to design methodology were retained.

Harry Jones

The U.S. Army applies violence with the goal of obtaining a better peace. Doing this well is difficult. Until recently, the Army generally assumed that it recognized a problem when it saw one and that, reactively, it had the means to solve it. In March 2010, the Army introduced design into doctrine with the release of *The Operations Process* (or Army Field Manual 5-0), which serves as a guide for planning and implementing military campaigns. As General Martin E. Dempsey, chairman of the Joint Chiefs of Staff, points out in the manual's foreword, the introduction of design into the Army planning process—design defined as "a critical and creative thinking methodology to help commanders understand the environment, analyze problems, and consider potential approaches"—highlights "the importance of understanding complex problems more fully before we seek to solve them." The endorsement of design thinking as an approach to problem solving in the Army is not merely useful and smart; it is a morally significant step toward obtaining a better peace.

The Army's operational environments are more complex and uncertain than ever before, and military-campaign planning has become increasingly difficult. Enter design: it might seem like a minor addition to the Army's suite of planning tools, but as design-thinking expert Roger Martin asserted in *Design Observer*, the introduction of design into FM 5-0 is "quite a leap forward" from the manual's previous iteration.[1] As a career Army officer, I want to argue that FM 5-0 represents, perhaps inadvertently, an important moral step in our thinking about how to use violence when required. The very idea of using violence "well" may seem at best a perversion and at worst an oxymoron; nevertheless the Army has to apply violence well for at least two reasons.

First, just-war theorists have always maintained that noncombatants in a war zone retain the right not to be harmed. When the Army fights at its best, it takes great care to avoid harming civilians. Design, when applied to war planning, creates possibilities for better uses of violence—or, better yet, for

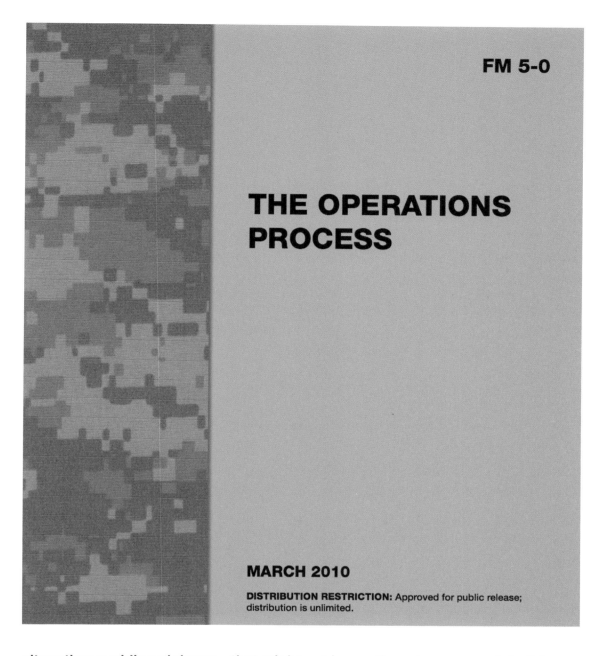

FM 5-0

THE OPERATIONS PROCESS

MARCH 2010

DISTRIBUTION RESTRICTION: Approved for public release;
distribution is unlimited.

altogether avoiding violence—that might not have otherwise emerged. In this way, we better fulfill our duties of care. Second, the very nature of design forces us to look more deliberately at the various stakeholders in any given circumstance and to work harder at understanding those who will be affected by whatever course of action the commander ultimately chooses. Design thinking requires us to question our understanding of the perceived problem before taking action. Attempting to see the conflict from the perspective of all those involved pushes us toward a truer appreciation for what is at stake and for whom. Insofar as we in the Army use violence in service of the United States, we must do so with utmost care—our duty is to understand exactly what kind of violence is required in any situation. This is much more difficult than using violence indiscriminately. The upshot, however, is that we are more likely to solve the right problem, to competently fulfill our duties, and to better align the effective and the ethical.

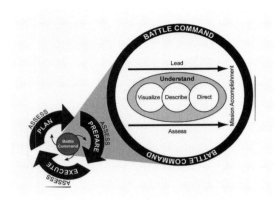

Diagram from *The Operations Process* outlining the various activities performed during military operations

The addition of design to FM 5-0 is more than a cosmetic update. The manual has already been superseded by Army Doctrine Reference Publication (ADRP) 5-0, which refined what is now referred to as the "Army design methodology." And, if design thinking sticks, it will have positive ramifications far beyond military-campaign planning as we seek to accomplish our missions under substantial fiscal constraints and with a smaller force. Design thinking is a crucial tool for enabling the U.S. Army to fulfill its duty to serve the American people by applying violence when necessary. It requires that violence be imposed smartly and proportionally, and that we take into account the human rights of all relevant stakeholders. Accomplishing the mission under these constraints is difficult to be sure. But design, if understood and implemented well, gives us a powerful tool to meet our goals successfully and ethically.

The views expressed here are those of the author and do not reflect the official policy position of the U.S. Military Academy, the Department of the Army, the Department of Defense, or the U.S. government.

Harry Jones is a lieutenant colonel in the U.S. Army who has served in both Iraq and Afghanistan.

1. Roger Martin, "Design Thinking Comes to the U.S. Army," *Design Observer*, May 3, 2010, http://designobserver.com/feature/design-thinking-comes-to-the-us-army/13478.

Q: Is the use of design thinking by the U.S. military morally significant?

COMMENT 1. Luke Baker:
In prescriptive military fashion, this field guide codifies the very processes by which we identify problems, plan solutions, and effect actions for the most preferable outcome. It comes as a surprise that best practices drawn from design methodology have not been explicitly employed by military campaigns prior to this moment, even as they were being identified by design theorists and practitioners. After all, the designer's tenets of efficiency, suitability, and solution-oriented creative thinking seem tantamount when it comes to protecting and preserving Earth's most valuable resource; that is, human life itself. As a grave act, it is my feeling that human violence should be meted out sparingly, and only when truly required to uphold the greater good for all. If design thinking aids universal military operations in running better campaigns with positive contribution to the art of war cannot be overlooked.

COMMENT 2. Andrea Morales:
It seems almost absurd to me to have to say this, but the thought alone of American military forces claiming that war is a step towards peace, especially in the context of "design thinking," is laughable.

. . . If the U.S. military can be defined as a force "for obtaining better peace," then the nature of its acts would rely not on violence itself, but on the predefinition and building of consensus surrounding a systematic state of well-being. This is where I think the use of "design thinking" is misguided.

Design thinking should, in theory, not only guide possible interventions, but also frame issues. In that sense, even before violence is chosen as the instrument to create change, the application of military force should be called into question by all people claiming to be exercising design thinking. It seems, from the article, that this is not the case in the Army Field Manual, as design thinking becomes an afterthought to be applied DURING field tactics and specifically in the context of enacted violence.

In a nutshell, though I support the inclusion of design thinking as a possible step toward creating [conscientiousness] among the military of the systematic problems that are created and reproduced by applying violence to violent issues, it seems as though the design methodologies being applied are limited to tactical scenarios. Is it really design thinking if the possible solutions to the design challenges are already framed inside violence? My guess would be no.

Annihilate

To seek out total obliteration of an obstacle or adversary by any means available, whether human made or naturally occurring.

Mountaintop Removal
(Various designers, c. 1970s)

Mountaintop-removal mining (MTR), which evolved in the 1970s out of conventional strip-mining techniques, has become the predominant method of extracting coal in North America. Largely concentrated in the Appalachian Mountains, MTR makes use of thousands of tons of explosives each day to remove the layers of rock and soil above a mountain's coal seam. MTR drastically changes and destroys the surrounding landscape, despite streamlining the traditional method of coal extraction. In the United States, approximately 40 percent of electricity is generated by burning coal, a process that contributes to the excessive build up of greenhouse gases in the earth's atmosphere. Concerns over straining the U.S. power grid have added to the tensions between coal companies and environmental agencies. Although MTR provides access to untapped coal used to fuel the country, its severe environmental and social impact render the practice abominable for many.

Laura Antrim Caskey

When I was a child, my family would often drive through the northeastern United States for family vacations and field trips. On one particular trip, when I was six years old, I had recently watched the newly released *King Kong* (the 1976 version with Jessica Lange), and the ape's death had especially upset me. I felt great sadness for the vulnerable beast who was cruelly captured and displayed in a cage, and who then toppled to his death from the roof of the World Trade Center. As we drove along, the gently sloping Appalachian Mountains appeared often on the horizon. Staring out the window at them, I imagined they were parts of King Kong—his face in profile, his body laying in repose, his enormous elbow propped up on a table. Now it seems that King Kong has been chopped up into tiny bits.

The aerial images of West Virginia's Guyandotte Mountain and Coal River Valley belie the on-the-ground horror of the situation. Looking down on the transmogrified landscape, I feel disconnected. The images defuse the brutality of the ruthless cancer metastasizing over the hills, creeks, and communities. We are able to document our destruction using human know-how and billions of dollars of sophisticated technology. What will we do with all this information?

This most recent exploitation of Appalachia has a 150-year history: in the late 1800s and early 1900s, land speculators and coal agents acquired massive tracts of land through deceptive contracts known as the "broad-form deed." Countless Appalachians unwittingly signed away their land and mineral rights for a pittance, some marking only an *X* for their signature (and revealing that illiteracy no doubt gave the speculators a powerful advantage). As the area's railroads expanded, so did the coal-mining industry, most of it deep underground. Underground mining leaves the mountain in place while the mineral is extracted and removed through tunnels and shafts. The excavation work is highly dangerous—so dangerous, in fact, that it helped spark the American labor movement and the implementation of some of the first child-labor laws. But its impact on the topography of the surrounding landscape, and thus on the people who live there, does not compare to the devastation wreaked by today's mountaintop-removal coal mining.

The broad-form deed came back to haunt Appalachians when surface mining started up in Kentucky in the 1950s. Newly developed earth-moving machinery made surface mining both less expensive and higher yielding than underground methods, yet another step toward mechanization where machines replace humans. Coal agents, eager to access the black carbon rock, returned to take the resource-rich land that legally belonged to them; the mining industry's plan to dominate the region moved forward relentlessly. But surface mining, unlike underground mining, devastates the landscape—and with it the lives and livelihoods of those who depend on it for income and for sustenance. Appalachians witnessed these new mining operations "ruin their farms and fields and streams," as claimed in a 1965 petition quoted in the *New York Times.*[1]

In the eyes of the mining industry, Appalachia was most valuable as a resource colony; its residents were merely getting in the way. Without any available recourse, the residents organized in protest. Doris Shepherd, an early demonstrator against strip-mining in Kentucky, described it thus: "It was just rampant rape-and-run. I don't know how [the mining companies] could justify what they did. . . . And a lot of them, as soon as they filled their pocketbooks, they left; they left us to deal with the problems—the ruined land, the polluted air and the water. We're still dealing with that today."[2]

Despite its good intentions, the Surface Mining Control and Reclamation Act of 1977 (SMCRA), designed to regulate the controversial new mining processes, instead institutionalized the process known as mountaintop-removal or valley-fill mining. In mountaintop-removal mining, first hardwood forests are clearcut and burned; then ammonium nitrate and diesel fuel are used to blast apart the mountains to reveal the underlying coal seams. The pulverized mountain rock and rich soil are shoved into the adjacent valleys below, burying headwater streams that provide drinking water to the southeastern United States. Big yellow machines dig up the coal, layer by layer. The mountains fall and the valleys fill, leveling West Virginia. Even President Jimmy Carter, who signed the bill into law, expressed concern that it had been compromised during congressional negotiations: enforcement of the SMCRA was remanded to the individual Appalachian states rather than to the federal government, solidifying the practice of corruption and violence by coal interests and the politicians who backed them.

The continuum of government-sanctioned violence in this region stretches as far back as the forced relocation of nearly one hundred thousand Native Americans following the Indian Removal Act of 1830. Maria Gunnoe, a resident of Bob White, West Virginia, lives on the land her Cherokee ancestors first settled after following—and surviving—the Trail of Tears. The mountaintop-removal mine that invaded her backyard and threatened her family once again with displacement radicalized Gunnoe. Now an environmental activist, she has fought tooth and nail to end mountaintop removal, enduring and sacrificing much to protect her community.

Today an area roughly the size of the state of Delaware has been obliterated by mountaintop removal, burying with it thousands of miles of headwater streams and depopulating thousands of mountain communities. A strip-miner once told me cavalierly that mountaintop removal is no different than gutting a fish. That miner relished his ability to take down a mountain, even when all around him people cried for the destruction to stop. Is there any greater violence against a people than poisoning their water or fouling their air? It's no wonder then that Gunnoe, as with so many others whose ties to Appalachia's cherished lands go back as far as nine generations, is often heard to say, "What have we done?"

Laura Antrim Caskey is an independent photojournalist who has spent the last decade reporting on the human and environmental costs of mountaintop-removal coal mining in Appalachia.

1. Ben A. Franklin, "Strip Coal Mines Vex Kentuckians," *New York Times*, June 23, 1965, p.63.
2. John Cheves and Bill Estep, "Bombs and Bullets in Clear Creek," *Lexington Herald Leader*, June 22, 2013 www.kentucky.com/2013/06/22/2687942_bombs-bullets-in-clear-creek-knott.html.

Active mountaintop-removal coal-mining site, Coal River Valley, Edwight, West Virginia. 2009

Overleaf: Branch mountaintop-removal coal mine and 2.8 billion gallon coal-sludge impoundment, Guyandotte Mountain (aka Bolt Mountain), West Virginia. Marsh Fork Elementary School once sat directly below the impoundment. 2007

Q: Is violence to the earth any more acceptable than violence to humans?

COMMENT 1. William DePaulo:
Violence against the earth IS violence against people. Two dozen plus peer-reviewed health studies over the last decade document the encyclopedic adverse health impacts in communities near mountaintop-removal coal mines. From increased birth defects, decreased birth weights, and diminished educational attainment to increased cancer, cardiac and pulmonary disease, and significantly decreased life expectancy, the verdict is in: particulate matter released from MTR sites kills. My home state of West Virginia is fiftieth out of fifty-one states + D.C. in median income and [almost] dead last—yeah, fiftieth—in the rank of its educational system. But long before the health effects of MTR were documented, West Virginia was number one—first in the country—in deaths per one hundred thousand from particulate matter emitted from coal-fired electric plants (which generate more than 90 percent of the states' electric power). Instructive are the names of the states ranking two through six: Virginia, Pennsylvania, Kentucky, Ohio, Indiana. Step back from that six-state map: What are you looking at? The footprint of mega-utility American Electric Power, the largest purchaser of coal on the North American land mass. Violence against the earth IS violence against people. Period. Paragraph. Full stop.

Mine Kafon
(Massoud Hassani, 2011)

As a child in Qasaba, a village between Kabul and Jalalabad in war-torn Afghanistan, Massoud Hassani made toys out of whatever materials he could find. Among his favorites were rolling objects powered by the wind, which he raced with other children. Often these toys would be blown into nearby minefields, where they could not be retrieved. Many of Hassani's friends were injured or killed by land mines, and, years later, while in design school in Eindhoven, the Netherlands, Hassani payed tribute to their memory by making the toys once more— only bigger, heavier, stronger, and designed to be intentionally released onto minefields. Easy to transport and assemble on site, Mine Kafon (*kafon* means "explosion" in Dari) rolls across the ground, detonating the mines in its path and, with an interior GPS chip, recording the safe area cleared. If it detonates a mine, the object is partly destroyed, but its bamboo and biodegradable-plastic parts may be easily salvaged and reassembled into another Mine Kafon, ready for deployment. Once an industrial scale of production is achieved, one Mine Kafon could cost as little as forty dollars to produce, whereas current de-mining methods and materials can cost as much as a thousand dollars per mine. Hassani has been testing Mine Kafon with the Dutch military.

Jody Williams

Elegant and simple. A beautiful object. At first look, it seemed a mistaken proffer—more a retro-modernistic ceiling light or a dandelion gone to seed than an object related to violence. Yet despite its deceptive design, Massoud Hassani's Mine Kafon is neither light nor flower. As its name implies, it is related to mines. Land mines. Infernal, indiscriminate weapons of war created to explode on contact and mutilate human beings. Created to sow terror and destruction.

Also simple—but lacking elegance or beauty—some land mines have been described as having a deliberately toylike design to attract and blow up children, which may or may not be true. But how poetic that an object designed to destroy these explosive devices actually is inspired by a toy, one from Hassani's childhood. How elegant that he transformed his memories of youthful days playing alongside his brother with simple, handmade toys that were carried by the wind, into an object that can harness nature and blow over land mines, destroying them with no loss of life or limb.

Song Kosal was six years old and working in a rice paddy in Cambodia with her mother. Deep in the water of the paddy, where it was impossible to see the bottom, she stepped on a land mine, shattering her leg up to her knee and leading to amputation. It sounds like a tragic story that could only have a tragic ending, but Kosal is made of more than bone, blood, and tissue; she has an indomitable spirit.

Not many years later, in 1992, nongovernmental organizations came together to create the International Campaign to Ban Landmines, which was instrumental in pressing governments to do what they should have done anyway: negotiate the 1997 Mine Ban Treaty, an international agreement prohibiting the use, production, trade, and stockpiling of antipersonnel land mines. Kosal, along with other land-mine survivors, became a powerful advocate for the ban. She raised her voice for more resources dedicated to helping survivors and their families, so that some day we would all walk in a world free of land mines.

Often responses to violence are simple—if we chose to open our minds to them.

Jody Williams received the Nobel Peace Prize in 1997 for her work to ban land mines through the International Campaign to Ban Landmines, which shared the Peace Prize with her that year.

Above and overleaf: Massoud Hassani (Dutch, born Afghanistan, 1983). Design Academy Eindhoven (The Netherlands, est. 1947). Mine Kafon. 2011. Bamboo and biodegradable plastics, 87 x 87 x 87" (221 x 221 x 221 cm)

Q: Indiscriminate, insidious, obstinate, and ready to detonate years after a conflict has ended—is the land mine the cruelest weapon?

COMMENT 1. Herb:
. . . As a commander, how do you protect your own men so that you are not writing a thousand letters to the parents of dead soldiers the following day? You use mines. They slow an enemy and can funnel them into kill zones where a small force has a chance against an overwhelmingly large force. Now I know my argument will be hated. It is an emotional subject. Everyone thinks mines are awful and should be banned. The problem is, when you ban mines you give any aggressive nation with a large army a tremendous advantage. Mines are important in helping a smaller force defend itself against an invader. . . .

M855A1 Enhanced Performance Round
(U.S. Army Armament Research, Development and Engineering Center, 2010)

Since the mid-1990s, the U.S. Department of Defense has been seeking a lethal, lead-free bullet to replace its longstanding standard-issue NATO round: the 5.56 x 45 mm (.223 caliber) M855. Developed for the M-16 family of weapons, and in wide use since the 1970s, the M855 was in recent years criticized by troops for its poor lethality and unreliability. Military and government officials were also increasingly concerned that the M855's lead slugs were polluting soil and ground water at small-caliber firing ranges. In 2010, the U.S. Department of the Army began replacing its M855 rounds with the M855A1 Enhanced Performance Round. Designed over a period of five years at the U.S. Army's Picatinny Arsenal in New Jersey (although not without legal dispute from Florida-based Liberty Ammunition over its patent), the M855A1 is the same size and weight as its predecessor, but ostensibly improves on its velocity, range, and consistency. Importantly, the M855A1 contains a copper slug, earning it the moniker "green bullet" and ensuring it does not contaminate food or water supplies, only its intended target.

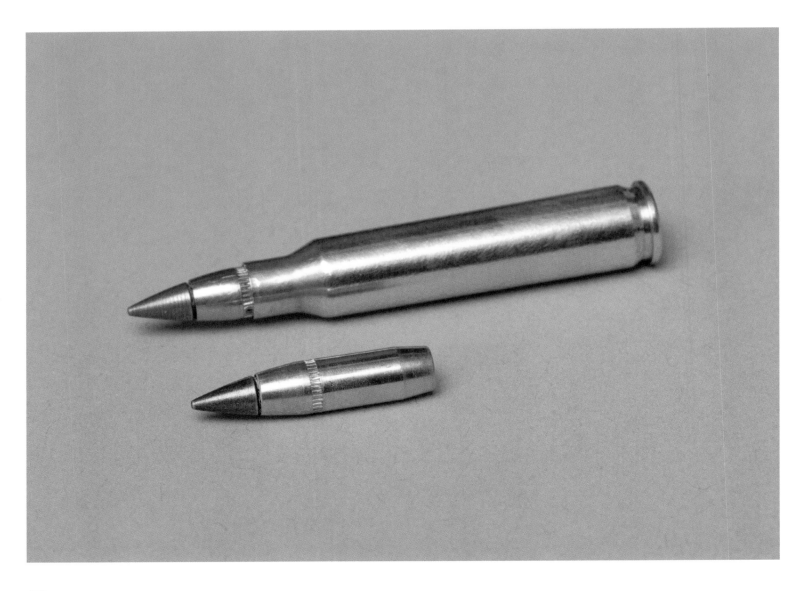

Army Armament Research, Development and Engineering Center (USA, est. 1977). Department of Defense (est. 1949), previously National Military Establishment (est. 1947), preceded by Department of War (est. 1789). M855A1 Enhanced Performance Round (also known as the "green bullet"). 2010. Steel penetrator, bronze tip, copper jacket, copper slug, brass case, 1 ¾ x ¼" (4.5 x 0.6 cm)

Clive Dilnot

I came late to this party. Assigned the object "green bullets," which—and here I quote from the original invitation—"are lead-free, good for the environment, but still deadly when used properly," I hesitated to write.

Partly, I envied the language of the invitation. Who could improve on its irony? (Or, at least, I assumed it as such since the conjunction of these clauses could not, surely, be written with a straight face.) But design, we know, is a curious field. Like the Catholic Church of old, it encourages—even demands—(false?) innocence of its participants.

The title of this project does not escape this. It is not, one should note, design *as* violence. The conjunction "and" carefully preserves the separation, and thus the absolution, of design. To be sure, the title toys with the connection. It teases, suggests slumming or playing on the other side. But the words do not "penetrate," "infiltrate," or "breach" (more language from the initial invitation and the *Design and Violence* website): "violence" and "design" preserve their respective positions. Decorum is maintained.

True, the *Wikipedia* entry on "bullets" includes a section on design. But we know, do we not, that this is not "real" design. Real design—our design, your design—does not engage with such things.

But to return to my assigned topic: green bullets. What can we say about them? In fact, they are nothing but the product of a larger increase in the market price of lead in the last few years relative to that of copper, of which they are made. They are cheaper, in other words.

They are also more truly lethal. Good for the environment they may (not) be. But they kill even better. Copper allows for a lighter bullet, hence for a larger carrying capacity by the average GI, and thus a faster rate of fire.

Firing is, after all, significant. Bullets, we could say, wish to be shot. This is what they ask us to do with them. And the world has many. You and I—meaning the global population at large—pay for at least fourteen billion of them to be made each year.

And more of them are getting fired. Yet, one wonders, at what? The rate at which U.S. armed forces fire rounds of small-bore ammunition has doubled over the last five years. One astonishing statistic is that since 2002, U.S. forces have fired an estimated 250,000 rounds for every insurgent killed in Iraq and Afghanistan. Perhaps this is why the Department of Homeland Security is currently hoarding more than 1.6 billion rounds in its arsenal. To put that figure in perspective, during the height of active battle operations in Iraq, U.S. soldiers were using 5.5 million rounds of ammunition each month. An arsenal of 1.6 billion bullets is enough to sustain an Iraq-scale war for twenty-plus years in the United States.

But the nation's gun owners, too, are hunkering down, hoarding. Sales of domestic ammunition are booming. Americans' bullet of choice is increasingly the "hollow-point," so called because of the small dip in its tip. When a hollow-point enters the body, the dimple causes the bullet to open up umbrella-style and fragment. One often touted advantage of the design is that it decreases the chance of the bullet passing through the attacker and striking loved ones.

It also ensures that almost any shot to the torso will be fatal. Cavitation, caused by the kinetic force of weapons-grade bullets as they rip through and out of the body, is how the modern bullet destroys the body. The children murdered in Sandy Hook had appalling internal and exit wounds. Almost none of them could have survived the traumatic shock even if their vital organs had not been hit. As *Wikipedia* explains, insightfully, "Ballistic trauma is sometimes fatal for the recipient, or causes long term negative consequences."[1] Indeed. That is, after all, the point.

The astonishing casualty rate of the U.S. Civil War—six hundred thousand dead with a population of a little over thirty million—was a direct consequence of the rate of fire allowed by the modern rifle. Together rifle and bullet offer a temptation that cannot be resisted. Here is an account from the diary of an officer on one of Welsh explorer Henry Morton Stanley's expeditions in Africa, circa 1887:

"It was most interesting, lying in the bush watching the natives quietly at their daily work. Some women were making banana flour by pounding up dried bananas, men we could see building huts . . . boys and girls running about, singing. . . . I opened the game by shooting one chap through the chest. He fell like a stone. . . . Immediately a volley was poured into the village."[2]

The rifle made all the difference in the colonial wars. Until around 1830, the weaponry deployed by colonial powers and indigenous peoples exhibited near parity. By the end of the century, this was no longer the case. At the battle of Omdurman in 1898, in the Sudan, the British counted forty-seven killed and 382 wounded. The Mahdists, on the other hand, counted ten thousand killed and thirteen thousand wounded. The disproportion was entirely technological.

Was all this the product of design? Of course. The modern small-bore rifle was a product of careful evolution. No one who has ever fired a rifle can deny the exquisite pleasure of placing the bullet in the target, live or dead. Here is an instrument perfectly attuned to the desire for effect at a distance—for action that one both is and is not responsible for. We know that killing at a distance is essentially irresponsible; this is part of vestigial horror we feel at mass-bombing campaigns, at the use of nuclear weapons, and, today, at the ever-expanding program of drone assassinations. Yet, at the same time, we excuse ourselves. The bomb, we say, *leans toward* being dropped; the rifle, and the bullets that fit so snugly in its breech, want to be fired. Both gun and bullet urge us to prove their (and our) capabilities by squeezing the trigger and hitting the target. Bullet and rifle conjoin in perfect partnership. They are designed to do so.

In that sense, there is no "and." There is no disconnection; the conjunction does not apply. It is not design *and* violence but violence by design—violence by and through design.

Clive Dilnot is professor of design studies at Parsons The New School for Design.

1. "Ballistic Trauma," *Wikipedia*, last modified on December 15, 2014, http://en.wikipedia.org/wiki/Ballistic_trauma.
2. The story is recounted in Adam Hoshschild, *King Leopold's Ghost* (New York: Mariner Books, 1998), p. 99.

Q: Can violence ever be sustainable?

COMMENT 1. Raphael Sperry:
Thank you, Clive, for these thoughts. It's hard to add to them, but I can echo them with a piece I recall from the BBC quoting a spokesperson for [British] weapons manufacturer BAE [Systems] touting its green bombs and land mines: "We all have a duty of care to ensure that from cradle to grave products are being used appropriately and do not do lasting harm." [See "BAE Goes Big on 'Green' Weapons."] Again, one must wonder at the sincerity behind the choice of words.

COMMENT 2. Kelsey:
As I understand the question, it's asking whether there is some form of violence that is beneficial to the environment. I come from a rural area where there has to be some cutting back of growth, burning of grasses, weeding out of certain crops to favor others, and culling of certain animal populations in order to maintain a harmonious ecosystem. It's a balance between Man's will and Nature's, but I believe that evolution itself has always needed some "violent" acts—they're part of Darwin's description of natural selection, even though we may shy away from this idea. However, applying this thinking to the human landscape rather than to "nature" demonstrates the way in which most of us prize human life above all and apply to it a completely different moral code. Violence to nature, or as a part of the natural world, is the stuff of David Attenborough documentaries and, as such, is presented as entirely reasonable and ecologically balancing. Violence toward humans, on the other hand, can never be "sustainable" to someone with any kind of moral compass—and yet, it still occurs so often, as Dilnot describes, despite the good nature of most of us, and because of the dark nature of a few.

COMMENT 3. Colleen Doyle:
As Dilnot points out, heightened environmental stewardship was surely not the impetus for the switch to copper, but rather the consideration of resource material, manufacturing costs, and efficiency of intended use. . . . The name itself is the only designed element that discerns the bullet ecologically speaking, but who is the audience of this assigned attribute and why should the U.S. military promote it? Does the term "green bullet" allay scrutiny about the volume of ammunition used in training and combat? Does it do anything to exonerate the designer, producer, or user of violent intent if we believe that green bullets fight pollution while fighting the enemy? In a 2013 article about its manufacturing, posted to the U.S. Army website by the Picatinny Arsenal military research and manufacturing facility, there is no mention of the bullet's greenness. But the article does reference environmental policy: "The M855A1 EPR's new bullet design provides soldiers with better hard-target penetration and more consistent soft-target performance at increased distances. Additionally, because it's lead-free, the M855A1 allows training exercises to occur on ranges where lead projectiles are no longer permitted." Here it seems the shift to copper is spurred by environmental compliance, not ecological conviction. By definition, design is the purpose or intent behind an idea, action, or object. The discipline is not independent of its impact. The nickname "green bullet" only confounds our understanding of that impact.

How to Kill People: A Problem of Design
(George Nelson, 1960)

That the act of killing is an important design problem underpins the now classic *How to Kill People: A Problem of Design*, architect and industrial designer George Nelson's twenty-minute film on the evolution of weaponry from prehistoric times to his contemporary moment. Originally produced for the humanities-focused television series *Camera Three*, which aired on CBS from the mid-1950s through the late 1970s, Nelson's narrated history of the relationship between design and violence was made all the more devastating for its calm and measured delivery. Against the backdrop of the Cold War arms race and the postwar fetishization of conspicuous consumption, Nelson surveys the ways in which design has throughout history brought beauty and efficiency to artifacts of human violence. Nelson begins the program by examining a simple, handheld rock, whose efficacy as a weapon requires physical proximity between attacker and victim. For Nelson, the rock demonstrates a central tension in weapons design: one must be close enough to inflict harm without being so close as to put oneself in danger. Nelson concludes the program by considering the rocket launcher and the atom bomb, two weapons whose power derives in part from the great distance between those who operate them and those who suffer their consequences. Nelson had a wide-ranging and prolific career that encompassed architecture and design criticism, curating, and teaching as much as it did architectural, product, graphic, and industrial design. *How to Kill People* was billed by *Camera Three* host James Macandrew as the chapter Nelson did not include in his 1957 book *Problems of Design*; later, the lecture was adapted and published in the January 1961 issue of *Industrial Design* magazine. In light of today's drone-fired missile attacks and mediated warfare, Nelson's lecture was profoundly prescient; its concerns should continue to interest designers, and all of us, in the present day.

Alice Rawsthorn

There are many reasons to admire George Nelson. For a pillar of the mid-twentieth-century U.S. design establishment, he had an unusually enlightened interest in the social, environmental, and human impact of design. He championed the work of more gifted friends, like the Eameses and Buckminster Fuller, and lent the latter a desk in his New York studio whenever he needed one. I even quite like his Bubble lights.

But Nelson also had his flaws, and his 1960 short film *How to Kill People: A Problem of Design* is among them. It consists of a twenty-four-minute soliloquy, which he begins by arguing that devising lethal weapons is one of the three roles in which design enjoys the "unquestioning support" of society—the others being homemaking and fashion. Nelson then delivers a lively potted history of weaponry design, illustrating his points by brandishing a rock, a club, and other suitably menacing props.

Not that his arguments are wholly wrong. Weapons have indeed played a pivotal part in design history, starting with the prehistoric men and women who attached sharpened stones to sticks to defend their caves against predators. Designing ever deadlier armaments has since been essential to the success of fearsome warlords through the ages, and pioneered new models of manufacturing. Thomas Jefferson was so impressed by the ingenuity with which the late-eighteenth-century French armorer Honoré Le Blanc standardized the design of his muskets that he submitted a report on Le Blanc's methods to the U.S. government.

Nor does the film founder solely because of Nelson's antediluvian views, like his infuriating presumption that designers are invariably male, or that their greatest aspiration is to produce "works of art." Such gaffes date his film as indelibly as his *Mad Men* smoker's cough, but the most troubling aspect of *How to Kill People* is its morality.

George Nelson (American, 1908–1986). *How to Kill People: A Problem of Design.* 1960. 16mm film (black and white, sound), 20 min.

HOW TO KILL PEOPLE

A PROBLEM OF DESIGN

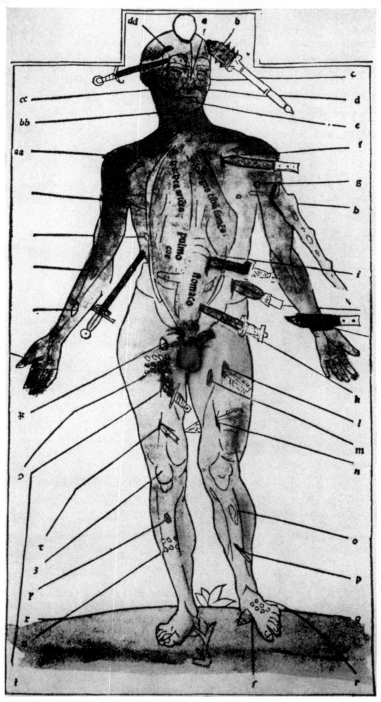

One problem is Nelson's apparently unquestioning conviction that governments are entitled to go to war, and that society will support them. Equally disturbing is his insistence on distinguishing between what he calls "the respectable kind of killing" (his euphemism for government-sanctioned warfare) and "murder." He seems so dazzled by the colossal investment in the design of military gizmos that he assumes everyone else is too. And he fails dismally to address one of the most important, albeit tortuous aspects of the design of weaponry or anything else: the designer's moral responsibility toward the outcome of his or her work.

At no point does Nelson question whether so many designers should invest so much of their time and energy on armaments. The answer will be determined by each individual's beliefs. If, like him, you consider war—and the slaughter it can cause—to be justifiable, why would you object to designing the most efficient means of ensuring victory? But if you are opposed to warfare, surely you will feel the same about designing its tools, even those that are intended for conflicts whose objectives you may deem to be laudable, like the overthrow of vicious tyrants. Given the virulence of the illegal arms trade, what's to stop them from subsequently being used malignly?

The same question of conscience applies to every area of design whose outcome is potentially damaging, from health to the environment. Not that designers should automatically be held responsible for the unintended consequences of their work unless they could reasonably be expected to have anticipated them. And how could they not in the case of a combat drone, assault rifle, or supercavitating torpedo?

One positive point Nelson might have made in defense of weaponry design is that some militaristic innovations are subsequently put to benevolent use. The leaps in computer technology in the years after World War II were fueled by the wartime investment in devising new systems of code-breaking and theoretical bomb testing, just as millions of people have benefited from the advances in the design of wheelchairs and prosthetic limbs, originally intended to assist military veterans. Do the benefits justify the suffering and destruction caused by earlier incarnations of the same technologies? Again, the answer is a matter of individual conscience and is as complex as every other judgment relating to the design politics of warfare.

Nor does Nelson ask whether it would be more productive to focus the design resources currently expended on "how to kill people" on "how to stop killing people." The answer to that question is an unambiguous "yes," or would be if society could be persuaded to see design differently. Public perceptions of design have evolved since Nelson made his film in 1960, but are still prone to muddles, clichés, and the irritatingly pernicious presumption that design is primarily a styling tool.

Not until there is a consensus that design has much more to offer—by applying the design process strategically to help to develop more effective alternatives to military conflict, for example, or to create fairer, more productive societies whose citizens are less likely to fall prey to tyranny—will we derive the full benefit of design's power to save lives, rather than to destroy them.

Alice Rawsthorn writes about design in the *International New York Times*, which syndicates her articles worldwide.

Q: Design for war and weaponry often spurs further innovations and adaptions for the greater good. Can this perverse relationship ever be reconciled? Do the benefits justify the suffering and destruction caused by earlier incarnations of the same technologies?

COMMENT 1. Julie Lasky:

Alice, with Hiroshima and Nagasaki only fifteen years behind them, I believe the TV audience of 1960 found the title of this program as shocking as we do today. They, too, I am certain, were poised between disbelief ("He can't be serious!") and indignation ("Or is he?"). And I think, with his deadpan drone and smoker's hack, Nelson, that old fox, was playing to their outrage.

One giveaway is at the beginning when he enunciates three categories of design: fashion, housewares, and tools for killing people (as if he didn't participate himself in a much more nuanced universe). But the real ironic clobber comes at the end with his discussion of advances in weapons of warfare:

"We have designed war and its instruments to the point where we have not only re-created the boredom and the tedium of peace, we have also made the weapons incomprehensible. . . . Is it any wonder that in every medium of entertainment we have shifted from the respectable kind of killing to stories of murder? How else can we reintroduce the personal element into the activity that has been man's favorite throughout all history?

"If legalized killing should ever be brought to an end, the newest designs tell us why: it has become too impersonal to be interesting and too complex to be comprehensible."

He concludes with the hope that designers brought to such a pass would turn to other pursuits. "Personally," he says, "I think it would be nice if that something else has to do with people."

Can we doubt that everything that leads to that final invocation of humanity is a very dark joke?

Natural Deselection
(Tim Simpson, 2006)

The term "natural selection" was first introduced and given popular currency by British naturalist and geologist Charles Darwin (1809–1882) in his *On the Origin of Species* (1859). The book describes a key mechanism of the evolutionary process whereby organisms that carry the biological traits to succeed in their environment are necessarily favored in terms of reproductive and genetic continuance. Designer Tim Simpson's Natural Deselection, part of his 2006 thesis show at London's Royal College of Art, plays with the process described by Darwin to call attention to those that don't make the cut. His experiment pits three flowering plants against one another in a race to the top. The plant that grows to a predetermined height first trips a sensor, triggering shears poised at the stalk base of the competitor plants. The last plant standing possesses the superior biological design to survive in this particular environment. Simpson's darkly subversive work bluntly demonstrates how evolutionary science, a field of inquiry that radically enlightened the world in many ways over the last 150 years, can be manipulated to create artificially designed hells.

JC Cahill

Life causes death. Death causes life. These are fixed rules of nature, applying to all organisms.

The slice of bread eaten this morning came at the cost of at least fifty lives, each the product of a broken or nonexistent home. The fifty baby wheat plants required for our bread each had a father both unknown and absent and a mother left alone to nourish the growth and development of her offspring. The infant mortality associated with our sustenance does not end when the bread enters our mouths, but continues until it exits our bodies. The glutenous goodness of our breakfast is broken down with the help of countless numbers of microbes residing in our gut, giving their lives in the service of our digestion. Life causes death. Death causes life.

When did the violence in our morning routine begin? Was it when we first domesticated wild grasses, altering their genetic makeup to meet our needs? Was it when we introduced forced breeding programs in which we plant row after row of wheat babies, selecting from them a small group to breed and re- produce, while killing and discarding unwanted youth? Did violence begin even further back, when our heroic predecessors ripped apart wild and native grass- lands with their plows, converting complex and diverse ecosystems into planta- tions of uniformity? Perhaps instead, the ends justify the means, as this vegetal genocide (phytocide?) allows those with bounties of land and water to feed those without. Or is violence against plants an impossibility, as plants are not like us, and it is we who decide what is violent? Would our view of the morality of these actions differ if plants were capable of expressing behavioral complexity? What if potentially violent actions were conducted by plants, not people? Enter Tim Simpson and his project Natural Deselection.

Three sunflower plants grow in individual pots. The first plant to reach a specified height trips a sensor, whereupon garden clippers snap shut, dealing lethal blows to the slower-growing neighbors. As a one-off botanical interven- tion, we have expensive gardening. But let us consider what happens next, when the victor is rewarded with the opportunity to mate with other survivors. In Simpson's world, there is no safe haven for the young, and the victors' off- spring are themselves thrust into this arena of death. Over time, these botanical

Tim Simpson (British, born 1982). Natural Deselection. 2006. Potted sunflowers, sensors, mechanical shears, retort stands, 47 ⅛ x 23 ⅜ x 23 ⅜" (120 x 60 x 60 cm); video (color, silent), 1:48 min.

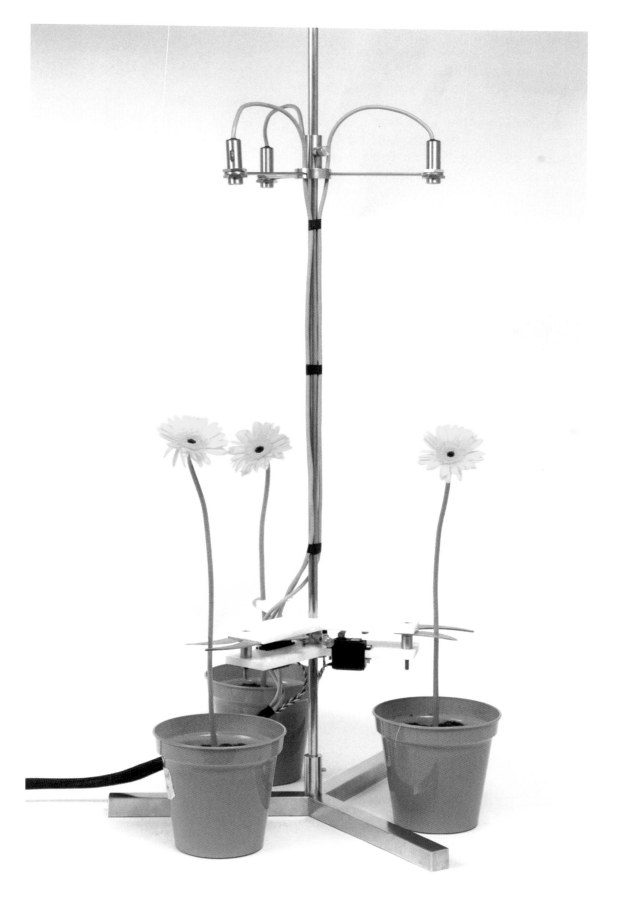

gladiators evolve, with selection favoring the fast and the tall. The victors trade away growth of leaves, flowers, and roots in exchange for taller and thinner stems. Outside of the arena, they would perish, unable to do more than grow tall; inside they are rewarded with food, sex, and survival.

Where is the violence in Simpson's world? On the surface, Simpson's arena is barely different from plant-breeding programs where humans select and reward plants that express desired traits, killing those that do not. However, although the processes are the same, the intent is not. We must kill to survive, and in doing so, we alter the evolutionary outcomes of those around us. We rationalize this by assigning to the lives of different organisms a value different from our own; we soften what we do by using words such as "harvest" and "seed," not "kill" and "baby." But, in the end, we kill to survive. I see little violence in these acts, just necessity.

In contrast, Simpson's arena of death follows in the human tradition of killing for sport—it's a dog fight in garden pots. The violence lies not in the actions of the plant, whose successful growth causes the death of two others, but lies instead in the creation of the circumstances that causes such mortality. The plants have no means to prevent their babies from being collected, no means to alter where they are planted, nor any perception that their basic life functions will cause the death of other plants. They have no power to control their circumstances, and thus no ability to exert violence upon others. Instead, violence is performed consciously only by the outside agent: Tim Simpson.

But these are just plants, we might say—our food, furniture, and fibers. It is easy to forget, or to choose not to know, that plants are living and breathing organisms capable of profoundly complicated physiological and behavioral processes. Despite their essential value to our lives, we devalue theirs. Plants have been around for a very long time and will likely persist well after humans have gone extinct. Though plants will forever carry the evolutionary legacy of their treatment during the brief Anthropocene era, they may experience some pleasure in having outlived their captors.

JC Cahill teaches at the University of Alberta, where he heads the Lab of Experimental Plant Ecology.

Q: Why does watching something as "natural" as natural selection in action horrify and fascinate us?

COMMENT 1. Sam:
As human beings, we are not only capable but compelled to use morality (think about how people feel about amoral sociopaths and tell me I'm wrong). For our social networks to work and human beings to survive, we have to work together, which means we're invested in moral rules, like Thou shalt not kill, etc. This sensibility works really well with regard to other humans, but when one thinks in a particular mode, it can become very different to think outside of it. This is probably one of the main reasons why watching Natural Deselection is horrifying and fascinating. Animals and plants don't behave the same way we do, nor do they think the same way. It's also very easy to anthropomorphize everything in the world, so when we see a lion eat a gazelle or something, we imagine how they both feel, thus triggering our horror and fascination.

Sequence from Tim Simpson's Natural Deselection. The plant that grows to a predetermined height first trips a sensor, triggering shears poised at the stalk base of competitor plants.

Serpentine Ramp
(Temple Grandin, 1974)

Animal-rights activist and scientist Temple Grandin created the Serpentine Ramp to ensure the humane treatment of livestock raised for beef production. Grandin's first ramps, designed in 1974, were used on ranches and feedlots for herd vaccinations and, soon after, in slaughterhouses. The ramp's semicircular turns take advantage of the movement cattle naturally make in groups, and prevent them from being spooked by either the workers or the abattoir up ahead. Walking nose to tail, the cows march their way through to the kill floor without the use of prods or noise, and without panicking or injuring themselves. To demonstrate the efficacy of her designs, Grandin closely observed cattle in pasture and in her vaccination and slaughterhouse chutes. Blood samples from the cattle revealed that cortisol levels (a stress hormone) were comparable in each of the three locations. She believes that design is never a substitute for livestock managers who support low-stress handling, and she advocates for video auditing to prevent employees from abusing animals. In an email to the curators, Grandin wrote, "People forget that nature is very harsh, especially when predators attack. The big cats kill their prey first, but the canids (wolves and hyena) may rip the guts out of a live animal. We owe the animals we use for food a life worth living and a painless death."

Ingrid Newkirk

"Stunned" is the word that springs to mind as I contemplate the Serpentine Ramp, the slaughterhouse chute designed by Temple Grandin, with its snakelike reticulation and its oxblood paint. If it works, if all goes well—as well as things can go when a living being is lured toward a violent death—then the cow will end up stunned, courtesy of a pneumatic device pressed against her forehead. Not unconscious but stunned, disoriented but fully sensate, her brain scrambling to make sense of things before she is hoisted up by a chain. It's a stunning sight: every pound of her immense weight hanging by one ankle, as she dangles and twirls like a leaf snagged on a fencepost.

It's also stunning to realize that, in the U.S. alone, some thirty-three million cows—about ten times the number of visitors who file through The Museum of Modern Art each year—will experience this slaughter chute firsthand, or a similar but less welcoming version of it. Perhaps one designed with less rigor, maybe thrown together with pieces of corrugated sheeting, much as a child might nail together some planks to make a tree house. These thirty-three million cows— each an individual with her own thoughts and worries—will stumble through this or that chute each year, unless people begin to relate to who's on their plate at a far faster rate.

Who? It is now thought that cows convey messages to each other via subtle facial expressions, and as reported in the *Sunday Times*, studies show that "cows have a secret mental life in which they bear grudges, nurture friendships and become excited over intellectual challenges."[1] They have a secret death, too, because almost no one but migrant workers and meat inspectors has ever visited a slaughterhouse.

Is it stunning to learn the perspective of People for the Ethical Treatment of Animals (PETA) on Temple Grandin's designs—not just her various iterations of the serpentine chute, but also her kosher slaughter pen, a narrow stall designed to render more humane slaughter that adheres to the requirements of the Jewish faith, and all her efforts to make slaughter a slightly less upsetting process for animals such as cows, who are so shortsighted that they shy away from a paper cup? Surely, PETA *must* condemn an object that contrives to lure hapless animals to a bloody end. But no, puritanism has no place in war, and the human race, which fancies itself as compassionate, decent, and thoughtful, is engaged in an unjust war against the animal nations. No matter how bright, sensitive, and interested in life cows may be, they are seen as raw materials for hamburgers and handbags, steaks and satchels, reduced to the sum of their flesh, blood, and skin. In war, real choices, not lofty philosophical positions, are what count. Ask me which I would prefer: my mother frog-marched by guards into a concentration-camp gas chamber, or led in the chamber gently without her realizing fully what lies ahead, and the answer is simple. If wishes were horses, my mother and the cow would both be out in a flower-filled meadow—one grazing happily, the other gathering mushrooms for soup.

But slaughter is the current reality, and design makes a difference. The right design can mean that a cow doesn't get kicked in the face by the man on the rail because she hesitated at a blind corner and turned back in a panic, setting off ripples of fear in the other cows, who then trembled and turned back, too, clogging up the line and slowing down the process of converting cows into cuts of meat. And it can mean, too, that she will step calmly forward, toward the man with the chain, unwittingly drawn into the realm of violence and into an experience that she could never have imagined—her own death. What is especially stunning to me, though, is that so many people do not yet know how very easy it is to reject violence, to decide to walk past the meat case and, instead, eat for life.

Ingrid Newkirk is founder and president of People for the Ethical Treatment of Animals (PETA) and its international affiliates, and author of over a dozen books on the philosophy of animal rights.

1. Jonathan Leake, "The Moody Life of Cows," *Sunday Times*, February 27, 2005, http://www.thesundaytimes.co.uk/sto/news/uk_news/article100199.ece.

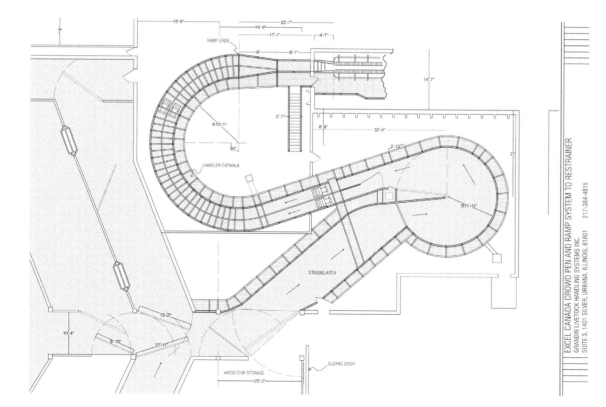

Temple Grandin (American, born 1947) of Grandin Livestock Handling Systems (est. 1980). Serpentine Ramp (reproduced architectural drawing). First designed in 1974, design modifications ongoing. Various materials, dimensions variable

Overleaf: Dual single-file serpentine chute under construction

Single-file serpentine chute and crowd
pen with revolving gates and poured-
concrete fence

Q: Can we design a violent act to be more humane?

COMMENT 1. Erich:
As far as I am concerned, anybody living in a first-world nation, particularly anybody generally able to subsist, can lay no claim whatsoever to moral absolutism. But then, no matter where you go, there you are. So, if we are to live this way, the best that we can do (if we want to maintain any claim to morality) is to make concessions. PETA's support of these innovations may at first seem contradictory to its mission, but it is also a pragmatic concession to make an improvement in the short term while continuing to fight a larger fight.

COMMENT 2. Alicia:
I hope that after seeing Grandin's design, people will think harder about the fact that cows (and chickens, pigs, and fish) all feel pain, fear, love, and joy, just like the dogs and cats we share our homes with. Learning that it is important to keep cattle calm before their violent deaths should inspire people to think about the fact that animals value their lives and don't want to die. In the developed world, where we can go to the grocery store and buy a veggie burger or a pound of beans, there is absolutely NO reason to force any animal to endure the horrors of factory farming and slaughter just to satisfy someone's fleeting taste for their flesh. Go vegan.

COMMENT 3. Lucy P:
My dad had a plaque hanging in his office that said "There's no right way to do a wrong thing." I tend to agree with that sentiment, but in cases like this, where we are dealing with such a massive "wrong" . . . the least we can do for the animals who are killed for meat is to make their lives and deaths a bit less painful and terrifying.

COMMENT 4. Christina:
I think . . . designing slaughter chutes to comfort cows right before they are murdered is shocking, and yet speaks to the wider human condition. We want to be absolved of guilt and not witness the slaughter of animals who experience pain, fear, and love to satisfy our selfish desires. These chutes help us accomplish this while granting some measure of peace to the animals who are about to die for us.

COMMENT 5. Rebecca:
There is nothing "humane" about animal exploitation. Nor can there ever be. Hint: that's why it's called exploitation. And for supposed animal-rights advocates to line up to give this project a stamp of approval only consolidates the belief that enslaving and killing another sentient being is somehow concomitant with ethical treatment, and the belief that the interests of the vulnerable can be used as means to our ends provided they are not tortured "too much" (as if one could substitute ethics for mathematics, or measure it out). Making people feel more comfortable with abusing animals is the very opposite of any stance for the end of animal use. There is no middle ground. True animal-rights activists must categorically reject such moves in practice as well as in theory, if they are to reach the nonvegan population and make any substantive progress toward ending animal use. Anything else confuses the issue. And that is certainly not needed. . . .

COMMENT 6. Jill:
I think PETA uses forums like this one that MoMA provided to educate people about the horrendous suffering that animals endure, in hopes that by having this discussion, some people will realize that they can indeed reject the violence and bypass the meat counter altogether, as Ingrid wrote.

Abolition is the goal, but unlike some other groups that are all talk and no action, PETA is out in the trenches, conducting undercover investigations at slaughterhouses and factory farms (and laboratories, circuses, animal-breeding mills, horse racetracks . . . you get the picture). PETA's investigations resulted in the first-ever felony convictions of farm workers for abusing pigs, and the first-ever felony convictions of farm workers for abusing poultry. A pig slaughterhouse in Mississippi that PETA investigated in 2013 just announced that it is shutting down. Sniping at a group because it embraces multiple approaches to ending animal suffering is counterproductive.

Euthanasia Coaster
(Julijonas Urbonas, 2010)

Between 2003 and 2007, designer and engineer Julijonas Urbonas ran an amusement park in Klaipėda, Lithuania, and garnered firsthand experience crafting situations that involve "gravitational aesthetics." Drawing from this experience, Urbonas created the hypothetical Euthanasia Coaster, a humane, elegant, and euphoric solution, as he outlines on his website, for those who have chosen to end their lives. Challenging the physical and psychological limits of the human body, this speculative roller coaster slowly ascends 510 meters (roughly 1,700 feet) into the air before launching its passengers through seven loops at a mind-boggling speed of 100 meters (328 feet) per second. Euthanasia Coaster is designed to give its riders a diverse range of experiences from euphoria to thrill to tunnel vision to loss of consciousness and, eventually, to the end result: death.

Antonio Damasio

At first glance, it appears possible that the intent behind Julijonas Urbonas's Euthanasia Coaster, a conceptual roller coaster engineered to kill its passengers, is to provoke horror followed by rejection; and that, although the Euthanasia Coaster seems both to bask in violence and to instigate it, Urbonas merely animates a disgraceful idea so that it can be repudiated more easily. Another conceivable reading is that Urbonas was simply indulging in flippant outrageousness for the sake of novelty and sensationalism.

One wishes either reading would apply to Urbonas's proposal, but on closer review, the evidence is not encouraging. The setting for the original presentation, a large-scale exhibition on the future of the human species titled *HUMAN+: The Future of Our Species*, is intriguing. It took place at the Science Gallery, Dublin, and featured a variety of futuristic pieces based on both reasonable and marginal readings of contemporary science. On the exhibition website (as elsewhere), Urbonas describes the Euthanasia Coaster as follows: "Thanks to the marriage of the advanced cross-disciplinary research in space medicine, mechanical engineering, material technologies and, of course, gravity, the fatal journey is made pleasing, elegant and meaningful. Celebrating the limits of the human body, but also the liberation from the horizontal life, this 'kinetic sculpture' is in fact the ultimate roller coaster."[1] Here Urbonas highlights not the horror, as we might expect, but rather the elation and exhilaration of the experience. (Unfortunately, the likelihood of any pleasure and euphoria being produced is low; nausea and discomfort would be more probable.) And in a video interview he gave at the time of the exhibition, Urbonas suggests that his creation would be helpful in dealing with problems such as "overpopulation" and "living too long" without any apparent flippancy.[2]

Those who react to the design with concern can be accused of lacking a sense of humor, of being unable to read irony and satire where irony and satire may have been intended—in brief, of being spoilsports indifferent toward innovation. But the blame surely must rest with the design and concept. Death and comedy are to begin with strange bedfellows. Their marriage requires abundant doses of expository justification, strangeness, a little bit of hamming, and redemption—as when, in Mozart's opera *Don Giovanni,* the murdered Commendatore comes back to dispatch Giovanni into hell, an event followed by the merriment and moral rectification of one and all. Euthanasia is death,

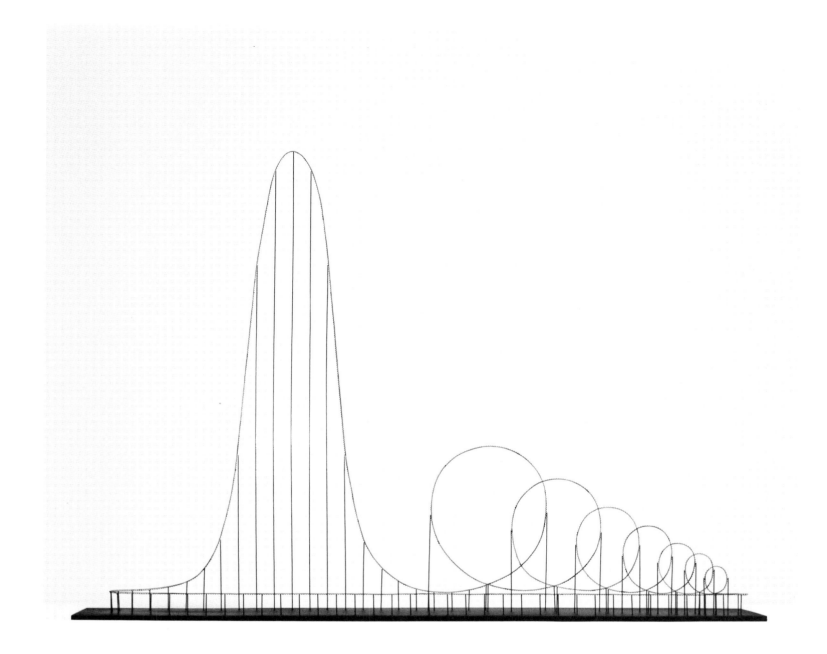

Julijonas Urbonas (Lithuanian, born
1981). Design Interactions Department
(est. 1989), Royal College of Art (UK, est.
1837). Euthanasia Coaster. 2010.
Scale model in etched brass, black matt
acrylic paint, carbon fiber, plywood,
39 ⅜ x 53 ¹⁵⁄₁₆ x 12 ⅝" (100 x 137 x 32 cm);
black sand, 33 lb. (15 kg); framed technical
drawing, 35 ⁷⁄₁₆ x 49 ¼" (90 x 125 cm)

Julijonas Urbonas. Design Interactions
Department, Royal College of Art.
Euthanasia Coaster. 2010

but death compounded by myriad questions regarding the circumstances in which its assistance may or may not be acceptable; there is nothing even faintly comedic about it or its organized versions. As the population ages and birth rates decline, as resources dwindle and advanced societies accept high unemployment as the norm, it is possible, albeit troubling, that social and political systems intent on solving the problems of old age, disease, defeat, and discontent might resort to technically intricate solutions; that the Euthanasia Coaster could, under these circumstances, become the Execution Coaster.

On the one hand, there would be little new in such a development. For the past century, even as violence has generally declined—a welcome trend that signals some human maturity—elaborate modes of institutional killing have emerged, all relying on the miserable scientific backing of physics, chemistry, and medical science. Our own varied methods for carrying out the death penalty are in effect public endorsements for these scientifically ornamented means to ending human life. On the other hand, were the Euthanasia Coaster, or designs like it, adopted as a final solution for a suffering humanity, the novelty would reside in the sweeping scale at which such a killing machine would have to be institutionalized.

The Euthanasia Coaster is not at all fun as art, and it is preposterous as a technical device. Curiously, it does work as provocation, regardless of authorial intent. So be it. Mostly it is sad, sad, sad.

Antonio Damasio is university professor, David Dornsife Professor of Neuroscience, and director of the Brain and Creativity Institute at the University of Southern California in Los Angeles.

1. Julijonas Urbonas, "Euthanasia Coaster," *Human+: The Future of Our Species*, Science Gallery, Trinity College Dublin, accessed December 22, 2014, https://dublin.sciencegallery.com/humanplus/euthanasia-coaster. See also the designer's website, http://www.julijonasurbonas.lt/p/euthanasia-coaster.
2. Julijonas Urbonas, video interview, "Euthanasia Coaster," *Human+: The Future of Our Species*, Science Gallery, Trinity College Dublin, accessed December 22, 2014, https://dublin.sciencegallery.com/humanplus/euthanasia-coaster.

Q: Is euthanasia a form of violence or a form of compassion?

COMMENT 1. mycosys:
Your post extends from a singular premise—that death is necessarily a tragedy. As somebody who is in pain every day, I do not believe this is the case. Sometimes life is the tragedy. When one's only experience is overwhelming pain, it is a tragedy to be prevented release. For many there is only one option for release and that is the final option. I feel it likely that one day in the distant future I may choose this option myself. Doing so through the experience of something so amazing that the human body cannot withstand it sounds a whole lot better to me than a boring gray room.

To remove all violence from humanity would be to utterly sanitize life, to remove the experience of anything but grays. Certainly the specter of interpersonal violence is undesirable, but I WISH to be violently happy, violently sad, violently moved. I wish to feel violent acceleration and violent relief. Conflating violence with anything that challenges us is to remove all value from the human experience, to paint the world gray.

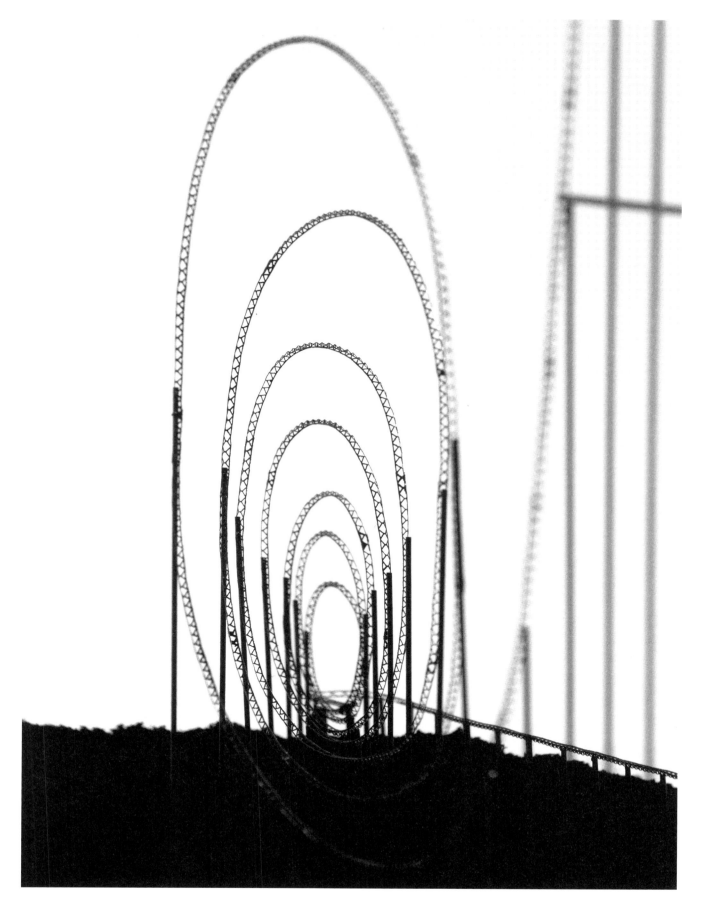

Beetle Wrestler
(Natalie Jeremijenko, Leigha Dennis, Lee von Kraus & Chris Woebken, 2008)

Beetle Wrestler, an interactive-design environment, updates the metaphor for empathy that suggests walking a mile in the shoes of another—in this case, the shoes of the rhinoceros beetle. The rhinoceros beetle is proportionally one of the strongest species in the animal kingdom, its male members capable of lifting 850 times their own weight with their sharp two-inch-long horns. This strength is used first to win female mates and then to control access to them. Beetle Wrestler pits the Hercules Beetle (Dynastus Hercules)—the largest in the rhino-beetle family—against a human, who clips her head into a helmet-like device with a mounted display. The display scales the wearer to beetle proportions in size and strength, allowing her to imitate the beetle's range of movements and engage her insect opponent in battle. As the designers describe it, Beetle Wrestler proposes "an architecture of reciprocity," allowing humans to better understand the heightened state of combat in the insect world. Beetle-wrestling matches have long been a popular past time for elementary school students in Japan, where the insects are kept as pets and celebrated in festivals, video games, and cartoons. Beetle Wrestler turns a spectator sport into a participatory exercise, while also cleverly flagging present-day technological hubris. The project links the fields of art, design, performance, science, and ethics, and asks whether we can ever understand the experience of another living creature, insect or otherwise. Natalie Jeremijenko is the director of the Environmental Health Clinic at New York University, where she developed Beetle Wrestler in collaboration with Chris Woebken, Lee von Kraus, and Leigha Dennis.

Natalie Jeremijenko (Australian, born 1966),
Leigha Dennis (American, born 1984),
Lee von Kraus (American, born 1981), and
Chris Woebken (German, born 1980) of
Environmental Health Clinic (USA, est.
2007). Steinhardt School of Culture,
Education, and Human Development
(USA, est. 1890). New York University
(USA, est. 1831). Beetle Wrestler. 2008.
Motors, plastic, metal, electronics,
72 x 24 x 30" (182.9 x 70.0 x 76.2 cm)

Hugh Raffles

Imagine for a moment that you are the beetle. Not the beetle-wrestling woman in the minimalist loft with the lo-tech gadgets and the trippy helmet and the exotic pet and the starring role in the multispecies art project. Imagine instead that you are the beetle.

Maybe you raised beetles like this when you were growing up in Japan. Maybe you trained them to fight in your village in Thailand. Or, maybe, wherever you're from, you've had other reasons to spend time observing and interacting with them. Maybe you worked in a zoo or a pet store. Maybe you're one of those people for whom sympathy with other creatures comes easily.

You're here on the table, though you don't know why. The table lacks features, there's nowhere to hide. The table lacks contours, there's nowhere to climb. The surface is unstable, so it's hard to get traction. The room lacks shade, and the light is relentless.

And this thing that's coming at you. It's huge and powerful, lunging at your head. It grapples. It wants to fight; though you don't know why.

Try to imagine that you are the beetle. It's not possible. You can try to imagine it, but you can't get close. You're physically too different. Your sensoria don't correspond. You occupy an entirely different world, not only in temporal and spatial scale and experience but in texture and chemistry. The signals you receive are not the same; the signals you send don't translate. Even if you could somehow build a body of similar sophistication—and you couldn't—it would provide no insight into the qualities and forms of the animal's perception. There is no reciprocity, architectural or otherwise; there is only contact. There is no prosthetic to bridge difference; there is only what departs one side as a philosophical game and arrives on the other as . . . well, we'll never know.

Dive into the ocean and shimmy a little fishlike. Take off in a plane and soar part bird. Enter a tunnel and feel the mole stir inside you. Stand still in the forest until the fluids rise in your veins.

Lie on the summer grass and let your skin rustle in the breeze.

Hugh Raffles is an anthropologist at The New School whose work explores relationships among people, animals, and things.

Q: Can design ever allow us to understand the violence we humans bestow upon other living creatures?

COMMENT 1. Pamela:
I've always imagined that one of the legendary warrior cultures of the insect world (a world rife with wondrous warrior cultures, surely) is that of the beetle. Perhaps that all has something to do with having to share the planet with us. If design can do anything to get humans to even consider, never mind understand, the intensity of the violence we humans bestow upon other living creatures, it's doing important work.

COMMENT 2. Isabella Brandalise:
Raffles's argument makes sense—[this] highly speculative project does not allow us to truly put ourselves in a beetle's shoes. What it does instead is open a space for discussion and imagination. By creating the opportunity to perform as a Kafkaesque dystopian figure, the project's role becomes not only a trigger to begin multiple conversations concerning issues like violence and otherness, but also to discuss design as a player in facilitating these debates or even promoting aggressions. The absurdity of such a hybrid and disruptive living form (or rather artifact) makes us leave our comfort zones and enter a space of disquietude and questioning. No, we definitely cannot understand our capability for violence. However, it may be a chance to speculate and envision alternative scenarios.

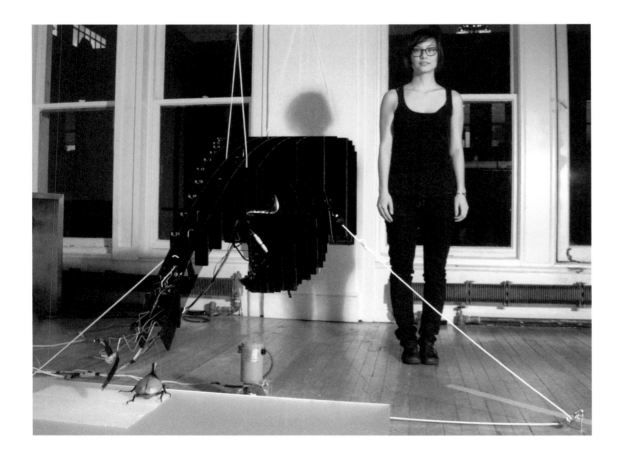

Natalie Jeremijenko, Leigha Dennis,
Lee von Kraus, and Chris Woebken of
Environmental Health Clinic. Steinhardt
School of Culture, Education, and Human
Development. New York University.
Beetle Wrestler. 2008

Salty's Dream Cast Casino
(Designer unknown, 2013)

Controversy over the link between violent video games and violence in society is in no way new. Electronic gaming has been connected to violence ever since the earliest interactive electronic games, designed in the late 1940s to simulate World War II missile drops, were played on cathode-ray tube monitors. Since then, however, game design has evolved radically. Today's games offer a broadened range of experiences, including new forms of interactivity—such as massive multiplayer online games—and of narrative engagement, ramping up the stakes for both designers and players alike. Enter *Salty's Dream Cast Casino,* otherwise known as *Salty Bet,* a free game that allows players to place virtual bets on live competitive fights between (often wildly mismatched) video-game characters. (The game's designer is unknown, going only by the name Salty.) The combatants are sourced from M.U.G.E.N., a freeware 2-D fighting-game engine designed by Elecbyte. The meaning of the original acronym is claimed lost by its creators, but the word *mugen* translates from its original Japanese as "infinite," and perhaps refers to the endless character customizations the engine enables. This continuous live stream of A.I.-controlled M.U.G.E.N. fights is hosted by Twitch, the Amazon-owned video network for real-time coverage of electronic gaming. In *Salty's Dream Cast Casino,* bets are made in an invented currency called "Salty Bucks"; no real money is used or paid out. An eclectic mixture of rock, rap, and video-game music provides the sonic backdrop, while a chat screen of trash talk among those placing bets scrolls rapidly alongside the fight.

Jamin Warren

In the grand arc of gaming history, there are only two single-player games of note: solitaire and golf. Perhaps even those who excel at this pair are unaware of the larger gaming conversation at work. At their best, both encapsulate a singular encounter between humans and a set of rules. But primarily, games are played with others.

That games developed primarily as social functions is perhaps unsurprising; however, with the development of arcades in the late 1970s and early 1980s, games became objects of social pariahdom. Arcade culture was bedecked in the robes of vice and violence, operated by the same proprietors of peep shows and slot machines. They were played by outcasts in the darkest corners that suburban malls would allow.

Every arcade was blessed with its own rites of performance and pageantry. Quarters lined up quietly along the lower lip of console cabinets claimed spots for the next round. Finishing moves or moments of brilliance were accompanied by a wide variety of dances and sequences, ranging from nervous, expectant fidgets to no-handed two-step at a bested opponent's side. This social atmosphere allowed games—and gamers—to express themselves in public.

The king of the arcade was undoubtedly the fighting game. Games like *Street Fighter* and *Mortal Kombat* were the purest expressions of competitive excellence. Battles hung in the balance until the game's final seconds. Although fighting games no longer hold the esteem and popularity they once did, there's something delightfully quaint about their continued existence. In an age of drone warfare, the proximity and purity of hand-to-hand combat lives on in the minutiae of combos and the rhythms of tapped buttons.

It is against this history of game-mediated violence that the brilliant *Salty Bet* emerges. A clever amalgam of the oldest values of video games with the contemporary aid of Internet-enabled voyeurism, *Salty Bet* exists as testament to the new truth of Internet gameplay: real-time algorithmic spectacle. The game

removes human agency from the equation entirely, pitting two bots in a death match against each other while the entire ordeal is live-streamed. Currency ("Salty Bucks") is doled out and wagered. All players are spectators and vice versa. An entirely new language of games emerges.

Salty Bet's existence is curious for many reasons. Much like Bitcoin, that other problematic, distributed Internet form, the creator of *Salty Bet* is still unknown. And where Bitcoin found its voice on Reddit, *Salty Bet* has generated its own reflexive inner sanctum inside the game itself, rife with its own language. To wit, just watch the chat box alongside each match turn blue with its own pastiche of profanities, emoticons, and expressions of frustration. The game essentially taps into the same manic energy that animates the Barclays Center during a Brooklyn Nets game. And true to Nets games, the matches are wildly inconsistent, as the fighters have mismatched abilities. The Coca-Cola polar bear fights Little Miss Powderpuff. An avatar of the figure in Edvard Munch's painting *The Scream* faces off against Super Mario. *Salty Bet* chafes dangerously at the edges of fair use, playing fast and loose with copyright and trademark. (Ronald McDonald, for example, is one the best fighters in the *Salty Bet* universe.)

A large part of *Salty Bet*'s appeal is its reclamation of something that has been lost since kids first retreated indoors to play during the 1990s PC video-game boom. In the last twenty years, game designers have focused most heavily on the mediated space: the place where the image is presented in cinematic form. Marketing that extolled the virtues of games and gameplay requiring technical proficiency over narrative and ludic pleasures bombarded players; in reaction, the players turned their attention to the fictional space that lives in our minds and haunts us in our sleep. Perhaps counterintuitively for a game predicated on a fight to the death, the social space where players interact with each other—both within the game as they place bets and draw pairs, but also outside the game when the fighting talk and fantasy combat pairings are discussed—is the part of video-game design that *Salty Bet* reawakens. It is voyeuristic violence, but one where "no holds barred" means less rampaging through Miami à la *Grand Theft Auto: Vice City* and more nostalgia for the way *The Legend of Zelda*'s Link outwitted Ganon.

Salty Bet speaks more broadly to our new relationship with Internet machinery; we ask games to play against themselves for our enjoyment (a strange form of respect, perhaps). These interactions in code have proven to be wildly popular and entertaining, suggesting that algorithms are able to generate, of their own accord, something akin to human sport. Games may never be the same again.

Welcome to *Fight Club*, reimagined in code.

Jamin Warren founded video-game arts and culture company Kill Screen.

Q: Does violence in video games have a correlative or causal relationship to violence IRL (in real life) or are they completely unrelated?

COMMENT 1. Andrea Morales:
. . . Beyond the voyeuristic pleasure that *Salty Bet* can provide to the spectators, perhaps what terrifies us most is that an algorithm can continue being violent even after its creator is gone.

Video games are just one instance where we wonder if human violence can be spawned without its human origin—the point where true creation would exist among dynamic systems.

Designer unknown. In partnership with Twitch (est. 2011). *Salty's Dream Cast Casino.* 2013. Video-game software, fighting characters sourced from M.U.G.E.N. (est. 1999)

Ninja Star
(Various designers, documented from the eleventh century)

The term "ninja star" (or "throwing star") is a colloquial appellation for a class of disc-shaped Japanese weapons, *shashuriken,* designed to be thrown in combat. Small enough to fit in the palm of the hand, the effectiveness of these small projectiles, which rotate in the air en route to their target, is contingent in part on the element of surprise. Shashuriken are part of a larger family of concealed, palm-sized weapons, *shuriken,* that includes dart- or spear-shaped blades. During the Edo period in Japan (1615–1868), close-at-hand combat materials, such as rocks and large stones, were replaced by metal ironstones (*tesutsubute*) forged into geometric shapes. It is suggested that shashuriken evolved from this lineage and were eventually deployed in various martial-art traditions, although the history of these weapons is not well documented and difficult to parse. The *shashuriken's* mythologization in various pop-culture narratives as essential to the ninja assassin's arsenal—as in the 1960s classic eight-part Japanese film series, *Shinobi no Mono* (known in English as *Ninja, a Band of Assassins*), or Quentin Tarantino's 2003 schlocky action thriller *Kill Bill*—only contributes to this uncertainty. In recent years manga, video games, and other forms of popular culture have exhibited the ninja star in action; dipped in poison to effect a slow, lingering death, for instance, or deployed dexterously to fell an unsuspecting opponent. The design included here, authorless and available cheaply online, is a prop for role-play rather than for killing; its spikes however are still sharp enough to prove deadly.

Brian Ashcraft

Silent. Sharp. And oh so deadly. That's the shuriken, or ninja star, of the popular imagination. *Shuriken* (手裏剣) literally means a "sword that's hidden in hand." It is just one of the many weapons in the ninja's vast repertoire, which also includes bows and arrows, smoke bombs, an array of blades, and tactical stealth. But during the 1980s, few things captured the attention of kids like these lethal projectiles.

While ninja lore has long been popular in Japan, the cloaked assassins experienced a popularity boom during the 1980s in the United States, a natural evolution of the martial-arts movie craze. While the 1970s saw Bruce Lee's *Enter the Dragon* (1973), the 1980s ushered in a glut of B movies like *Enter the Ninja* (1981), which worked throwing stars into its box art, and *Pray for Death* (1985), its poster featuring a ninja cloaked in a face cowl with a shuriken stuck right above the brow. These flicks were eager to thrill martial-arts-hungry American audiences with ninja assassins. We saw shuriken flung in comic books and cartoons like *Teenage Mutant Ninja Turtles*. We even chucked virtual ones in video games like *Ninja Gaiden*. It was no accident that one of the most desired G.I. Joe figures was the ninja Storm Shadow, who proudly displayed two shuriken in his waist sash.

By the time I was eight or nine, I knew one thing for sure: I must have a ninja star. I wanted one just like the by-then-iconic throwing stars I saw in movies and video games. Sure, I was young and naive. I didn't know about the shuriken's true history. I didn't know that the ninja star actually came in an array of styles, from square to X-shaped. Not all throwing stars were even, well, *thrown*; some were used for slashing and stabbing. Historically, shuriken were used more often for slowing down enemies at close range than for killing them at a distance, like in *American Ninja 2*. I didn't know that so much of ninja iconography had been created as late as the nineteenth century by Japanese artists and writers—despite that *ninjutsu*, the art of the ninja, had existed for centuries prior. Artist Katsushika Hokusai, for instance, is often credited with first depicting ninja in their iconic black outfits, a costume apparently inspired by the dark

Right and overleaf: Various designers. Ninja Star. Documented in Japan from the eleventh century. Various materials, dimensions variable

clothing of kabuki stagehands. So much of what we know about the ninja, and in turn shuriken, is intertwined with fantasy, which explains why these stealth assassins continue to capture the imagination.

My parents wouldn't let me buy a metal shuriken, fearing, perhaps smartly, that I'd accidentally slice myself. Not disheartened, I saved up my allowance for a practice set of foam stars. "Practice" entailed my jumping on the bed and tossing the stars around my bedroom. I thought I was pretty badass. That is, until a friend procured what he called a "real" ninja star. By "real," he meant it was metal and could injure.

The silver metal glistened when he took it out of the black velvet box. The star was stabby-stabby sharp, and we did what any kids would do: we took it outside to throw at a tree.

The shuriken felt heavy in my hand, and I was already visualizing how it would slice through the air. I remember awkwardly rearing back in a wind-up to let it rip, flinging my wrist forward and watching the shiny star flop down in the dirt in front of me with a thud. I felt slightly embarrassed. This sort of thing didn't happen to martial artist Shô Kosugi in *Revenge of the Ninja* (1983). Heck, this wasn't even like chucking those foam stars around my bedroom. My friend's effort wasn't much better. We ended up jabbing the star in the tree's bark, pretending that we'd unleashed a magnificent throw—just like we had seen in the video games we played and the movies we watched.

Perhaps I wasn't throwing the star correctly. Perhaps this particular model needed to be used at close range. Perhaps I didn't know what I was doing. What I did know was that reality could be such a letdown.

Brian Ashcraft is a senior contributing editor for video-game website *Kotaku* and a columnist at the *Japan Times*.

Q: Does the grace, elegance, and rigor of martial arts incite a more extreme violence?

COMMENT 1. Pasquale Robustini:
Both [the Japanese terms] *budo* and *bujutsu* have been translated into English as "martial arts," but they are two very different things. Bujutsu (*bu*=war/*jutsu*=technique or art) includes all the techniques studied by old Japanese warriors to use in real combat during wars—*ninjutsu, kenjutsu* (sword combat), *jujutsu, aikijutsu,* etc. Budo—*judo, kendo, aikido, iaido, karatedo, kyudo*—was developed later as a means to train body, mind, and spirit. Violence is not included in budo (*do*=way, path); the goal is self-improvement, not winning in a combat.

Ninja Star

Glassphemy!
(Macro Sea, 2010)

Environmentally responsible design does not necessarily signify sanctimony and abnegation. The New York City-based developer Macro Sea, for instance, whose self-described mission is to "create unexpected value in underutilized places," argues that environmental responsibility should simply become a normal part of life, and thus be integrated through design into daily rituals and actions, including those that allow us to blow off some steam. Macro Sea conceived Glassphemy!, a bulletproof-glass recycling tower installed in a Brooklyn parking lot, as a way to reinvigorate the recycling process. Participants at one end of the tower stand on a high platform where they are encouraged to grab locally sourced bottles and, in a liberating burst of eco-aggression, hurl them toward the wall of theatrically lit onlookers on a lower platform below. An on-site bicycle-powered tumbler then pulverizes the glass, to be later refashioned into decorative lamps, and for use as environmental fill.

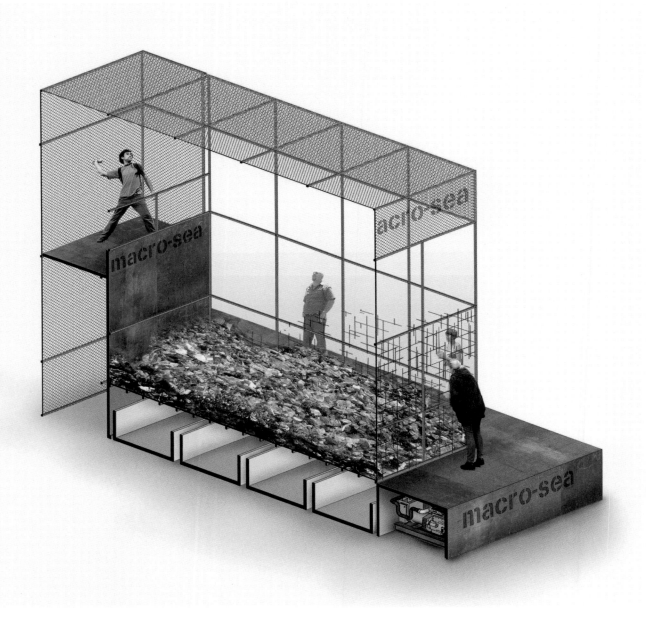

David Belt (American, born 1967) of
Macro Sea (USA, est. 2007), Vamos
Architects (USA, est. 2007), John
Wischmann (American, born 1964),
Paul Maiello (American, born 1966),
and Jason Krugman (American, born
1983). Glassphemy!. 2010. Plexiglass,
steel, wood, responsive light installation,
and glass bottles, 20 x 8 x 16'
(6,000 x 2,500 x 5,000 cm)

Geoff Manaugh

The images are clear, though only partially lit and half-hidden in shadow: they show adults, sometimes in couples, sometimes alone, throwing bottles. They are surrounded by shattered glass inside a structure of some sort, a kind of arena; other people are cheering them on. The audience members are lively, standing outside the structure and pressing their faces up to its transparent walls so as not to miss even a second of what's happening inside. They watch the destruction, enthusiasts of this mad energy, this apparently open invitation to wreck things. There are more people waiting in line, holding yet more bottles, impatient but thrilled. In these images of Glassphemy!, an installation by real-estate developers Macro Sea, we see not just two minutes of hate, but an entire evening's worth, a bottle-breaking binge, and the whole town is involved.

But it's not vandalism, despite the piles of sharp edges and shards. It's a festival: a setting aside of the rules to wreak carnivalesque destruction. And it arrives with the unsettling suggestion that we need outlets like this: architecturally framed free zones, ritual sites of violence and energy expenditure stretching far beyond mere exercise; some riotous, shared occasion that lets us find equilibrium again. We have a metabolic need, the project implies, to assault the world, as if energies long buried will always seek unrestrained release.

Or not, of course.

Perhaps it's all just a joke. Perhaps it's just another long, boring Saturday in the city somewhere, and you've got some bottles to break. You would have thrown them out anyway, or put flowers in them, or lined them up on your windowsill like a college student. Instead you can flail your arms like a baby and throw things; you can watch old bottles burst open into flowers of glass. And it's all because the day didn't go your way or maybe you had nothing better to do (and neither did your best friend). You can hurl your frustrations out with a smile. It's no wonder everyone in the photos is laughing.

Glassphemy! is the furthest possible thing then from a riot or revolution; it's probably the safest place to be in the city. Charge admission and it's a new commercial sport, no different from bowling. Like darts, your grandparents might play it. Just wear a pair of gloves.

But the confusion—Is it a dangerous outburst? An odd evening out with the kids?—reveals a secret in the end. It doesn't matter where the energy comes from if you can make something from it, from this debris—if you can forge new forms from the chaos. You break things down to rebuild later; in this case, melting shining piles of ruins into something pliant and beaten, rolled in ovens and massaged into something unexpected. Bottles become jewelry becomes art. The rage—Or was it celebration?—was just an intermediary moment in this cycle of exchange.

Geoff Manaugh is a freelance writer, curator, and architecture blogger based in Brooklyn, New York.

Q: Is this rage, celebration, or just an intermediary moment in a cycle of exchange?

COMMENT 1. Cameron Tonkinwise:
. . . Given the energy involved in getting glass recyclate into a washed and sorted form suitable to become food-grade packaging again for your boutique wine or artisanal beer or hipster kombucha, you may as well just wash the intact bottle and reuse it. We no longer do this, not because recycling is less eco-impacting than washing for reuse, but because handling glass in ways that afford reuse involves human labor, and human labor is expensive and local, not globally industrializable. . . .

COMMENT 2. David Belt:
. . . Glassphemy! was designed to be an installation that responded to what I saw as the extreme hypocrisy of the use of recycling as a "guilt reliever" of a certain class of consumer. . . . We decided we wanted people to throw bottles at each other and then have to deal with the aftereffect, the smashed glass. We wanted it to be a recycling of emotion rather than just materials. It was meant to be a visceral experience. . . .

AK-47
(Mikhail Kalashnikov, 1947)

The AK-47 (Avtomat Kalashnikova) was designed by Soviet military engineer Mikhail Kalashnikov and debuted in 1947. Building on previous assault-rifle technologies, Kalashnikov developed the AK-47 to be lightweight, easy to handle, durable, and cheap to produce. The rifle became standard issue for the Soviet Union's military in the late 1940s and redefined modern warfare in the latter half of the twentieth century. The AK-47 allows its operator to alternate between single-cartridge-shot and fully automatic modes with ease. This feature, when combined with the rifle's industrial production in countries outside of what is now Russia, has facilitated mass killing with a scale and rapidity unmatched by any other weapon. Once a tool of state control, the AK-47 is today the tool of choice for insurgents seeking to destabilize governments and institutions. It is estimated that there are between seventy-five and one hundred million AK-47s worldwide, many of them ersatz.

China Keitetsi

On June 27, 2014, the Museum of Modern Art's *Design and Violence* team spoke with China Keitetsi, an international campaigner for the rights of child soldiers. A former conscript herself, Keitetsi is the author of *Child Soldier: Fighting for My Life*,[1] a memoir describing her brutalized adolescence as a soldier in Uganda's National Resistance Army beginning in the late 1980s. After ten years, she escaped to South Africa, and later made her way to Denmark, where she currently lives. Wary of provoking disturbing memories, the team sent Keitetsi a list of questions in advance of the conversation. The interview was conducted by telephone, with Keitetsi making final edits to the transcript.

Design and Violence: Thank you for taking the time to speak with us.
China Keitetsi: I am happy to be talking about this subject with you, but it's not easy to be reminded of your past, you know? I live in Denmark now. I think about how lucky I am because I don't see a gun everyday on the streets of Denmark. I feel like I was given another chance—like I was dead and in hell, and now I am back, alive.

D&V: We've explained a little about *Design and Violence* in advance of this conversation. One of the designs we're including in the project is the AK-47. The illustration on the cover of your book shows a small child holding this weapon. How central was the gun to your experiences as a child soldier? How central is it now to your memories of that time?
CK: When I was there, it meant a lot in my life. It was like my mother. It became a part of me, and I a part of it. It was my identity, my passport. Like, they ask you at the airport for your passport—at that time, if I had been asked who I was, I would have shown my gun. It became my mother; it was my friend, my protector. And yet, I still felt fear everyday [as a child soldier].

D&V: You write very powerfully about this in your memoir, as when you say, "We were told our guns were our mothers, our friends, our whole world, and we must rather lose ourselves than our guns." Can you expand on your feelings toward the AK-47 during your time as a child soldier?
CK: I'd get so frightened. I'd dream, and I'd think, I don't have the gun. If I woke up, and my gun wasn't there, I would become crazy because I knew I

would be punished. In Europe now, when a woman goes out, most of the time she makes sure not to forget her purse. It was like that for us. You could forget to wear clothes, but you could not forget your gun. Today, when I talk or think about it, when I see others [in the media] carrying guns, I look down on them, and I feel shame that I carried one too. I look at women I see around me today, perhaps drinking margaritas or pink drinks. Fine hands, fine fingers, fine nails. I look back, and I realize how different I was. I try to distance myself as much as I can from the gun because it makes me feel that I am not a woman.

D&V: According to the *New York Times,* the weapon's designer, Mikhail Kalashnikov, a Russian general and military engineer, has said that he designed the AK-47 to protect his homeland: "This is a weapon of defense . . . It is not a weapon for offense."[2] What are your feelings toward the AK-47 today?

CK: The gun can be easily carried by a child—even children as young as the age of six. When we carried them, they made a mark on the ground as we walked because we were too short [to hold the butt of the weapon up off the ground]. Kalashnikov should have changed the design. If this man cared, he should have made it heavier so that only an adult man could lift it.

D&V: How does the AK-47 and your memory of it continue to affect you in the present, despite your being removed from it in time and space?

CK: I knew my weapon more than I did my parents; I was more with my gun than my family. The experience of carrying it leaves you with a fate that is not sealed. It leaves you desperate for love. And most of the time, you don't even know where you will get that love from. I lost my parents, and I lost my sisters in the Rwandan genocide. I work hard every day to find something to smile about, to be happy about. But you are never the same again after an experience like that. It is not only the gun. You can be apart from the weapon, but the abuse and

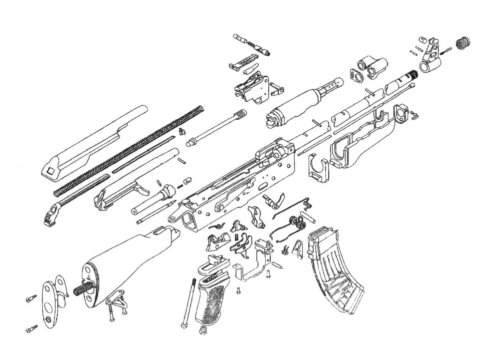

Mikhail Kalashnikov (Russian, 1919–2013). AK-47 7.62 x 39 mm Assault Rifle (exploded-view drawing). 1947. Wood, steel, dimensions variable

Overleaf: Mikhail Kalashnikov. AK-47 7.62 x 39 mm Assault Rifle. 1997

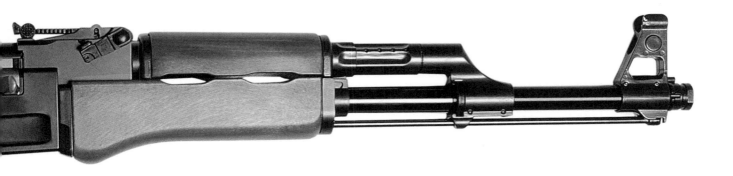

Members of the U.S. Air Force 447th Expeditionary Security Forces Squadron train Iraqi airmen to fire AK-47s, Baghdad, Iraq. 2011

the humiliation are also weapons and these are harder to move away from. I don't know if that's part of your project, but it's important.

One woman, a psychologist, told me at a conference that once you are a child soldier, you never recover. And my answer to her was: I think that if you are left in the same place where you did all the bad things with that gun, it takes longer to recover. Because every time you look at the gun, the places you used it, your mind travels back. But I am in Denmark. Here, I don't see AK-47s every day.

D&V: As you said, you now live in Denmark with your family. How has your experience influenced your hopes for your children and for the future?

CK: For the first time in my life, I have someone who loves me unconditionally. I have a five-year-old girl and twin boys who are a year old.

D&V: Congratulations! That's wonderful.

CK: Thank you, yes. It gives me hope. After holding an AK-47, I looked down on myself. You judge yourself. Always, I will be different than others. But having my own children and family means I get some pride back. It is the first real peace for me. It has made me grateful for life. I feel lucky to bring them up, and I feel it as a privilege. I don't think I can thank God enough that they will never have to know what I left behind, what it is like to live in fear. They will always have freedom.

China Keitetsi was born in Uganda where, at the age of nine, she was recruited by Uganda's National Resistance Army (NRA).

1. China Keitetsi, *Child Soldier: Fighting for My Life*, ed. Ruth Friedland (Bellevue, South Africa: Janaca, 2002).
2. C. J. Chivers, "Mikhail Kalashnikov, Creator of AK-47, Dies at 94," *New York Times*, December 23, 2013, http://www.nytimes.com/2013/12/24/world/europe/mikhail-kalashnikov-creator-of-soviet-era-ak-47-weapon-is-dead-at-age-94.html.

Q: What responsibility do designers bear for the products they design?

COMMENT 1. Harry Rhoades:
It depends on the product. If you design a weapon, you must acknowledge that the weapon, even if created for defense, could easily be used for offense. And while you are not responsible for actions of everyone in the world, you did provide further means to violence that formerly did not exist. I also think if a product is successful and used as intended, it's likely that designers are happy to take responsibility for the impact on the world—and, crucially, vice versa.

End

The Design and Violence Debates

Can design mitigate or eliminate the inherent violence of the slaughterhouse? Should the experience of pain transcend gender boundaries? Should the tools of production be made accessible such that we are able to print weapons from the comfort of our own homes?

In March and April 2014, six months after launching *Design and Violence* as an online curatorial experiment, we (organizers Paola Antonelli and Jamer Hunt and I) staged three debates at The Museum of Modern Art, moving the project from the digital to the physical agora. Each debate centered on a provocative project featured on the *Design and Violence* website: The Liberator, crypto-anarchist Cody Wilson's 3-D-printed pistol and its corresponding downloadable design; Menstruation Machine, designer Sputniko!'s wearable device that emulates the pain and bleeding of a five-day menstrual period; and the Serpentine Ramp, animal scientist Temple Grandin's curved chute designed to reduce the stress of cattle en route to the slaughterhouse. Each debate featured speakers engaged with issues germane to the design under examination, generating passionate manifestations of the arguments, concerns, and questions raised online—and allowing us to bypass the sometimes stilted back-and-forth discussion in the comment threads.

The event format honored the spirit of the Oxford-style debate: one motion, one moderator (Antonelli and Hunt switched off in this role), one speaker for the motion and one against. Each participant presented a ten-minute opening statement foregrounding either the merits or flaws of the proposed motion. In order to outline the extremities of the discursive spectrum, we encouraged debaters to forgo nuance in their opening remarks (in some cases, against their own personal convictions). We then devoted the remainder of the event to shading in the vast and complicated gray areas, with the moderator prompting discussion between debaters and opening the floor to audience questions. Although we covered only serious topics, we maintained a degree of levity by administering an informal audience poll at the beginning and again at the end of each program, comparing how opinions had shifted throughout the course of the discussion. Unlike a traditional debate, the point was not to establish winners and losers, but to facilitate fiery, intense, multifaceted dialogue.

The inaugural event took The Liberator as its catalyst and centered on the motion *We cannot limit open-source design, even when we do not support every consequence.* Liberator-creator Wilson argued for the motion—indeed, for his belief in the inevitable triumph of individual actors over any government or state—while technology columnist Rob Walker argued against it (although, in the ensuing discussion, professed unbridled admiration for The Liberator as a design provocation). The unambiguous harm unleashed by well-designed weapons and the limits of gun laws took a backseat to broader discussions about the nature of open-source design—what it is and who it is for—and the ethics of design, a discipline whose mantra "first, do no harm" is compromised or contravened more often than is perhaps admitted. The question of "should" verses "can" was raised by many in the room, with both speakers admitting that although open-source design projects *can* be limited (and have been successfully—online plans for The Liberator were retracted after legal threat by the U.S. government) neither could imagine how meaningful regulation might occur. Walker's claim toward the end of the session succinctly summed up the general consensus: "If you think [untraceable guns] are a bad idea, you can't be for open-source design without limits. Period. And if [you're for] open-source design without limits . . . then you have to support the idea of an untraceable 3-D gun printed in someone's garage."

The second debate, inspired by Menstruation Machine, offered the motion *Design's potential to transcend gender boundaries is limitless.* Mickey Boardman, editorial director of *Paper* magazine, supported the motion, while Chris Bobel, author of *New Blood: Third-Wave Feminism and the Politics of Menstruation* (2010), argued against it. Hunt acted as moderator. Speakers and audience members explored the potential of design, whether speculative or applied, to allow us to move beyond our own biology, not only to empathize with others but also to experience their pain. Participants questioned whether design's potential could ever truly be limitless when its iterative processes take place within the larger spectrum of human experience, including entrenched prejudice and fear. Both Boardman and Bobel ultimately tempered their general enthusiasm for the motion with Bobel highlighting the dangers of "experiencing something partial, which you interpret as total . . . authoriz[ing] you to speak for another."

The third debate took the Serpentine Ramp as its focus. The motion, *Design can allow us to humanely include animal products in our diet,* was perhaps the most fiercely contested of the series. With Antonelli in the role of moderator, Nicola Twilley, author and editor of the blog *Edible Geography*, argued for the motion, while animal-rights activist Gary L. Francione argued against it.

Nicola Twilley (left) and Gary Francione (right) debate Temple Grandin's Serpentine Ramp and the motion *Design can allow us to humanely include animal products in our diet.* April 17, 2014. The Museum of Modern Art, New York.

Cody Wilson, Paola Antonelli, and Rob Walker discuss the motion *We cannot limit open-source design, even when we do not support every consequence* during the question-and-answer session at the inaugural *Design and Violence* debate. March 27, 2014. The Museum of Modern Art, New York

Both the debate speakers and the audience members wrestled with the notion that humans have used animals as food products for millennia. Twilley argued that design could serve this dietary tradition by rendering livestock farming more humane and by enabling humans to empathize more closely with their nonhuman counterparts. Francione, a longstanding advocate for the equal rights of animals and humans, argued that, at least for the audience members gathered at MoMA, killing another living being in order to satiate their dietary needs is ethically unjustifiable. Both speakers floated facts and figures in support of their respective positions, but the issue of consumption was incontestable: in the United States, we collectively consume over 25 billion pounds of cattle meat annually, propping up a beef industry worth around $85 billion a year. Authors such as Michael Pollan (*The Omnivore's Dilemma*, 2006) have fostered public awareness of our individual and collective relationships with the animals we eat, and the debate benefitted from audience members obviously engaged and well versed in the contemporary discourse. Earlier the same week, PETA president Ingrid Newkirk responded to Grandin's Serpentine Ramp on the *Design and Violence* site, highlighting the great American appetite and proposing that we might instead choose to, as she puts it, "bypass the meat counter." Her suggestion, supported by Francione, as well as many of the audience members, was that the most humane design would be one that reconceives not the slaughterhouse but *us*—ideally to want and need less of everything, including animal products.

In each case, the debates left avenues of discussion open and motions unresolved. As the *Design and Violence* project has highlighted in all its incarnations, violence is experienced through many forms of design as part of daily life. Whether felt immediately or in the remove of the relentless twenty-four-hour news cycle (itself a peculiar violence), violence is at once a shared shadow over our collective humanity and, because of its ubiquitous, quotidian nature, often strangely invisible. Design can simultaneously be to the benefit of some and the detriment of others. Each of the debates demonstrated emphatically that the world is neither inherently "good" nor "bad," as we all know—and neither is design.

Michelle Millar Fisher
Curatorial Assistant, Department of Architecture and Design

Acknowledgments

A project of this scope is necessarily the work of diverse colleagues, friends, volunteers, and obliging acquaintances who have played roles both inspirational and invaluable. First and foremost, we wish to thank the myriad designers, manufacturers, artists, and producers featured on the *Design and Violence* website, as well as the many authors who thoughtfully responded to the complex works under investigation. We owe the success of this experimental project to their enthusiasm, cooperation, and, above all, their extraordinary contributions. Steven Pinker, author of *The Better Angels of Our Nature* (2011)—an astounding meditation on the cultural evolution of violence—and Cody Wilson, creator of the 3-D-printed pistol The Liberator (2013), are worthy of special recognition; their provocative work precipitated our exploration of violence and its varied intersections with contemporary design.

Our deepest gratitude goes to the many authors whose outstanding essays appear online but, simply for reasons of space, could not be included in this book: Jad Abumrad, Christina Agapakis, Kalpona Akter and Liana Foxvog, Geoffrey Batchen, Carolyn Birdsall, Andrew Blauvelt, Amy Ellenbogen and Derick Scott, Gregg Easterbrook, Ingrid Fetell, Milton Glaser, Marta Gutman, Ricky Jackson, Maira Kalman, Christopher Kilmartin, Jennifer Leung, Mark Mahoney, Christoph Niemann, Christian Parenti, Talan Skeels-Piggins, Bruce Sterling, Superflux, Amy Taubin, Torolab, Alex S. Vitale, Graham Westgarth, and Mabel O. Wilson. We also wish to recognize the contributions of the many individuals who extended and enriched these conversations by commenting on the website. As the selection of their critical insights in these pages surely attests, their participation was key to realizing the project's full potential.

Over the course of the project, a few talented individuals contributed essential ideas, formative research, and stalwart support; they deserve special recognition. The project was born in 2012 with a proposal drafted in collaboration with Kate Carmody, formerly Curatorial Assistant in the Museum's Department of Architecture and Design. Her contributions to the project's initial concept and checklist, and her conviction in the viability of the online experiment, cannot be understated. Meagan Durlak came on board in the summer of 2013 as Research Assistant from the Transdisciplinary Design graduate program at Parsons The New School for Design in time for the project's launch. Michelle Millar Fisher, Curatorial Assistant in the Museum's Department of Architecture and Design, ably took the reins in early 2014 and has masterfully managed the online project, this publication, and all related public programming. Her ideas and insights, zeal and intelligence, dedication and creativity are reflected in every aspect of *Design and Violence,* not least of which includes the overwhelming majority of curatorial statements authored for the website and for this publication. We have also benefited from the matchless assistance of three brilliant interns: Melinda Zoephel, Kristina Parsons, Ala Tannir, and Steffi Duarte have contributed indispensable research and support.

From the project's initial stages, we were fortunate to receive guidance from key allies who engaged in discussion both on and off the website and encouraged others to get involved. In particular, we thank Susan Yelavich and her students from the graduate program in Design Studies at Parsons The New School for Design. Yasmin Green and Anna de Paula Hanika at Google were early champions of the project and generously invited us to exhibit a prototype at the 2013 Google Ideas summit Conflict in a Connected World.

The various iterations of *Design and Violence* generated intense and productive collaborations between many people and organizations. The project lives on the web thanks to Arrow Root Media, who oversaw the site's development, and to Shannon Darrough, Director, Department of Digital Media, who supervised its design. Shannon and his team ensured that the design matched the project in tone. We are grateful to designer Luke Keller for the site's initial design and to Allegra Burnette, formerly Creative Director in the Department of Digital Media, for her ideas and recommendations. Jason Persse, Manager, Department of Marketing, has carefully and thoughtfully edited each weekly online post. We owe special mention to the team at WeTransfer, especially CSO Damian Bradfield and artist Nelly Ben Hayoun, who supported our project with wallpaper space on their site, connecting new audiences to the conversation.

The success of our spring 2013 debate series is due in no small part to our extraordinary roster of speakers: Cody Wilson, Rob Walker, Mickey Boardman, Chris Bobel, Nicola Twilley, and Gary L. Francione contributed expert analysis with passion and precision. We thank Charlie Kalinowski, Manager, Audio/Visual Services, and his team for their essential support, as well as our wonderful colleagues in the Department of Education, in particular Pablo Helguera, Director, Adult and Academic Education; Sheetal Prajapati, Assistant Director, Learning and Artists Initiatives; and Susannah Brown, Associate Educator, Courses and Seminars, who tirelessly orchestrated complex event logistics.

In MoMA's Department of Publications, we owe thanks to Christopher Hudson, Publisher, for supporting the book from the first proposal. We are also grateful to David Frankel, Editorial Director; Chul R. Kim, Associate Publisher; Marc Sapir, Production Director; Matthew Pimm, Production Manager; and Genevieve Allison, Rights Coordinator. We would also like to thank our editor, Sarah Resnick, who sensitively handled the complex transition from web to print, and our brilliant designer, Shaz Madani; we could not be more delighted with her restrained and elegant layout, which makes this publication even more incisive.

In the Museum's Library, we wish to thank Jennifer Tobias, Librarian, and Megan Williams, Kress Fellow, for their enthusiastic research assistance. Victor Samra, Digital Media Marketing Manager, and Gretchen Scott, Building Project Digital Media Marketing Manager, have tirelessly promoted the *Design and Violence* project through MoMA's social-media channels. In the Department of Communications, we would like to thank Kim Mitchell, Chief Communications Officer; Paul Jackson, Communications Manager; and Meg Montgoris, Publicist, who have extended the reach of this project and lured the press with their efforts. In the Department of Graphic Design, we thank Ingrid Chou and In-Hee Bae. We were floored by the extraordinary generosity of our colleague Ravi Iyer, Project Manager, Department of Information Technology, who called manufacturers in India at all hours of the night to help us secure image permissions.

A project such as this requires of its proponents a substantial leap of faith, and colleagues in the Department of Architecture and Design and at Parsons

The New School for Design have championed the venture from the outset, even when its experimental nature precluded easy or immediate grasp of any final product. Worthy of special acknowledgment are the Museum's Board of Trustees and senior curatorial, exhibitions, and administrative staff for their willing encouragement in launching this experiment. We thank Ronald S. Lauder, Honorary Chairman, and Agnes Gund, President Emerita, as well as David Rockefeller, Honorary Chairman; Robert B. Menschel, Chairman Emeritus; Donald B. Marron, President Emeritus; Jerry I. Speyer, Chairman; and Marie-Josée Kravis, President, for their unwavering support of the Museum's curators in all endeavors. We are grateful to Glenn D. Lowry, Director, for being an enthusiastic advocate and allowing us to break new ground. Ramona Bannayan, Deputy Director, Exhibitions and Collections; Peter Reed, Senior Deputy Director, Curatorial Affairs; and Nancy Adelson, Deputy General Counsel, were each integral to the success of this venture.

Last, and anything but least, we wish to thank those closest to home, our endlessly patient and always inspiring partners in life—Judith and Larry—as well as Felix and Ivy, our intrepid photographic models. This has been an incredibly instructive and moving project. With this publication we hope to advance two years of discussion and debate and to provide a clearer understanding of the stakes at the intersection of design and violence.

Paola Antonelli and Jamer Hunt

Contributors

Ahmed Ansari, p. 88

Ahmed Ansari teaches courses in design and in science and technology studies in Karachi, Pakistan. His academic interests involve exploring the philosophical and political implications of designed artifacts, and what design (always human-centric) can learn from disciplines that deal with the nonhuman. When not teaching, he spends most of his time traveling around the country evangelizing design research at workshops and lectures for local organizations, and consulting with local start-ups. Of particular fascination to him are the child laborers in Karachi's Saddar Market, who ingeniously use whetstones to buff scratched phone screens, making them as good as new for less than two dollars.

Ayssar Arida, p. 74

Ayssar Arida is a practicing "urbatect," writer, educator, and entrepreneur. His award-winning work ranges from digital design to large-scale city planning and strategy, including video-game development and toy design. He is author of the influential book *Quantum City* (Oxon, U.K., and New York: Architectural Press, 2002) and cocreator of urbacraft, the hackable urban-design construction toy. In 2013, in Beirut, he founded Urbatecture, the first urban-design-thinking agency, after running Q-DAR design agency in London and Paris for thirteen years. Ayssar holds a master of arts in urban design with distinction from Oxford Brookes University and a bachelor of architecture from the American University of Beirut.

Brian Ashcraft, p. 206

Brian Ashcraft is a senior contributing editor for the video-game website *Kotaku* and a columnist at the *Japan Times*. His work has also appeared in *Popular Science*, the *Guardian*, and *Metropolis*. Ashcraft was previously a contributing editor at *Wired*. Ashcraft is author of three books: *Arcade Mania!* (Tokyo: Kodansha International, 2008); *Japanese Schoolgirl Confidential* (North Clarendon, Vt.: Tuttle, 2014), with Shoko Ueda; and *Cosplay World* (Munich: Prestel, 2014), with Luke Plunkett. He is currently writing a book on Japanese tattoos for Tuttle. Originally from Texas, Ashcraft has called Japan home since 2001. He lives in Osaka with his wife and three sons.

Alison Bancroft, p. 108

Alison Bancroft is a writer and cultural critic, specializing in interdisciplinary approaches to modern culture and media. Her interests include art, design, and culture; also psychoanalytic thought, sex, and gender. She is the author of *Fashion and Psychoanalysis: Styling the Self* (London: I.B.Tauris & Co Ltd, 2012)—her first book, and a topic that she has published and spoken about widely—and is now working on her second book. Bancroft holds a doctorate from the University of London.

JC Cahill, p. 184

JC Cahill teaches at the University of Alberta, where he heads the Lab of Experimental Plant Ecology. Research in the lab addresses a diversity of fundamental questions in plant ecology. Cahill takes a broad approach to research, with interest in plant behavioral ecology, competition, plant-pollinator interactions, insect and mammalian herbivory, evolutionary and functional ecology, climate change, and mycorrhizae. Curious and open-minded, Cahill and his students study whatever sounds fun and interesting. He is adept at presenting hard science to the general public in a fun, inviting, easy-to-understand manner.

Laura Antrim Caskey, p. 165

Laura Antrim Caskey is an independent photojournalist. Caskey has spent the last decade reporting on the human and environmental costs of mountaintop-removal coal mining in Appalachia. In 2010, Caskey published *Dragline*, an award-winning photojournalistic exposé of the conflict between the coal industry and residents of West Virginia's coal river valley designed to educate people and spur them to action. Caskey distributed thousands of copies of *Dragline* across the planet in partnership with Climate Ground Zero, a grassroots organization, whose campaign of nonviolent civil disobedience she chronicled. Her photographs have been published in the *New York Times*, the *Wall Street Journal*, *Rolling Stone*, the *Smithsonian*, and *Nature,* and featured in documentary films, including *The Last Mountain* (2011).

Gabriella Coleman, p. 134

Gabriella Coleman is an author and professor. Trained as an anthropologist, she holds the Wolfe Chair in Scientific and Technological Literacy at McGill University, Montreal. Her research, teaching, and writing covers the ethics and politics of digital activism and computer hackers. She is the author of two books: *Coding Freedom: the Ethics and Aesthetics of Hacking* (Princeton, N.J.: Princeton University Press, 2012) and *Hacker, Hoaxer, Whistleblower, Spy: The Many Faces of Anonymous* (New York: Verso, 2014)

Antonio Damasio, p. 194

Antonio Damasio is university professor, David Dornsife Professor of Neuroscience and director of the Brain and Creativity Institute at the University of Southern California in Los Angeles. Damasio has made seminal contributions to the understanding of brain processes underlying emotions, feelings, decision making, and consciousness. He is the author of numerous scientific articles and the recipient of many awards. He is also the author of *Descartes' Error: Emotion, Reason, and the Human Brain* (New York: G.P. Putnam's Sons, 1994), *The Feeling of What Happens: Body and Emotion in the Making of Consciousness* (New York: Harcourt Brace & Company, 1999), *Looking for Spinoza: Joy, Sorrow, and the Feeling Brain* (New York: Harcourt Brace & Company, 1999), and *Self Comes to Mind: Constructing the Conscious Brain* (New York: Vintage Books, 2010).

Clive Dilnot, p. 176

Clive Dilnot is professor of design studies at Parsons The New School for Design. Originally educated as a fine artist, he later studied social philosophy with Polish sociologist Zygmunt Bauman. Apart from design topics, Dilnot has also written and taught in fields ranging from aesthetics and art theory to photography, the decorative arts, museums and their framing of objects, the economics of the current crisis, and the question of how we can contend with the world we have made. A coauthored book, *Design and the Question of History*, is forthcoming in from Bloomsbury Academic in 2015.

Aminatta Forna, p. 84

Aminatta Forna is the award-winning author of the novels *The Hired Man* (London: Bloomsbury Publishing, 2013), *The Memory of Love* (London: Bloomsbury Publishing, 2010), and *Ancestor Stones* (London: Bloomsbury Publishing, 2006) and the memoir *The Devil that Danced on the Water* (London: HarperCollins Publishers, 2002). She is professor of creative writing at Bath Spa University in the United Kingdom. She has acted as judge for a number of literary awards, most recently for the 2013 International Man Booker Prize. In 2003, Forna established the Rogbonko Project to build a school in a village in Sierra Leone. The charity now runs a number of projects in the spheres of education, sanitation, and maternal health.

William Gibson, p. 154

William Gibson's first novel, *Neuromancer* (New York: Ace Books, 1984), won the Hugo Award, the Philip K. Dick Memorial Award, and the Nebula Award in 1984. He is credited with having coined the term "cyberspace," and having envisioned both the Internet and virtual reality before either existed. His other novels include *Pattern Recognition* (New York: G.P. Putnam's Sons, 2003), *Spook Country* (New York: G.P. Putnam's Sons,

2007), *Zero History* (New York: G.P. Putnam's Sons, 2010), and his most recent, *The Peripheral* (New York: G.P. Putnam's Sons, 2014). He lives in Vancouver, British Columbia.

Elizabeth Grosz, p. 52
Elizabeth Grosz is the Jean Fox O'Barr Women's Studies Professor in Trinity College of Arts and Sciences in the Women's Studies and Literature programs at Duke University. She is the author of *Sexual Subversions: Three French Feminists* (Crows Nest, New South Wales: Allen & Unwin, 1989) and, most recently, *Becoming Undone* (Durham, N.C.: Duke University Press, 2011).

António Guterres, p. 144
António Guterres became the tenth U.N. High Commissioner for Refugees on June 15, 2005. Guterres was elected by the U.N. General Assembly to a five-year term. In April 2010, the General Assembly reelected Guterres to a second five-year term. As High Commissioner, Guterres heads one of the world's foremost humanitarian organizations providing protection and assistance to millions of refugees, returnees, internally displaced people, and stateless persons. The UNHCR has twice won the Nobel Peace Prize. Some 88 percent of its staff work in the field, often in difficult and dangerous duty stations.

John Hockenberry, p. 19
John Hockenberry is host of public radio's live morning news program *The Takeaway*. An Emmy and Peabody Award–winning journalist, he is a former correspondent for NBC News, ABC News, and NPR, and has traveled the globe reporting on a wide variety of stories in virtually every medium for more than three decades. He has written dozens of magazine and newspaper articles, a play, and two books, including the novel *A River Out of Eden* (New York: Anchor Books, 2001), and the best-selling memoir *Moving Violations: War Zones, Wheelchairs, and Declarations of Independence* (New York: Hyperion, 1995), which was a finalist for the National Book Critics Circle Award.

Christopher L. Heuertz, p. 26
Christopher L. Heuertz is an activist fighting for freedom and justice among some of the world's poorest people. He has worked alongside organizations in Bolivia, India, Moldova, Romania, and Thailand to establish small businesses and microenterprise initiatives as alternative incomes for women working in the sex industry. He has been featured in publications such as the *Washington Post* and has contributed to the book *Sexually Exploited Children: Working to Protect and Heal* (Pasadena, Calif.: William Carey Library Publishers, 2013). Chris has also been a featured speaker at numerous anti-human-trafficking events. He is the cofounder of Gravity, A Center for Contemplative Activism.

Arianna Huffington, p. 128
Arianna Huffington is the chair, president, and editor in chief of the Huffington Post Media Group; a nationally syndicated columnist; and the author of thirteen books. In May 2005, she launched the *Huffington Post*, a news and blog site that quickly became one of the most widely read, linked to, and frequently cited media brands on the Internet. In 2012, the site won a Pulitzer Prize for national reporting. In 2006, and again in 2011, she was named to the "Time 100," *Time* magazine's list of the world's one hundred most influential people. She holds an master of arts in economics from Cambridge University.

Harry Jones, p. 160
Harry Jones is a lieutenant colonel in the U.S. Army who has served in both Iraq and Afghanistan. He is currently assigned to the U.S. Military Academy at West Point as an instructor of philosophy. He teaches an introductory course on philosophy and ethics where special attention is given to the subject of war and morality. He is currently working at the intersection of creativity and ethics and is exploring various ways the military can learn from designers. He holds an MA in philosophy from the University of Virginia.

China Keitetsi, p. 214
China Keitetsi was born in Uganda. At the age of nine, she was recruited by Uganda's National Resistance Army (NRA). There, she was given a new name, "China"—her instructor interpreted her visage as Asian—and a gun. In 2004, Keitetsi founded the African Child Soldiers and War Victims Charity, a center to help reintegrate orphans and former child soldiers. She currently lives in Denmark.

Nama Khalil, p. 148
Nama Khalil is an artist and academic. In her work, she explores notions of "otherness" while attempting to speak for herself as an Other, acting as mediator between subject and viewer. Her work has been exhibited in numerous galleries, including in Cleveland, Ohio, and in both Dearborn and Ann Arbor, Michigan, as well as in online exhibitions. She received her master of arts in Middle East studies from the University of Michigan, where she is currently pursuing a doctorate in sociocultural anthropology. Nama's academic work has focused on transnational Islam, media, cultural production, and visual culture in Egypt, and identity politics and art in Arab American and Muslim American communities.

Angélique Kidjo, p. 96
Angélique Kidjo is a Grammy Award–winning Beninoise singer-songwriter and activist. She has been recognized as an iconic figure by the BBC and the *Guardian*, and is the first woman to be listed among "The 40 Most Powerful Celebrities in Africa" by *Forbes*. Kidjo has been a UNICEF Goodwill Ambassador since 2002 and vice president of the International Confederation of Societies of Authors and Composers (CISAC) since 2013. For a number of years, Kidjo has been campaigning for Africa for Women's Rights, a campaign launched by the International Federation of Human Rights (FIDH). She is the cofounder of the Batonga Foundation, which supports both secondary-school and higher education for girls in Africa so they can assume leadership roles and create change.

André Lepecki, p. 100
André Lepecki is an associate professor at the Department of Performance Studies at New York University and artistic professor at Stockholm University of the Arts. He is author of *Exhausting Dance: Performance and the Politics of Movement* and editor of several anthologies, including *Dance* for the Whitechapel series Documents of Contemporary Art. In 2008, he cocurated and directed a "re-doing" of Allan Kaprow's *18 Happenings in 6 Parts*. Commissioned by Haus der Kunst, Munich, and presented at Performa 7, *Happenings* received the International Association of Art Critics Award for Best Performance.

Lev Manovich, p. 22
Lev Manovich is the author of *Software Takes Command* (New York: Bloomsbury Academic, 2013), *Soft Cinema: Navigating the Database* (2005), and *The Language of New Media* (Cambridge, Mass.: The MIT Press, 2001); the latter was described as "the most suggestive and broad ranging media history since Marshall McLuhan." Manovich is a professor at The Graduate Center, CUNY, and a director of the Software Studies Initiative, which analyzes and visualizes culture-related big data. In 2013, he was named one of *Complex* magazine's "25 People Shaping the Future of Design."

Nivedita Menon, p. 57
Nivedita Menon is a professor at the Centre for Comparative Politics and Political Theory at Jawaharlal Nehru University, Delhi. She writes with a feminist perspective on political theory and contemporary politics and has published widely in both Indian and international academic journals. Menon regularly contributes to debates on current issues in newspapers and on the team blog *Kafila*. Her books are *Seeing Like a Feminist* (New Delhi: Penguin/Zubaan, 2012), the edited volume *Sexualities* (London: Palgrave MacMillan, 2007), *Power and Contestation: India Since 1989* (London: Zed Books, 2007, coauthored with Aditya Nigam), and *Recovering Subversion: Feminist Politics beyond the Law* (Champaign, Ill.: Permanent Black/University of Illinois Press, 2004). Menon also translates fiction between Hindi, Malayalam, and English and has been involved in a wide range of political and social movements.

Geoff Manaugh, p. 210
Geoff Manaugh is a freelance writer, curator, and architecture blogger based in Brooklyn, New York. He is the author of *BLDGBLOG* (http://bldgblog.blogspot.com), a long-running exploration of spatial ideas from archaeology to urban planning and science fiction to geology; and he is currently exploring the relationship between burglary and architecture for a new book forthcoming from Farrar, Straus and Giroux. He has curated exhibitions at the Nevada Museum of Art and New York's Storefront for Art and Architecture.

Ingrid Newkirk, p. 188
Ingrid Newkirk is founder and president of People for the Ethical Treatment of Animals (PETA) and its international affiliates, and author of over a dozen books on the philosophy of animal rights and its practical application, including *The Compassionate Cook, or, Please Don't Eat the Animals* (New York: Warner Books, Inc., 1993) and *Making Kind Choices: Everyday Ways to Enhance*

Your Life Through Earth- and Animal-Friendly Living (New York: St. Martin's Press, 2005). She is the subject of the 2007 HBO special *I Am an Animal: The Story of Ingrid Newkirk*.

Bruce Nussbaum, p. 48

Bruce Nussbaum is the author of the book *Creative Intelligence: Harnessing the Power to Create, Connect, and Inspire* (New York: HarperCollins Publishers, 2013). He blogs, tweets, and writes on innovation, design, and creativity. The former assistant managing editor for *Business Week* (now *Bloomberg Businessweek)*, he is professor of innovation and design at Parsons The New School for Design. Nussbaum also previously served as a Peace Corps volunteer in the Philippines.

Steven Pinker, p. 140

Steven Pinker is Johnstone Family Professor in the Department of Psychology at Harvard University. Until 2003, he taught in the Department of Brain and Cognitive Sciences at the Massachusetts Institute of Technology. He conducts research on language and cognition, writes for publications such as the *New York Times*, *Time*, and the *New Republic*, and is the author of seven books, including *The Language Instinct* (New York: William Morrow and Company, 1994), *How the Mind Works* (New York: W.W. Norton & Company, Inc., 1997), *Words and Rules: The Ingredients of Language* (New York: HarperCollins Publishers, Inc., 1999), *The Blank Slate: The Modern Denial of Human Nature* (New York: Viking Penguin, 2002), *The Stuff of Thought: Language as a Window into Human Nature* (New York: Viking Penguin, 2007), *The Better Angels of Our Nature: Why Violence Has Declined* (New York: Viking Penguin, 2011), and his latest *The Sense of Style: The Thinking Person's Guide to Writing in the 21st Century* (New York: Viking Penguin, 2014).

Camille Paglia, p. 122

Camille Paglia is the University Professor of Humanities and Media Studies at the University of the Arts in Philadelphia, where she has taught since 1984. She is the author of six books, and her third essay collection is under contract to Pantheon Books.

She has written numerous articles on art, literature, popular culture, feminism, politics, and religion for publications around the world. Her essay "Theater of Gender: David Bowie at the Climax of the Sexual Revolution" was commissioned by the Victoria and Albert Museum for the catalogue of its exhibition of Bowie costumes, which opened in London on March 2013 and is touring internationally.

Hugh Raffles, p. 198

Hugh Raffles is an anthropologist at The New School whose work explores relationships among people, animals, and things. His writing has appeared in academic and popular venues, including *Granta*, *Public Culture*, *Natural History*, *Orion*, and the *New York Times*. His most recent book, *Insectopedia* (New York: Pantheon Books, 2010), was selected as a *New York Times* notable book and will be published this year in French and Chinese. In 2010, he received a Whiting Writers' Award. He is currently working on an ethnography of rocks and stones.

Alice Rawsthorn, p. 180

Alice Rawsthorn writes about design in the *International New York Times*, which syndicates her articles worldwide. She is also a columnist for *Frieze* magazine and a prominent public speaker on design. Her latest book, *Hello World: Where Design Meets Life* (2014), explores design's influence on our lives. Described by the curator Hans Ulrich Obrist as "panoramic in scope, passionately argued and highly addictive to read," *Hello World* is published by Hamish Hamilton in the U.K. and in multiple foreign-language editions. A graduate in art and architectural history from Cambridge University, Rawsthorn was awarded an OBE (Officer of the Order of the British Empire) in 2014 for services to design and the arts.

Leslie Savan, p. 46

Leslie Savan is a writer and critic currently blogging about media and politics for the *Nation*. A three-time Pulitzer Prize finalist for her *Village Voice* column about advertising, Savan is the author of *Slam Dunks and No Brainers: Pop Language in Your Life, the Media, and, Like . . . Whatever* (New York: Vintage Books, 2005) and *The Sponsored Life: Ads, TV, and American Culture* (Philadelphia: Temple University Press, 1994). She has been widely published, including in the *New York Times Magazine*, the *New Yorker, Salon,* and the *Huffington Post.*

Shira A. Scheindlin, p. 64

Shira A. Scheindlin is a United States District Judge for the Southern District of New York. She was nominated by President Bill Clinton in 1994. She also has been a member of the Judicial Conference of the United States Advisory Committee on the Federal Rules of Civil Procedure (1998–2005). She is known for her intellectual acumen, demanding courtroom demeanor, aggressive interpretations of the law, and expertise in mass torts, electronic discovery, and complex litigation. During her tenure, Judge Scheindlin has presided over a number of high-profile cases, many of which advanced important new positions in the common law. Judge Scheindlin issued two notable and highly publicized rulings in 2013 in regards to New York City's controversial stop-and-frisk procedures: one found the NYPD's procedures unconstitutional, and the other ordered the city to implement reforms under the supervision of a court-appointed monitor.

Anne-Marie Slaughter, p. 118

Anne-Marie Slaughter is the president and CEO of New America and the Bert G. Kerstetter '66 University Professor Emerita of Politics and International Affairs at Princeton University. She has written or edited six books, including *A New World Order* (New Jersey: Princeton University Press, 2004) and *The Idea That Is America: Keeping Faith with Our Values in a Dangerous World* (New York: Basic Books, 2007), and is a frequent contributor to a number of publications, including the *Atlantic* and *Project Syndicate*. In 2012, she published "Why Women Still Can't Have It All" in the *Atlantic,* which quickly became the most read article in the history of the magazine and helped spark a renewed national debate on the continued obstacles to genuine full male-female equality.

Raphael Sperry, p. 68

Raphael Sperry, AIA, LEED AP, is president of Architects/Designers/Planners for Social Responsibility (ADPSR), and the first architect to receive a Soros Justice Fellowship from the Open Society Foundations. He researches the intersection of architecture, planning, and human rights, with a special focus on prisons and jails, and advocates for design professionals to play a larger role in supporting human rights in the built environment. Sperry has taught courses on green architecture, building systems, and building energy use. He holds a master of architecture from the Yale School of Architecture and a bachelor of arts summa cum laude from Harvard University.

Gillian Tett, p. 36

As assistant editor and columnist, Gillian Tett writes two weekly columns for the *Financial Times*, covering a range of economic, financial, political, and social issues throughout the globe.

Winner of several reputable awards—the most recent of which is a Society of American Business Editors and Writers award for best feature article in 2012—she is the author of *New York Times* bestseller *Fool's Gold: How Unrestrained Greed Corrupted a Dream, Shattered Global Markets and Unleashed a Catastrophe* (London: Little, Brown, 2009). Before joining the *Financial Times* in 1993, Tett was awarded a PhD in social anthropology from Cambridge University based on field work in the former Soviet Union.

John Thackara, p. 60

John Thackara is an British writer, philosopher, and event producer. He writes online and in books about examples of what a sustainable future can be like; he uses these examples in talks and workshops for cities, universities, and business; and he organizes social harvest festivals in which project leaders share experiences with each other. Thackara is the author of a widely read column at *Design Observer* and of the best-selling book *In the Bubble: Designing in a Complex World* (Cambridge, Mass.: MIT Press, 2006). He is a visiting professor at the School of Visual Arts in New York and the Ambedkar University, Delhi, in India, and a member of the Design Commission of the U.K. Parliament.

Judith Torrea, p. 78

Judith Torrea is an award-winning investigative blogger, journalist, and author who has covered the Mexico-U.S. border for sixteen years. Her work focuses on women's-rights issues, such as femicide, human trafficking, and immigration. Torrea's work spotlights some of the most dire human-rights cases in Ciudad Juárez and analyzes the impact of the war on drugs on marginalized and poor communities. Her book *Juárez en la sombra: Crónicas de una ciudad que se resiste a morir* (Mexico City: Aguilar Press, 2011) was released in Latin America and Spain. A pioneer blogger in conflict zones, Torrea is the author of the respected blog *Ciudad Juárez, en la sombra del narcotráfico* (*Ciudad Juárez: In the Shadow of Drug Trafficking).*

Rob Walker, p. 40

Rob Walker is a technology and culture columnist for *Yahoo Tech*. He is also a contributor to *Design Observer* and writes the Workologist column in the Sunday Business section of the *New York Times*. His most recent book, coedited with Joshua Glenn, is the collection *Significant Objects: 100 Extraordinary Stories about Ordinary Things* (Seattle: Fantagraphics, 2012).

Jamin Warren, p. 202

Jamin Warren founded video-game arts and culture company Kill Screen. Formerly a culture reporter for the *Wall Street Journal*, he serves as an advisor to The Museum of Modern Art's Department of Architecture and Design. Jamin also hosts the PBS web series *Game/Show*.

Carlotta Werner and Johanna Sunder-Plassmann, p. 30

Carlotta Werner and Johanna Sunder-Plassmann are a German product-designer and media-artist team. Their collaboration began as artistic directors for Turkish Nobel laureate Orhan Pamuk's Museum of Innocence, a museum in Istanbul inspired by his 2008 novel of the same name. Other projects include the design of charcoal stoves for use in West Africa and adapted for local cooking behaviors, as well as the documentary film *Istanbul Collecting*, which follows the designers as they seek out Istanbul's hidden collections of cinema tickets, toys, and diving helmets in preparation for the Museum of Innocence. Through their study of the emotional value assigned by individuals to everyday objects, the team aims to better understand social environments. Currently, they are working on an exhibition about hacked objects emerging in political protests worldwide.

Jody Williams, p. 170

Jody Williams received the Nobel Peace Prize in 1997 for her work to ban land mines through the International Campaign to Ban Landmines, which shared the Peace Prize with her that year. Beginning with her protests of the Vietnam War, she became a life-long advocate of freedom, self-determination, and human and civil rights. Since the launch of the Nobel Women's Initiative in January 2006, Williams has served as its chair. The initiative is made up of six women recipients of the Nobel Peace Prize who support the work of women around the world to achieve sustainable peace with justice and equality.

Cintra Wilson, p. 126

Author, performer, and disgraced *New York Times* fashion critic Cintra Wilson is the author of three books denouncing the hypocrisies of our age, including *A Massive Swelling: Celebrity Re-Examined as a Grotesque, Crippling Disease* (New York: Viking Penguin, 2000). Her articles can occasionally be found in exceptionally brave magazines. Her fourth book, *Fear and Clothing: Unbuckling America's Fashion Destiny*, will be published by W.W. Norton & Company.

Shandra Woworuntu, p. 26

Shandra Woworuntu is a legislative lobbyist in Washington, D.C., and an advocate on behalf of anti-human-trafficking groups. In 1998, she lost a job as a financial analyst in her native Indonesia due to political turmoil. Soon after, she responded to an opportunity to work in the hotel industry in Chicago. In 2001, upon arriving in the United States, Woworuntu was kidnapped and forced into prostitution; eventually she escaped her captors. Woworuntu now works to bring to justice those who engage in criminal trafficking with the help of Safe Horizon, a victim-assistance agency in New York. In 2014, she also established Mentari, a support group to empower trafficking survivors. Woworuntu holds a degree in finance and bank management.

Susan Yelavich, p. 113

Susan Yelavich is an associate professor and director of the MA Design Studies program in the School of Art and Design History and Theory at Parsons The New School for Design. A Fellow of the American Academy in Rome, Yelavich was awarded the Academy's Rolland Prize in Design in 2003. Her newest book is *Design as Future-Making* (London: Bloomsbury Publishing, 2014); she is also the author of *Contemporary World Interiors* (London and New York: Phaidon, 2007). In addition she is an independent curator; her most recent exhibition was *Deep Surface: Contemporary Ornament and Pattern* at the Contemporary Art Museum in Raleigh, North Carolina, in 2011. Previously, she was the assistant director for public programs at Cooper Hewitt, Smithsonian Design Museum in New York.

Index

Abbott, Tony, 88
Abumrad, Jad, 15
Adams, CJ, 135–37
Agid, Shana, 143
Alkalay, Shay, 126
Arendt, Hannah, 9, 11, 143
Ashurbanipal (king), 88
Attenborough, David, 179
Auger, James, 44, 61
Baker, Luke, 162
Balkind, Harriett Levin, 46–47, 47
Beachell, Henry M., 50–51
Bell, Rebecca, 59
Belt, David, 210, 212–13, 213
Benítez, Nuria, 97
Bentham, Jeremy, 68
Berry, Wendell, 60
bin Laden, Osama, 84
Boardman, Mickey, 221
Bobel, Chris, 54, 221
Borlaug, Norman, 48
Bouazizi, Mohamed, 30
Boudica (queen), 88
Boxer, Barbara, 58
Brandalise, Isabella, 199
Bridle, James, 14, 128, 129–33
Brown, Meredith, 152
Burdick, Anne, 44
Burton, Michael, 13, 60–61, 62–63
Bush, George W., 11, 78
Cadora, Eric, 141–42
Calderón, Felipe, 78
Caravaggio, Michelangelo Merisi da, 126
Carter, Jimmy, 166
Cervantes, Miguel de, 79
Chandler, Robert F., 50–51
Chideya, Farai, 143
Choy Ka Fai, 100–1, 102–7
Clair, Patrick, 22–24, 23, 25
Damasio, Antonio, 13
Darwin, Charles, 179, 184
DeBarge, Flotilla, 123
Dempsey, Martin E., 160
Dennis, Leigha, 198, 198, 200–1
DePaulo, William, 167
Diallo, Amadou, 66
Diller, Elizabeth, 14, 113, 115–17
Donatello, 126
Doyle, Colleen, 179
Duarte, Steffi, 37
Eames, Charles, 180
Eames, Ray, 180
Erdoğan, Recep Tayyip, 30
Evans, Walker, 144
Forsythe, William, 100
Foucault, Michel, 68
Francione, Gary L., 221, 221–22
Fretto, Mike, 26, 28–29
Fuller, R. Buckminster, 180
Galliano, John, 108, 110
Gates, Guilbert, 22
Gaynor, Kari, 26, 28–29
Gentileschi, Artemisia, 126
Gibson, William, 15
Grandin, Temple, 13, 188, 189–92, 193, 220–22
Grayson, Saisha, 101
Gulkarov, Simha, 47
Gunnoe, Maria, 166
Guterres, António, 13

Haddix, Sam, 85
Harara, Ahmed, 152
Hargreaves, Ian, 129
Harvey, Laurence, 123
Hassani, Massoud, 13, 170, 171–75
Hedren, Tippi, 123
Hijikata, Tatsumi, 101
Hirsch, Tad, 26, 28–29
Hitchcock, Alfred, 123
Hohensee, Nara, 75
Hokusai, Katsushika, 206
Holt, Tom, 139
Ijeoma, Ekene, 13, 144, 144, 146–47
Jackson, Brooks, 46
Jafarinaimi, Nassim, 129
Jarvis, Jonathan, 36–37, 37–39
Jaskot, Paul B., 73
Jefferson, Thomas, 180
Jennings, Peter R., 50–51
Jeremijenko, Natalie, 198, 198, 200–1
Johnson, Lyndon B., 50–51
Kalashnikov, Mikhail, 10, 214–15, 215–18
Kawakubo, Rei, 108
Keitetsi, China, 13
Kelly, Walt, 66
Kidjo, Angélique, 13
Kiem, Matt, 90
King, Rodney, 66
Knight, Nick, 118, 120–21
Kosal, Song, 170
Kosugi, Shô, 207
Krugman, Jason, 210, 212–13
Kurgan, Laura, 141–42
Lange, Dorothea, 144
Lange, Jessica, 165
Langner, Ralph, 23
Lasky, Julie, 183
Le Corbusier, 74
Lee, Bruce, 206
Leibniz, Gottfried Wilhelm, 101
Lincoln, Lizzie, 110
Lutz, William, 47
Macandrew, James, 180
MacPhee, Josh, 31
Maiello, Paul, 210, 212–13
Marcos, Ferdinand E., 50–51
Martin, Roger, 160
Martinussen, Einar Sneve, 128
McCarthy, Mary, 9
McMahon, JP, 155
McMillen, Colin, 135–37
McQueen, Alexander, 108
Mer, Yael, 126, 127
Miller, Nancy K., 148
Modi, Narendra, 58
Mogelson, Luke, 88
Morales, Andrea, 162, 203
Moyer, Katherine, 125
Mozart, Wolfgang Amadeus, 194
Munch, Edvard, 203
Nelson, George, 180, 181, 182–83, 183
Nelson, Josh, 26, 28–29
Newkirk, Ingrid, 13, 222
Newton, Helmut, 124
Niemann, Christoph, 15
Nirbhaya, 57
Nitta, Michiko, 13, 60–61, 62–63
Obama, Barack, 58
Ocasla, Vincent, 74, 74–75, 76–77

Paglen, Trevor, 15, 154, 155–59
Papanek, Victor, 10
Parsons, Kristina, 27
Parsons, Tim, 61
Pemberty, Juan Pablo, 125
Persse, Jason, 24
Pinker, Steven, 9, 13
Pollan, Michael, 222
Postman, Neil, 61
Rael, Ronald, 78–80, 79, 81–83
Reinfurt, David, 141–42
Rhoades, Harry, 49, 218
Robustini, Pasquale, 207
Rollins, Adriel, 26, 28–29
Russell, Catherine M., 58
Salahuddin, Hussain, 129
Salty, 202, 204–5
San Fratello, Virginia, 78–80, 79, 81–83
Scalia, Antonin, 46
Scheindlin, Shira A., 13
Scofidio, Ricardo, 14, 113, 115–17
Serres, Michel, 100
Shehab, Bahia, 148, 149–51, 152, 153
Shepherd, Doris, 166
Simpson, Tim, 184, 185, 186, 187
Sisi, Abdel Fattah el–, 152
Snowden, Edward, 134
Sperry, Raphael, 66, 179
Sputniko!, 14, 52, 53–54, 220
Stamets, Paul, 60
Stanley, Henry Morton, 178
Steinem, Gloria, 126
Sterling, Bruce, 80
Tacitus, 88
Tarantino, Quentin, 206
Taylor, Elizabeth, 123
Thackara, John, 13
Tolaas, Sissel, 118, 120–21
Tonkinwise, Cameron, 90, 143, 213
Tougaw, Jason, 148
Twilley, Nicola, 221, 221–22
Urbonas, Julijonas, 13, 194, 195, 197
van den Berg, René, 108, 109–10
van der Vyver, Leanie, 108, 109–10, 110
van Herpen, Iris, 108
van Houdt, Joel, 88
Viégas, Fernanda, 135–37
Vivier, Roger, 108, 122, 122
von Kraus, Lee, 198, 198, 200–1
Walker, Rob, 220–21, 222
Wang, Melanie, 26, 28–29
Wang, Shenyangzi, 125
Wattenberg, Martin, 135–37
Williams, Jody, 13
Williams, Sarah, 141–42
Wilson, Cody, 40, 44, 220, 222
Winner, Langdon, 61
Wischmann, John, 210, 212–13
Woebken, Chris, 198, 198, 200–1
Woworuntu, Shandra, 13
Wright, Lee, 125
Yelavich, Susan, 19, 143

Copyright and Photographic Credits

ILLUSTRATION CREDITS

In reproducing the images contained in this publication, the Museum obtained the permission of the rights holders whenever possible. In those instances where the Museum could not locate the rights holders, notwithstanding good-faith efforts, it requests that any contact information concerning such rights holders be forwarded so that they may be contacted for future editions.

Courtesy Jamer Hunt: 20–21; courtesy Patrick Clair: 23, 25; © 2015 Public Practice Studio: 28–29; © 2015 Veronika Helvacioğlu: 32–33; courtesy action press/Zuma Press/Pinar Istek: 34; courtesy Daniel Müller: 35; © 2015 Jonathan Jarvis: 37–39; © Defense Distributed, photo: Lorenza Baroncelli: 41; © Defense Distributed, photo: Marisa Vasquez: 42–43, 45; courtesy HonestAds, inset photos © 2015 iStock: 47; courtesy International Rice Research Institute (IRRI): 49–51; courtesy Sputniko!, photo: Rai Royal: 53–54; © Pawan Kumar: 59; © 2015 Michael Burton and Michiko Nitta: 62–63; courtesy Jamer Hunt: 65, 66 (left), 67; courtesy Flickr Creative Commons/Hello Turkey Toe: 66 (right); © The Moline Publishing Co., photo: Todd Mizener: 68–71, 73; courtesy Vincent Ocasla: 74, 76–77; © 2015 Rael San Fratello: 79, 81–83; Public domain/courtesy U.S. Marine Corps: 85; courtesy Andrew Chittock: 86–87; courtesy Australian Customs and Border Protection Service: 89, 91–95; courtesy Volontaire for Amnesty International Sweden, photo: Niklas Alm/Vostro: 97–99; courtesy Choy Ka Fai: 102–7; courtesy Leanie van der Vyver, photos: Lyall Coburn: 109–10; courtesy Diller + Scofidio, photo © Michael Moran/OTTO: 115–17; courtesy Jamer Hunt: 120–21; © Victoria and Albert Museum, London: 122; courtesy the designer, photo: Shay Alkalay: 127; courtesy James Bridle/booktwo.org, photos: James Bridle: 129, 132–33; courtesy Roberta Mataityte/Lighthouse, photo: Roberta Mataityte: 130–31; courtesy Google Ideas; DDoS data © 2015, Arbor Networks, Inc.: 135–37; © 2015 Laura Kurgan, Spatial Information Design Lab, GSAPP, Columbia University: 141–42; courtesy United Nations High Commissioner for Refugees (UNHCR): 144, 146–47; courtesy Bahia Shehab: 149–51, 153; © Trevor Paglen and Altman Siegel, San Francisco/Metro Pictures, New York/Galerie Thomas Zander, Cologne: 155–59; Public domain/courtesy U.S. Army: 161–62; courtesy Laura Antrim Caskey: 167; courtesy Kent Kessinger: 168–69; © Hassani Design BV: 171–75; Public domain/courtesy U.S. Army: 176; courtesy Vitra Design Museum Archive/ID Magazine: 181; © CBS News Archives/Camera Three and BBC Worldwide Learning: 183; courtesy Tim Simpson, photo, Dominic Tschudin: 185; courtesy Tim Simpson: 187; courtesy Ala Tannir: 189; courtesy Temple Grandin: 190–92; courtesy Julijonas Urbonas: 195, 197; courtesy Natalie Jeremijenko, Chris Woebken, Lee von Kraus, Leigha Dennis: 198, 200–1; courtesy saltybet.com: 204–5; courtesy Jamer Hunt: 207; courtesy Flickr Creative Commons/Daniel McMahon: 208–9; courtesy David Belt/Macro Sea, Vamos Architects, John Wischmann, Paul Maiello & Jason Krugman, photos: Chris Mottalini, drawings: Macro Sea + Vamos Architects: 210, 212–13; courtesy Jerry Lee Elmore: 215; © iStock.com/AlbertSmirnov: 216–17; courtesy U.S. Air Force/Flickr Creative Commons: 218; © 2015 Museum of Modern Art, New York: 221–22.

PRODUCTION CREDITS

Coproduced by the Australian Broadcasting Corporation and Zapruder's Other Films: 23, 25; Narration by John Levoff. Music by Brandon Au (DJ Sol Rising): 37–39; Creative advisor: Natalie Lam, Graphic Identity: Kishan Muthucumaru, Website production: Unit 9/Roll Studio, Website copy: Daniel Brill, Tagline: Don Levy: 47; Video Director: Yasuhito Tsuge, Video Production: AUG5, Inc., Japan, Product design assistance: Naoki Kawamoto: 53–54. Concept: Malin Åkersten Triumf/Yasin Lekorchi: 97–99; Concept, Design & Production: Hyperakt (Principal: Deroy Peraza, Senior UX Designer: Eric Fensterheim, Art Director: Josh Smith, Design Strategist & Account Manager: Ambika Roos) and Ekene Ijeoma, Desktop Development: Ekene Ijeoma, Mobile Development: Oak, Research and Writing: Ted Cava, Copyediting: Jenna Shapiro, Ambika Roos: 144, 146–47; Medical advisor: Dr. Michael Gresty, Spatial Disorientation Lab, Imperial College, London, Model making: Paulius Vitkauskas, Photography: Aistė Valiūtė and Daumantas Plechavičius, Video: Science Gallery, Trinity College Dublin, Video footage (human centrifuge training): William Ellis: 195, 197.